P9-CJL-461

Critical Issues in Educational Leadership Series
Joseph Murphy, Series Editor

Lessons from High-Performing Hispanic Schools:
Creating Learning Communities
PEDRO REYES, JAY D. SCRIBNER, and ALICIA PAREDES SCRIBNER, Eds.

Magnet Schools in Urban America: Magnet Schools
and the Pursuit of Equity
CLAIRE SMREKAR and ELLEN GOLDRING

Schools for Sale: Why Free Market Policies Won't Improve
America's Schools, and What Will
ERNEST R. HOUSE

Reclaiming Educational Administration as a Caring Profession
LYNN G. BECK

Cognitive Perspectives on Educational Leadership
PHILIP HALLINGER, KENNETH LEITHWOOD, and JOSEPH MURPHY, Eds.

Lessons from High-Performing Hispanic Schools

* * *

CREATING LEARNING COMMUNITIES

Edited by
PEDRO REYES
JAY D. SCRIBNER
ALICIA PAREDES SCRIBNER

Teachers College, Columbia University
New York and London

Published by Teachers College Press, 1234 Amsterdam Avenue, New York, NY 10027

Library of Congress Cataloging-in-Publication Data

Lessons from high-performing Hispanic schools : creating learning
  communities / edited by Pedro Reyes, Jay D. Scribner, Alicia Paredes
  Scribner.
     p. cm. — (Critical issues in educational leadership series)
    Includes bibliographical references and index.
    ISBN 0-8077-3831-X (cloth). — ISBN 0-8077-3830-1 (pbk.)
    1. Hispanic American children—Education—Texas—Case studies.
  2. Community education—Texas—Case studies. 3. Multicultural
  education—Texas—Case studies.   I. Reyes, Pedro. II. Scribner,
  Jay D. III. Scribner, Alicia Paredes. IV. Series.
  LC2674.T4L47   1999
  371.829′68073—dc21   98-51496

ISBN 0-8077-3830-1 (paper)
ISBN 0-8077-3831-X (cloth)

Printed on acid-free paper

Manufactured in the United States of America

06 05   8 7 6 5

Contents

Foreword

The literature is rich with accounts of the plight and demise of the Hispanic student. Many studies have been conducted to explain why so many Hispanic students are failing in schools. Their poor achievement has been linked consistently to a variety of sociocultural factors that propel Mexican American students to academic failure. The assumption of these findings is that the Hispanic child does not have the necessary competencies, values, and personal characteristics to succeed in America's schools.

Not much emphasis has been given to Hispanics who have overcome the obstacles and barriers impeding success. Most of the current research on Hispanic students has focused on how sociocultural factors contribute to their failure in school. These studies have helped to develop and justify acceptance of the dangerous, damaging, deficit model. In educational circles, this model often is referred to as the culturally different paradigm. It is accepted by many teachers and condoned by many school administrators as a way to explain why minority students fail to perform according to standards.

There are several implications inherent in this paradigm. The most obvious one is that those who accept it as an excuse for failure are implying, succinctly, that children who are culturally different are inherently less competent, less intelligent, less capable, and less motivated than the children of the more affluent dominant culture. It suggests that unless they change their culture, values, and physical appearance, they have little or no chance to be successful in school. Teachers who accept this paradigm also are saying that nothing is wrong with their pedagogy, teaching practices, or methodologies, or with the school system itself. Therefore, they will continue to operate the same way and students must learn to adapt to the programs available to them or fail. According to this approach, the solution for improvement is beyond the teacher's and school system's realm of influence and power.

EVIDENCE CONTRARY TO THE POPULAR BELIEF

The authors of this book argue that the current condition of education for Hispanic students need not exist. The high-performing Hispanic schools where the research reported in this volume was undertaken offer a much more optimistic picture.

These schools recognize students' needs and accept responsibility for providing leadership and support in planning, implementing, and evaluating quality instructional programs for those special needs students. Region One ESC is committed to working collaboratively with these districts in the development of programs, policies, and practices that will facilitate these students' attainment of state academic standards set for all Texas students.

In an effort to demonstrate our commitment to this end, Region One Education Service Center established the South Texas Institute for Educational Research and Development as a collaborative of the Texas Education Agency, Region One ESC, and Region One school districts. The research partners in this initiative include The University of Texas at Austin, the University of Texas–Pan American and Southwest Texas State University. This publication, a direct result of this Institute's research initiative, offers a message of hope for teachers and administrators across the country who are engaged in the teaching and learning process with Hispanic students.

We would like to thank and acknowledge the students, staff, and parents of the school districts that participated in this meaningful research endeavor—the Brownsville, Edinburg, La Joya, Laredo, McAllen, Pharr, San Juan, Alamo, Roma, San Benito, and Zapata Independent School Districts, located along the Texas–Mexico border of south Texas.

Sylvia R. Hatton, Ph.D.
Executive Director,
Region One Education Service Center

Ellen Gonzalez, Ph.D.
Associate Executive Director
Region One Education Service Center

Encarnación Garza, Jr., Ph.D.
Superintendent
Progreso Independent School District
Progreso, TX

Acknowledgments

The authors are greatly indebted to the leadership of the Texas Education Agency Region One Education Service Center who assisted us in every step of the research process, encouraged us in the writing of this book, and made it possible for us to gain access to schools participating in the study. Our gratitude accordingly goes to the current executive director, Sylvia Hatton, and associate executive director, Ellen Gonzalez, and to Roberto Zamora, a former special assistant to the State of Texas Commissioner of Education, and Region One Education Service Center Director. All three of these individuals were involved in the early conceptualization of our work, as were members of their Regional Advisory Council.

We also are indebted to the many faculty and students from The University of Texas at Austin, Southwest Texas State University, and The University of Texas–Pan American, which contributed to the various phases of our research. We are proud to say that many of the students are continuing their research as professors at major universities across the country.

We are happy to acknowledge a further debt to our friends and colleagues for their assistance in the development of this manuscript, especially Joseph Murphy, at Vanderbilt University, who prodded us to assemble the manuscript in the first place; Luis Moll, who encouraged us to explore nontraditional notions about schooling such as the "funds of knowledge"; and Eugene Garcia, whose work on student diversity and bilingualism inspired us to concentrate on the uniqueness of the Hispanic culture and student learning.

At Teachers College Press, Brian Ellerbeck and his colleague, Karl Nyberg, proved to be excellent partners in bringing this research to the field. Their overall guidance, careful and imaginative editing, accurate copyediting, and corrections converted a multiauthored manuscript into a book.

We have drawn on the expert administrative and secretarial assistance of Rhonda Manor, Anne Psencik, Sarah Jimenez, and Valerie Goldstein— supplemented by the help of Michelle Young, who is now an assistant professor at the University of Iowa, and who served as project coordinator.

Finally, we would like to extend our special thanks to the students, parents, community members, teachers, and school administrators who so willingly took time from their busy schedules to engage in lengthy interviews with our research staff. Without their cooperation and goodwill, this book would not have been possible.

PR
JDS
APS

CHAPTER 1

High-Performing Hispanic Schools: An Introduction

Alicia Paredes Scribner

EDUCATIONAL VULNERABILITY OF HISPANIC YOUTH

While educational reform movements of the past 2 decades have targeted improvements that largely benefit mainstream students, a major segment of culturally and linguistically diverse students faces almost impossible challenges in the process of acquiring an education. Is education truly accessible to all students in our country or is this only a prevailing myth? Unfortunately, the many arguments we hear in defense of reform programs designed to close the gap of increasingly discrepant test scores place the burden of responsibility on those students who represent a dramatically changing demographic composition in our society. In other words, social and demographic changes would appear to outdistance our ability to develop the technologies, practices, and capacity necessary to cope with classroom circumstances that are quite different from those of 20 years ago. Increasingly, teachers teach students who speak a variety of languages in their homes and communities. Some students come to school from homes with single working parents. Many come to school unprepared to learn or lack the prerequisite skills to benefit from instruction. Many of these students are from indigenous, minority families, and others have come to this country from Latin American countries with their families for a variety of reasons—some to seek a better way of life, others escaping political persecution.

Substantial evidence exists as to why Hispanic students fail in schools. Low expectations; archaic decision-making structures; ill-prepared teachers and administrators; lack of coordination among schools, parents, and communities on behalf of children; negative self-image; peer group pressure;

poverty; tracking; and other school policies are some of the major factors that contribute to the vulnerability of Hispanic youth (Cummins, 1984; Duran, 1989; Figueroa & Garcia, 1994; Garcia, 1994; Reyes & Paredes Scribner, 1995; Valencia & Aburto, 1991). The plight of the Hispanic student worsens with each advance in grade level, becoming particularly acute at the secondary level. Inappropriate and often poor instruction combined with repeated academic failure lead to feelings of alienation, lack of self-esteem, retention and ultimately being over age for grade level, and increasing instances of teenage pregnancy, gang activity, and other forms of socially deviant behavior. School professionals rarely involve parents in meaningful ways that would enhance the young Hispanics' chances of success in school. As a result, the school dropout rate soars for Hispanic students (Reyes & Paredes Scribner, 1995). In cities like San Antonio, Houston, Dallas, New York, Chicago, and Los Angeles, school districts report dropout rates in the 60% range for any given year in high school. These statistics refer only to those who matriculated in a particular school and who failed to complete the year (Reyes, 1990). A far greater number of student dropouts are unaccounted for due to attrition from public high school between ninth grade and expected graduation in the twelfth grade, 4 years later (Johnson, 1994).

Other problems contributing to the educational vulnerability of Hispanic youth can be attributed directly to teacher instructional practices, tracking, and curriculum organization. Because Hispanic students often are misdiagnosed and misplaced in the school's ability grouping structure, primarily as a result of limited English proficiency, they are stuck in a "Catch-22" of low expectations, inappropriate instruction, and unchallenging curriculum offerings. When teacher expectations are low, students become vulnerable. They lose interest, develop negative reactions, and perform poorly (Romo & Falbo, 1996). Moreover, curriculum often is structured to satisfy the needs of teachers rather than students (Moll, 1988). Teaching prescribed by the manual and basal text, rather than adapted to student needs, is the least challenging alternative. Students often disengage from the learning process because of exposure to piecemeal, superficial knowledge and culturally irrelevant curriculum material (Cummins, 1986; Garcia, 1994; Levin, 1986; Moll & Whitmore, 1993; Oakes, 1990; Tharp & Gallimore, 1988). When the curriculum and instruction fail the Hispanic student, learning problems are inevitable.

Students exhibiting learning problems often are referred for formal assessment, usually consisting of some form of standardized, norm-referenced testing. Standardized tests yield deficient profiles for Hispanic youth in language, cognition, memory, perception, learning ability, and aptitude (August & Garcia, 1988). The standardized testing industry has flourished in this country because of the large-scale use of the tests by educators looking for a quick and easy way to justify the sorting of students. Standardized tests shift the responsibility for relevant and appropriate teaching away from instructional personnel. Testing relieves the teacher from making instructional adaptations to individual student needs and evaluating individual student progress within the actual learning situation most familiar to students. Teachers soon learn to survive the micropolitical pressure induced by ill-informed school administrators, policy makers, and the larger community, by teaching to the test. If the students fail to make the grade, they are blamed for the deficit and the quality and appropriateness of instruction remain unquestioned.

The vulnerability of these children is further compounded because of the inadequate supply of professionals who share cultural identity with these students. Dynamic teachers who transcend language and cultural barriers can make a difference in the lives of Hispanic students (Garcia, 1994). As the population shifts to a majority-minority, only one teacher of color for every 10 White teachers is available, only 3% of all school administrators are Hispanic, and only 8% are African American (Digest of Educational Statistics, 1990). Moreover, these same shortages found among allied educational professionals exacerbate the vulnerability of Mexican American students. Lack of appropriately trained and culturally sensitive assessment personnel leads to psychoeducational practices that reinforce deficit assumptions for minority student performance (Paredes Scribner, 1995) and thus school failure.

Mexican American students, 90% of all Hispanic students, are increasing in numbers at a rate nearly 10 times greater than the overall population (U.S. Bureau of the Census, 1992). As indicated, these students are by far our most vulnerable. They are more likely to drop out of school than are other students. They disengage at an early age, resulting in an alarming statistic that has remained constant for the past 20 years. Only 5% to 6% of these students are graduating from our institutions of higher education, a condition that places profound limitations on their ultimate influence on social and educational policy in our society.

CURRENT CONDITIONS NEED NOT EXIST

We argue throughout this book that the current condition of education for Hispanic students need not exist. While most schools fail Hispanic students, some schools do not. The picture we show is far brighter and potentially far more optimistic than the tragic circumstances portrayed in the latest statistics on Hispanic youth. High-performing Hispanic schools, in fact, do exist and they have a strong impact on the learning conditions for Hispanic students. Located along the Texas–Mexico border region between Brownsville and Laredo, the schools included in the high-performing Hispanic schools differ from those schools that fail Hispanic students, as well as from what generally are referred to as mainstream effective schools. The high-performing schools are successful for Hispanic students who are predominantly low socioeconomic, bilingual, limited English proficient (LEP), and for English as a Second Language (ESL) students of Mexican American descent. Many are migrant students who are away from their schools for extended periods of time during the school year.

The schools we studied have been characterized as communities of learners where students come first, learning is fun, and everything begins in the classroom. They are making a difference even when faced with so-called "problem students"—migrant, bilingual, limited English proficient children, and children of the poor. Classroom experiences in the high-performing Hispanic schools are typified by teachers engaging students in a learning process that maximizes excellence and equity. Because teachers make no assumptions about why students cannot learn, no self-fulfilling prophecies prevail. Teachers, not students, are vulnerable. The case studies presented in this book document "best practices" associated with the key learning conditions found in these very special learning communities.

Within the classroom/learning context, for example, teachers were found to be empowered to adapt, modify, make culturally relevant, and match curricula to the unique needs of Hispanic students. Instruction was found to be interactive, active rather than passive, and student-centered rather than teacher-centered. Within the community, the home, and the school context, adults and other student peer group members shared common aspirations, goals, and visions of what ought to be expected of the Hispanic students in their respective school communities. Finally, researchers, focusing on the outcomes of the curriculum and instructional program, found that assessment was ongoing and advocacy-oriented. And above all else, teachers who work in these learning communities empower students to become excited about and responsible for their own learning. The authors hope that the case study results that follow will be used by those committed to creating learning communities that work for all Hispanic and non-Hispanic students in our society.

These classroom experiences for Hispanic students do not exist in a vacuum, however. These learning communities extend throughout and beyond the traditional schoolhouse. Classrooms in which the traditionally labeled "problem students" (the bilingual, LEP, migrant, poor children) achieve the highest levels of excellence are found in learning communities where the school district and school administrators allocate scarce resources as directly as possible to instruction, and in communities where collaboration among businesses, social service agencies, and schools is integrated into the learning environment. Family members are valued and respected full partners in the learning process. School principals care about children and seek to surround themselves with adults who care about children. In the high-performing Hispanic schools, an ethic of caring and learning prevails, power is shared, problems are solved collaboratively, and linguistically diverse students are celebrated. As communities of learners, everyone associated with the learning conditions of a school strive to do their best through growth and learning; have an idea about where they are and where they would like to be; achieve goals creatively, rather than reactively; and take risks to move beyond the margin of the status quo.

These learning communities do exist! And they do defy the odds! We have observed them in action. We have sought to understand why they differ from most of the schools serving Hispanic students from low socioeconomic, linguistically diverse backgrounds. In this book we share the findings of a major research and development initiative in Texas–Mexico border schools, schools incorporating new and successful programs and practices and achieving school-wide success in increasing student performance beyond state averages. As an introduction to the case studies included in this volume, we have provided in this chapter a brief overview of our argument about how certain conditions of learning can work for Hispanic youth, and about how we conceptualized our overall purposes, the case study method, and our interpretation of findings. The chapter concludes with a glimpse of the "best practices" our research team discovered in their individual case studies, followed by chapters presenting each case. The final chapter by Scribner and Reyes reframes our initial conceptual outlook and offers strategies for creating learning communities for Hispanic students through the implementation of proven programs and practices. We believe that the most important criterion for any school change must be its likely benefit to all students.

CONTEXT OF THE STUDY

This study was initiated in the fall of 1993 at The University of Texas at Austin in collaboration with the Region One Education Service Center and supported by the Texas Education Agency. Researchers were recruited from UT Austin, UT Pan American, and Southwest Texas State University. The area served by the Region One stretches along the Rio Grande from Brownsville to Laredo. Most of it is known as the Valley, an area in south central Texas that was populated by Mexicans long before Santa Ana's defeat in San Jacinto and Sam Houston's inauguration as first president of the Republic of Texas.

The Texas border region is defined as a 15-county area, extending almost 900 miles. Some 90% of the population reside in four counties with major metropolitan areas. A large segment of the population are immigrants from throughout Mexico, who are drawn to this area by the promise of jobs. In 1990, 35% of the population was under 18 years of age, compared with 20% in the rest of the country. Almost half of the Texas border children are under 18 years of age and live in poverty. Border counties continue to be some of the poorest areas in the United States. Almost 23% of the population in these counties are identified as migrant/seasonal farm workers. Unemployment exceeds 10% and underemployment is a significant problem (Romo & Falbo, 1996).

Mexican Americans living in this area have until recently enjoyed little political power, participation, or representation in local, state, or national governmental circles. While Mexican Americans have made unprecedented steps toward participating in Texas politics and policy making associated with the economic, social, and educational conditions, areas of the state, such as the Valley, remain unchanged (Montejano, 1996). Political inclusion has not been equated to economic assimilation and equal educational opportunity. Schools in the Valley have been among the most underfunded in Texas and the nation.

These schools enroll a population of approximately 277,720 students in 38 school districts. Of these students, 95% are Hispanic and 128,192 have been identified as limited English proficient. Seventy percent are from low socioeconomic backgrounds, 10% are recent immigrants from Mexico, and 20% are migrants (Snapshot, 1996). These learners bring unique challenges to the learning situation.

The Schools

Eight of these schools—three elementary, three middle, and two high schools—were selected for this study. Following is a brief overview of the school context for each of the effective border schools under investigation. The eight schools have been given fictitious names to protect their identities.

Calles Elementary School. Calles Elementary School is located in a border city with a population of approximately 90,000. The school has a population of almost 735 students, 87.3% Hispanic and 10.3% White. African American and Asian American students account for less than 2% of the total student population. Of the total student population, 63.65%

are identified as economically disadvantaged, defined as qualifying for free or reduced-cost lunch. In this school approximately 50% of the students are targeted Chapter I students. Approximately 23% of the students are identified as migrant students. Almost 16% of the students have been identified as disabled, according to federal guidelines set forth in the Individuals with Disabilities Education Act. Instructional personnel number 37 certified teachers and 12 paraprofessionals. In the school administration there are one principal, one facilitator (vice principal), and one-and-a-half counselors. Teachers' experience ranges from zero years for a first-year teacher to more than 20 years for three veteran teachers. The range in tenure is as broad as the range in total years experience. All teachers hold a bachelors degree and a teaching certificate. Three teachers hold a masters degree, and 30 teachers hold certificates or endorsements to teach bilingual education or ESL. Five teachers hold certificates for special education. The grades taught at Calles Elementary School are prekindergarten to grade 5.

Obregón Elementary School. Obregón Elementary School, a Blue Ribbon School, is in a school district located in the south central portion of the Lower Rio Grande Valley. There are approximately 890 students, 95% of whom are Hispanic and 5% White. No other ethnic group was represented at the time of the study. Of the total school population, 89% are considered economically disadvantaged, and 66% are considered LEP. Twenty-six percent of the Hispanic population is identified as migrant. Obregón Elementary School has an early childhood education program, prekindergarten, and kindergarten to grade 5. There are 50 teachers in the school, 26 of whom are bilingual/ESL endorsed. The school is administered by one principal and two facilitators (vice principals); there are two counselors, one librarian, three secretaries, and four custodians. This school is unique in that the pre-K and K teachers use the Montessori approach in their instruction, there is multiage grouping in pre-K to first grade, there is an after-school tutorial program, and there are Saturday classes. The latter are staffed by volunteer teachers who assist students in computer instruction.

Carranza Elementary School. Carranza Elementary School, like many of the other schools we studied, has a principal who has been in place for several years. There is one assistant principal. The school has a student population of 450 students, 326 of whom are classified as LEP. Ninety-five percent of the students are on the free-lunch program. The grade levels at this school are prekindergarten to fifth grade. Of the instructional personnel, 24 of the 31 teachers are certified in bilingual education. In the past 10 years, this school consistently has received distinguished or exemplary status in the state.

Madero Middle School. Madero Middle School is a school with a total enrollment of 991 students in grades 6–8. The student population is fairly evenly divided in the three grade levels. Ninety-six percent of the students are Hispanic, 3.4% are White, and 0.2% are African American. Approximately 83.8% of the student population are considered economically disadvantaged and 7% are LEP. There are 68 teaching professionals, 12 instructional and nine clerical paraprofessionals, five security guards, two counselors, one interdisciplinary resource person, two assistant principals, and one principal. At the time of the study, 14 teachers were working on their masters degrees. Madero Middle School is one of 58 mentor schools designated by the State of Texas.

Francisco Villa Middle School. Francisco Villa Middle School is another state-designated mentor school located in the Lower Valley region. The school has sixth, seventh, and eighth grades, with a total population of approximately 1,200 students. Ninety-four percent are Hispanic, 5.3% are White, and 0.6% are of other ethnic origins. The proportion of students who qualified as economically disadvantaged was 71%; the proportion of LEP students is 20%. Francisco Villa Middle School also has 6.4% of its students designated as gifted and talented. There are 93 teachers, two assistant principals, one principal, one instructional facilitator, and various special education programs. The staff has been fairly stable with very little turnover. For the past 4 years, the school has been organized by interdisciplinary teams consisting of reading, English, math, social studies, and science teachers.

Huerta Junior High School. Huerta Junior High School is also designated as a Texas mentor school. Dramatic growth has been experienced by this school in the past 5 years. During the 1994–95 school year, the school had a peak enrollment approaching 1,500 students in grades 7 and 8. As migrants return, projections are that this enrollment will surpass the peak enrollment of 1993–94. Ninety-six percent of the students are Hispanic and 4% are White. At least 75% of the student population are considered economically disadvantaged. About 20% of the students are migrants and 16% are considered limited English proficient. A total of 10 teachers have bilingual certificates, three of whom also are endorsed in ESL. In this school, students are assigned to academic teams and are heterogeneously grouped. One hundred percent of the students participate in the Accelerated Reader Program, which rewards students for reading and teaches them the value of reading. The majority of students also receive computer-assisted instruction in reading and math through Computer Curriculum Corporation. There are various activities and clubs sponsored and monitored by four grade counselors who give freely of themselves and are available for individual, group, and class counseling.

Benito Juarez High School. Benito Juarez High School became a ninth–tenth-grade-level campus in 1989. In 1992, the school's classrooms were remodeled and the school became a complete 4-year high school. Since then the school administration has done much to improve the morale and preparation of the faculty. Professional development activities have focused on the faculty members as persons, family members, and teachers. Of the school's 2,800 students, 99% are Hispanic, 75% receive free or reduced-cost lunch, 50% are classified as migrant, 7% are new or recent arrivals, and 4% are special education. Students are drawn from three towns in the district. The school itself is spread over 40 acres and has 160 professional staff and 60 paraprofessionals, including a large security staff. The current principal has been at the school for the past 5 years and was formerly principal of an elementary school in the district. The school governance structure is fairly hierarchical with six assistant principals each assigned specific administrative duties. The school operates under a site-based management plan whereby the faculty and staff make important decisions on budget, staff development, student incentives, and block scheduling.

Porfirio Diaz High School. Porfirio Diaz High School is a 4-year high school with approximately 700 students, 93.2% of whom are Hispanic and 6.8% White. Seventy-one percent of the students are identified as economically disadvantaged and 12% are identified as limited English proficient. At the time of the study, the dropout rate was reported at 1.7%, half the rate of the state. The breakdown of staff is as follows: 54 teachers, six professional support staff members, two administrators, and an educational aide. Forty-six percent of the teachers are females, 73% of the teachers are Hispanic, 22.8% are White, and 3.7% are classified as other. Slightly more than 60% of the teachers have 6 or more years of experience. Beginning teachers account for 9.8% of the staff; 26.8% have 1–5 years of experience, 13.7% have 6–10 years, 37.6% have 11–20 years, and 12.1% have over 20 years. Unique to this high school is the fact that it has three bilingual counselors who provide a variety of services to the student body. As the principal stated to the research team visiting this campus, "I want our counselors to counsel kids, not do paperwork."

THE RESEARCH METHOD

The authors of the chapters presented in this volume were asked to focus on various dimensions of the context of learning in those schools that were outperforming most schools in the attainment of state academic standards. Information about the context of learning was derived from a variety of sources representing conditions under which learning actually took place in the schools selected for this study. The overriding question that guided the researchers was, "What external, internal, and criterion performance conditions make a difference in student learning in the high-performing Hispanic schools?" Thus, the case studies presented in this volume focus on home and community educational contexts, classroom and school contexts, and the assessment context in which attempts are made to ascertain particular skills, attitudes, interests, beliefs, and other traits learned by the predominantly Mexican American students enrolled in the effective border schools.

Individual case studies were conducted to obtain information from which an in-depth, detailed, and comprehensive analysis could be undertaken. They provide descriptions of the learning conditions within and around individual school contexts, as well as some cross-case analyses that ultimately could enable other schools to be able to adopt selected "best practices" appropriate for their settings. Thus, the chapters presented in this volume offer a balance between unique variations within and generalizations found across these predominantly Hispanic schools. With the exception of the chapter concerning resource allocations, the qualitative case study was the preferred research strategy for understanding the ways in which people, programs, organizations, and practices were both similar and unique, as well as discerning the complex relationships among them (Patton, 1990; Stake, 1995).

A purposive sample was employed to select the schools included in this study. The logic of this sampling technique lies in the ability to select cases that exemplify issues of concern (i.e., learning conditions found in effective border schools) to the research project (Patton, 1990). The three elementary, three middle, and two high schools were selected on the basis of the following criteria: (1) school enrollment of 66.6% or more Mexican American students; (2) schools with well-above-average standardized test scores on the Texas Assessment of Academic Skills; and (3) schools that had received state and national recognition (e.g., mentor schools, blue ribbon schools).

Preinvestigation procedures included a literature review of "best practices" and a pilot study in two schools. Information and experiences gathered from these activities were used to develop and revise relevant protocol questions and to provide additional clarification of the context, culture, and overall climate of the schools we were to visit in our purposive sample. After the pilot studies, two research teams visited each of these schools for a minimum of one day. Research teams comprised principal investigators and research assistants and were organized around internal and external learning conditions.

Prior to our field visits we met with the principals of each of the high-performing Hispanic schools to inform them of the purpose of our visits and to collaborate in the final logistics for data collection. Background information was collected on the schools and their communities and was used to further refine and tailor our questions to specific campuses. Interviews were held with students, teachers, school site administrators, assessment personnel, parents and family members, community and business leaders, school board and central staff members, school custodians, cafeteria workers, and other staff members. Researchers attended meetings, observed students and faculty outside and inside classrooms, and gathered data using both formal and informal data collection techniques. Each team included Mexican American researchers who were bilingual and well grounded in multicultural research techniques. In addition, each research team met after the school visits for group reflection meetings to discuss and highlight similarities or contrasts in their findings.

Following the fieldwork phase, each research team began the process of data analysis and interpretation. This process consisted of reviewing taped and transcribed interviews, field notes and transcriptions of reflection meetings among the various teams, project directors, others from the field, and experts in various areas representing the internal and external learning conditions under investigation. Moreover, because of the uniqueness of each research area presented in this book, the chapters reflect both a common and an individualized approach to analysis and interpretation. For example, techniques used in analyzing statistical data from the state or local school districts were stressed more in some of the individual studies than in others, and similarly some stressed interviews in the natural setting of parents' homes, while others were conducted entirely at school, resulting in variations in contextual effects on the interpretation of findings. During the early stages, however, all field workers and principal investigators underwent rigorous training in multicultural research, qualitative data analysis, and interpretation techniques that were used throughout the studies presented in this volume.

As mentioned earlier, the high-performing Hispanic school initiative began with a comprehensive search of the literature for evidence of what works for Hispanic youth. This book represents phase two of the initiative, the research phase. In phase three, training modules have been developed as a result of this research and have undergone refinement and adaptation to the needs of Hispanic youth in schools throughout the State of Texas (Reyes & Scribner, 1996). The intent of these three phases is to bring the research findings reported here to the many schools whose student populations reflect the demographic characteristics of the high-performing Hispanic schools.

CREATING LEARNING COMMUNITIES FOR HISPANIC YOUTH

Collectively, the research findings reported in this book are irrefutable on one point: The disjuncture between the traditional mission of schools and the plight of linguistically and culturally diverse students need not exist. Throughout this book the authors examine conditions found in learning communities where all community members (adults and youth) strive to do their personal best through individual growth and mutual learning. Accordingly, a common theme that weaves its way through the case studies that follow can be of great help in keeping readers focused as they search for ways to create optimal learning environments for all students, particularly for those our schools traditionally have failed, the linguistically and culturally diverse students: "Establishing learning communities will take everybody striving for their personal best to create a successful learning environment for all, understanding each other's world view, and learning to work in teams in order to effectively create a shared vision (Reyes & Scribner, 1996)."

The learning community we propose is organized around four major dimensions: (1) collaborative governance and leadership; (2) community and family involvement; (3) culturally responsive pedagogy; and (4) advocacy-oriented assessment and quality control.

Collaborative Governance and Leadership

It takes resources and leadership to support a learning community effectively. Wagstaff and Fusarelli found leadership in high-performing Hispanic schools to emanate from a variety of sources within the learning community. Simply put, it can be concluded from this study that schools with adequate resources and strong collaborative cultures are not driven by state-mandated accountability measures. They emphasize accountability based on the belief that all children can learn and that the responsibility of administrators and teachers is to see that it happens.

Chapter 2 provides further evidence of our underlying premise that communities of learners strive for their personal best, practice team learning, and progress within the parameters of a shared vision. High-performing Hispanic schools exhibit a clear, coherent mission that is shared by all members of the learning community. In these schools, empowerment of all stakeholders, including administrators, teachers, and sometimes students, prevails. Moreover, a climate of innovation exists where promising new ideas and procedures can be tested for their efficacy to the mission of the school. All learning community members have the confidence to accept or reject innovations based on careful, critical, and collaborative reviews of them. It all boils down to, "Will this work for our students?" These schools manifest a culture of caring and responsibility for student academic performance. As one principal put it, "We have proved that living in an economically disadvantaged [area], that we can run with the best and our kids are just as smart; they just have not had the experiences that perhaps your kids and my kids have had." The bottom line is that each school engages students with enriched instructional materials previously limited to only a few, labeled gifted.

Community and Family Involvement

Parental involvement encompasses a multitude of complex phenomena. Scribner, Young, and Pedroza explored ways in which borderland parents and school personnel develop and sustain meaningful parent involvement. In Chapter 3, they present an in-depth view of how parents and professional staff hold distinctively different views regarding the meaning of parent involvement and different reasons for valuing parent involvement. Finally, how parent involvement is carried out has much to do with student age and grade level, size of school, community needs, and the nature and amount of communication, using strategies that stress personal contact, creating inviting learning environments, initiating opportunities for parent interaction, providing opportunities for formal and informal involvement at school and home, and building on the Mexican American culture, values, and experiences.

Brooks and Kavanaugh's Chapter 4 assists us in identifying some of the best practices in developing and maintaining school–community relationships in the high-performing Hispanic schools found in Region One of Texas. While the popular media portray this region as a homogeneous, impoverished area largely populated by people of Mexican descent, Brooks and her colleagues found the region to be far more demographically and historically diverse. The schools conceptualized their relationships with communities using three models, as follows: (1) the community as resource model, described as a relationship in which the community is perceived as a resource for funds, services, and volunteers; (2) the traditional community model, depicting culturally homogeneous communities in which strong Mexican American cultural identifications are upheld and a seamless relationship appears to exist with the school as a center of activity for the surrounding community; and (3) the learning community model, which represents a relationship in which the school is a community-based and self-empowering place in which personnel see themselves as solutions to their school's problems, and the development of the surrounding community as an important way of strengthening the schools.

Finally, findings reported in both Chapters 3 and 4, as well as other findings that will become apparent throughout the chapters to follow, challenge the assumption that "community" refers exclusively to the business, civic, and students' parents' communities. On the one hand, community, for the high-performing Hispanic schools, encompasses multiple layers of the larger community with which the schools interact, including the children's families, and within the local community—the district administration, the business and civic communities, as well as the larger context of state, regional, and federal governments. On the other hand, the concept of community can be limited to all those participating members of this larger context involved directly in learning for, about, and with Hispanic learners.

Culturally Responsive Pedagogy

After observing numerous outstanding classrooms, the authors of Chapters 5 and 6 were convinced that educators who embrace a culturally responsive pedagogy accept students as they are. The classroom teachers in the high-performing Hispanic schools do not believe in the bell curve; rather, they are strongly committed to the idea that all children can succeed at high levels. Within each of their classrooms and schools, everything is driven by the needs of children. The culture and first language of the child are highly valued. Collaboration, nonhierarchical (i.e., structurally flat) organizations, ample use of teaming, openness to new ideas, and high consensus on goals were among the factors characteristic of the high-performing Hispanic schools. But perhaps the most powerful finding pertaining directly to classroom learning was the incorporation of students' interests and experiences, the "funds of knowledge" they bring with them into the learning situation, whether it is reading, writing, mathematics, or other subject areas.

Chapters 5 and 6 address instructional programs in these schools. In the area of mathematics, academic achievement of Hispanic students is related directly to the quality and level of instruction they receive. Unfortunately, however, in most schools, little support is provided to limited English proficient students in subject areas such as mathematics, social studies, and science (McDonnell & Hill, 1993; U.S. General Accounting Office, 1994). Thus, in Chapter 5, Reyes and Pazey reveal a different story in the high-performing Hispanic schools. They found that the expectations for LEP students were challenged by teachers who organized and wrote their own curricula. Teachers developed thematic units, often meeting during the summer months to design lessons and develop time lines for the following academic year. Among the best practices identified by Reyes and Pazey were cooperative learning strategies, peer and cross-age tutoring, and language support instruction for students whose limited English skills interfered with understanding content. Finally, the three most common findings in class-rooms where student performance was beyond what is typical in Hispanic schools were (1) emphasis was placed on meaning and understanding, (2) mathematical skills were embedded in context, and (3) connections were made between subject areas and between school and life outside the school.

Rutherford, for example, in Chapter 6, focuses on his investigation of reading instruction and the strategies teachers in the high-performing Hispanic schools use for successful second-language acquisition. The teachers interviewed and observed used a whole language approach to literacy that took into account the interests, experiences, and language proficiency of their students. The teachers referred to the various instructional techniques they used to develop literacy, rather than a particular language arts or reading series. Calling on a variety of materials and instructional strategies, these teachers went beyond the traditional 45-minute reading period per day. Most teachers reported that they taught reading "all day long"! To make reading material, regardless of subject area, more comprehensible to students, teachers used the students' native language without hesitation. They worked collaboratively in order to help students meet expectations, often coordinating thematic units that incorporated their various content areas.

Advocacy-Oriented Assessment

The final chapter reporting the findings of our study focuses on assessment, which unfortunately in the case of Hispanic youth too often is misused. Until recently little attention has been directed toward the proper use of standardized assessment tools or the effectiveness of teacher-developed devices to assess limited English proficient students. Paredes Scribner found in her study that "best assessment practices" take into consideration the entire learning environment, the effectiveness of instruction, and the availability of resources and strategies needed to remedy students' learning difficulties. Staff in the high-performing Hispanic schools maximized resources by working closely through consultation and collaboration on behalf of students. The overall philosophy of these schools and the leadership of the principals facilitated growth and empowerment of teachers and assessment personnel.

In the schools discussed in this book, advocacy-oriented assessment took place. Alternative assessment procedures were used to reflect literacy learning across content areas. Teachers used standardized test scores only to provide information after a period of instruction during which interventions and modifications were provided. Teachers used portfolio assessment, curriculum-based assessment, whole language instruction, informal reading inventories, and informal procedures for assessing competencies and weaknesses in writing and spelling. Each student was expected to achieve at the highest level possible and no student failed in the effective border school.

IMPLEMENTING BEST PRACTICES FOUND IN THE HIGH-PERFORMING HISPANIC SCHOOLS

The closing chapter, "Creating Learning Communities for High-Performing Hispanic Students: A Conceptual Framework," is intended to provide not only insights, information, and hope, but also the inclination among those educators who read the entire book to think more deeply about transforming schools into better places, where all children, and particularly Hispanic youth, can flourish and reach their ultimate potential. Our hope is that we will excite teachers, principals, and all other members of the learning community to take action, become agents of change, and do what is morally right in fighting for high-impact schools. Finally, we believe the ideas in this book are both intellectually and practically oriented, providing both a framework and the strategies necessary for bringing about change in the learning conditions of Hispanic youth (and the larger population of students as well). This book will help those who read it to think more deeply about:

- Creating a community of learners through striving for personal best, identifying personal world views, practicing team learning, and developing a shared vision.
- Establishing a caring environment, governing for student success, and empowering the school community to foster collaborative governance and leadership.
- Building collaborative relationships with parents and empowering the surrounding community.
- Creating a culture of caring—an inclusive student-centered classroom culture—and cultivating funds of knowledge to nurture a culturally responsive pedagogy.
- Conducting advocacy-oriented assessments for appropriate and relevant language/psychoeducational evaluations of high-poverty, linguistically diverse students.

REFERENCES

August, D., & Garcia, E. (1988). *Language minority education in the United States: Research, policy and practice.* Chicago: Charles C. Thomas.

Cummins, J. (1984). *Bilingualism and special education: Issues in assessment and pedagogy*. San Diego, CA: College Hill.

Cummins, J. (1986). Empowering minority students: A framework for intervention. *Harvard Educational Review, 56*(1), 18–35.

Digest of Educational Statistics. (1990). Washington, DC: National Center for Education Statistics, U.S. Department of Education.

Duran, R. (1989). Assessment and instruction of at-risk Hispanic students. *Exceptional Children, 56*(2), 154–158.

Figueroa, R., & Garcia, E. (1994). Issues in testing students from culturally and linguistically diverse backgrounds. In F. Schultz (Ed.), *Multicultural education, 95/96* (2nd ed.; pp. 147–156). Guilford, CT: Duskin.

Garcia, E. (1994). *Understanding and meeting the challenge of student cultural diversity*. Boston: Houghton Mifflin.

Johnson, R. (1994, October). Attrition rates are going up: Texas rates higher than national average. *Intercultural Development Research Association Newsletter, XXI*(9), 6–9.

Levin, H. M. (1986). *Educational reform for disadvantaged students: An emerging crisis*. Washington, DC: National Education Association.

McDonnell, L. M., & Hill, P. T. (1993). *Newcomers in American schools: Meeting the educational needs of immigrant youth*. Santa Monica, CA: Rand Corporation.

Moll, L. C. (1988). Educating Latino students. *Language Arts, 64*, 315–324.

Moll, L. C., & Whitmore, K. F. (1993). Vygotsky in classroom practice: Moving from individual transmission to social interaction. In E. A. Forman, N. Minick, & C. A. Stone (Eds.), *Contexts for learning: Sociocultural dynamics in children's development* (pp. 19–42). New York: Oxford University Press.

Montejano, D. (1996). On the future of Anglo-Mexican relations in the United States. In D. Montejano (Ed.), *Chicano politics and society in the late 20th century* (pp. 234–257). Austin: University of Texas Press.

Oakes, J. (1990). *Multiplying inequalities: The effects of race, social class, and tracking on opportunities to learn mathematics and science*. Santa Monica, CA: Rand.

Paredes Scribner, A. (1995). Advocating for Hispanic high school students: Research-based educational practices. *The High School Journal, 78*(4), 206–214.

Patton, M. Q. (1990). *Qualitative evaluation and research methods* (2nd ed.). Thousand Oaks, CA: Sage.

Reyes, P. (1990). Factors affecting the commitment of children at risk to stay in school. In J. Lakebrink (Ed.), *Children at risk* (pp. 150–175). Chicago, IL: G. Anderson Publications.

Reyes, P., & Paredes Scribner, A. (1995). Educational reform, students of color, and potential outcomes. *The High School Journal, 78*(4), 215–225.

Reyes, P., & Scribner, J. (1996). *Creating communities for Hispanic youth: Training modules*. (Available from the University of Texas at Austin, SZB 310, Austin, TX 78712).

Romo, H. D., & Falbo, T. (1996). *Latino high school graduation*. Austin: University of Texas Press.

Snapshot. (1996). Texas Education Agency. Austin: Department of School Support Services.

Stake, R. E. (1995). *The art of case study research*. Thousand Oaks, CA: Sage.

Tharp, R. G., & Gallimore, R. (1988). *Rousing minds to life: Teaching, learning and schooling in social context*. Cambridge, UK: Cambridge University Press.

U.S. Bureau of the Census. (1992, September). *Census of population and housing: Summary Tape File 3A, 1990* (CD90-3A-54, CD-ROM). Washington, DC: U.S. Government Printing Office.

U.S. General Accounting Office. (1994). *Limited English proficiency: A growing and costly educational challenge facing many school districts* (Report No. GAO-HEHS-94-38). Washington, DC: Author.

Valencia, R. R., & Aburto, S. (1991). The uses and abuses of educational testing: Chicanos as a case in point. In R. R. Valencia (Ed.), *Chicano school failure and success* (pp. 203–251). New York: Falmer Press.

CHAPTER 2

Establishing Collaborative Governance and Leadership

Lonnie H. Wagstaff and Lance D. Fusarelli

The purpose of our study was to examine the governance, leadership, and administrative support patterns of high-poverty, high-performing schools. It was assumed, and the literature provided support, that the actions and behaviors of school administrators have an impact on school effectiveness and achievement. Some of these patterns promote student success, while others may not. It was the intent of this study to examine the behavior and leadership styles of successful school administrators for the purpose of assisting other administrators in educating students who traditionally have been ignored or undereducated by the school system.

COMMON THEMES

Several distinct themes common to all the schools emerged from the data. These themes reflected patterns of governance, styles of leadership, and patterns of administrative support common in effective schools along the border. Each will be examined in detail in the following section. Excerpts from the interviews are provided to highlight these themes.

Communication and Collaboration Among Administrators, Professional Staff, and the Community

Communication and collaboration were identified as essential elements of school success. Several members of numerous site-based, decision-making committees (SBDM committees) noted that the process of shared decision

Lessons from High-Performing Hispanic Schools: Creating Learning Communities. Copyright © 1999 by Teachers College, Columbia University. All rights reserved. ISBN 0-8077-3830-1 (pbk.), ISBN 0-8077-3831-X (cloth). Prior to photocopying items for classroom use, please contact the Copyright Clearance Center, Customer Service, 222 Rosewood Dr., Danvers, MA 01923, USA, tel. (508) 750-8400.

making itself facilitated open communication and collaboration by promoting the sharing of ideas among committee members, department heads, administrators, and teachers. One parent serving on an SBDM committee spoke for many when she stated, "They [administrators and teachers] do listen to what I have to say. Any recommendations that I made or any suggestions that I made were listened to." Several respondents noted that "you have to have effective communication to be successful."

This process of collaboration extended well beyond the parameters of site-based management. Effective schools were suffused with a high degree of coordinated planning and communication among teachers and staff. One school used a system of peer evaluations (a minimum of one every 6 weeks) to promote effective teaching strategies and techniques among the staff. One principal asserted that communication was an essential element in school success. She stated her belief that the school was effective because "we are developing a lot of communication tools." These included a calendar of events that was produced every week and given to all staff and put in student activity calendars and parent newsletters.

The principal noted that

> There is a better flow of communication. People know what is going on not only at the school but at the main office. Everyone in the school knows where the administrative staff is at all times. I want them to know where I am and what I'm doing and why I'm off this campus, because my job is to be here. People around the neighborhood know what is going on.

The most effective schools kept parents well informed about what was going on at the school. One teacher noted that "parents are always kept abreast of everything that is going on." Parents at one school were even given a copy of the school's report card. The principal at this school "makes it a point to get the parents involved."

A Clear Coherent Vision and Mission

The existence of a clear, coherent vision among administrators, teachers, and parents was found in the most effective schools in the study. "We all work together," one SBDM member said. "We all know that we are here for all the kids. We try to work for the whole school." Another SBDM member stated, "We focused on attitudes of everybody, the parents, teachers, and students. We took students to retreats to change the attitude of the school." Administrative leadership is essential for promoting a shared vision of the school. One principal remarked that "we are all working toward the same goal."

Leadership Styles of Effective Administrators

Principals of effective schools viewed themselves as facilitators whose job was to get teachers, parents, and students the resources they needed to achieve success. One principal stated, "My role is to listen to whoever comes to me and not try to make what they want impossible." Another principal stated, "I tend to be very much available for my teachers if they need something. If they need something, I try to get it for them. I try to let them know that I am here to support them." A third principal asked, "How can we [administrators] help you [teachers] serve this child?"

Effective administrators tended to be highly visible on campus and seemed always to be in motion rather than cloistered behind a desk from which they seldom emerged. One SBDM member stated:

> When administrators are out in the halls or in the classroom, visibility is high, the kids and the faculty see that, and it shows that they care. It helps with classroom discipline. It helps with the teachers. You stand a little taller and walk a little straighter.

The willingness of administrators to "go the extra mile" infused the entire staff. The degree of dedication found among the staffs (administrators, paraprofessionals, and teachers) of the most effective schools was extraordinary. Many teachers in these schools went so far as to give up their conference periods to offer additional instructional assistance to students. Some principals offered to compensate teachers for teaching extra classes, particularly those aimed at remediating students and preparing them for the TAAS test.

Principals of effective schools recognized the importance of building trust among staff, teachers, parents, students, and the community. One principal noted that "trust has got to be there for a school to have a good positive climate where kids feel safe and kids want to come. That's the foundation of any kind of good organization, that support and concern for each other."

Effective administrators understood that everyone had individual styles (both teaching and learning) and they were willing to accommodate these differences to achieve success. Principals in effective schools recognized the importance of building on the strengths of the staff and the students. "We try to do as much as we can to enhance whatever it is they do good," one principal stated. "We just build on that."

Effective administrators and school board members respected the professional judgment of teachers and staff and gave them the autonomy necessary to do their jobs effectively. Teachers consistently identified this as one of the most essential elements of school success. Effective administrators knew when to let go and provide the means for staff to solve their own problems. One principal stated:

> I think of myself more as a coach. I very much value the expertise of the people around me. I surround myself with people who are very competent in what they do. I treat them as professionals. I am not a watchdog-type principal. I try to treat my people as professionals and I try to deal with [them] professionally.

These administrators recognized that the teaching staffs were the key to school effectiveness. When asked what made their schools successful, one school board member replied, "I believe that teachers deserve the most credit." Another board member said, "Teachers make the difference." A principal went a step further and stated, "The leader needs to realize when he/she is in the way, when to step aside and let your people expand."

Humanistic Leadership

One principal described her leadership style as "humanistic" and expressed genuine concern for the values, capacities, and achievements of her students. Consistent with this approach was her belief that "if you intend to do something to kids, you meet with the kids." This principal turned her leadership style into a governance philosophy and expressed displeasure over those who did not consult with the students in decisions most affecting them. "What really bothers me is that some of the staff still believe that we are going to make a decision and tell the kids; that upsets me," she stated.

Principals of effective schools modeled the behavior they expected from teachers and staff. A principal stated, "I try to model what I say. I am a hard worker and I model that." One principal refused to do paperwork during school hours. Another principal said, "The number one thing is modeling that positive attitude and that commitment and that dedication toward children."

Empowerment of Professional Staff, Parents, and the Community

Some of the respondents suggested that site-based management contributed to school success by encouraging administrators to allow classroom teachers to make the most effective decisions for their students. One teacher on the SBDM committee stated that involvement in "the decision-making process is helping me in the classroom. I'm . . . able to make decisions for my students." A board member stated, "They [teachers] know what is going on. They can see that they make a difference; that if they have a problem, they will be heard. It is not like it used to be 7 years ago where they wouldn't say anything; they would be reprimanded; they would be fired; they would be intimidated."

Site-based management contributed to school effectiveness by placing the responsibility for school success at the campus level; principals, teachers, and parents were empowered to make fundamental decisions about what was best for their schools. One teacher stated, "I feel that it is very important that we as teachers or we as staff get involved in the decision-making process because it affects our students' success. It affects all aspects of the school function." Another stated, "It is incredible how teachers have been included in decision making. We are still a little overwhelmed . . . all of a sudden we have more power."

This process encouraged open communication and collaboration among participants and provided more opportunities for involvement in decision making. One SBDM member stated, "Everybody has a voice here. It might not be heard all the time, but everybody is given the opportunity to express themselves." Another commented that "it is nice to be involved in all the decisions that are being made for the school. It's nice and important." A parent serving on a committee stated, "If you have something to say, you are welcome to say it. They [administrators and teachers] will look at what we think."

Several members of the SBDM committee on one campus said, "Coming to SBDM, you learn what's going on in the school. It is very informative for the parents." Members of the SBDM committee at another school praised the principal for her willingness to listen and accept input from the committee. They stated that "she has been very good at listening to us. She gives us a lot of leeway and she wants a lot of input." One teacher on the SBDM committee summed up the feelings of many when he stated that "ultimately, SBDM, to be effective, is going to be based on the administrator's ability and willingness to listen and take input."

There were differences in the degree to which site-based management was practiced in each school. Most schools had been working with site-based management for less than 5 years, but one school had not developed campus guidelines and bylaws until the year of our study. Although there was variation as to the numerical representation of participants on the site-based management committees, all but one of the committees had teacher and parent representatives. Many included representatives from the community as well. One committee also had a student representative.

The site-based management committees had varying degrees of responsibility over discipline policies, attendance policies, personnel, budget, curriculum, and instruction. The frequency with which the campus SBDM committees met varied from school to school—they met once a month, every 6 weeks, bimonthly, or even once a week. Most district-wide SBDM committees met once a month or less often.

Whether the principal had formal veto power over decisions made by the SBDM committee varied from school to school and district to district. In one school, the school principal retained veto power over the decisions of the SBDM committee but this power was seldom used. One principal remarked that "I have not used it [the veto] yet in the 3 years that we have been a council." One principal retained veto power over committee decisions and did use it. However, on this campus, the principal was required to justify to the committee in writing when she did so.

On the other hand, on some campuses the principal did not have veto authority over committee decisions. An SBDM member at a school stated, "Many times we [the committee] will say no to the administration." Decisions at most of the schools were arrived at by consensus among SBDM members. At one school, decisions were made via voting. In case of a tie, the principal would cast the deciding vote.

Consistent with the literature, this study found that principals exerted tremendous influence over the extent to which decision making was spread throughout the school. One parent noted that "the administration now is more receptive [toward SBDM], more open, more flexible. I feel that I am being taken into consideration. Before I felt that it didn't matter how I felt."

Anyone could place items on the agenda; it was an open process, although the principal almost always had the responsibility for drawing up the agenda for the meetings. Agendas and meeting minutes usually were posted in the hallway. One campus distributed copies of the minutes of each meeting to the entire staff. "That way," said the principal, "everybody knows what happened at the meeting." On all the campuses, anyone could attend the SBDM committee meetings and voice concerns. However, only those duly elected to the committee could engage in the final decision-making process—voting or consensus finding.

District-level support was critical to the success of site-based management. One principal stated, "The school board has been very supportive of site-based decision making." Another commented that the district took a "hands-off" approach and did not try to micromanage schools in the district. This theme was reiterated by two board members who suggested that board members needed to understand that their job was to make district policy rather than administer the schools. "We let administrators, teachers, paraprofessionals, bus drivers, everybody do their own thing. It's a hands-off board," replied one board member. Another board member stated, "I do not want to be involved in managing the campuses." One board member stated, "Let administrators be administrators; let teachers be teachers. Stay away from them." School boards in effective schools supported the efforts of administrators and teachers and sought to provide, as one board member said, "the finances for whatever it is you need to achieve success."

In most districts, the superintendent and central office staff were open and accessible. School relations with board members most often were described as collegial. However, all the districts placed some restrictions on site-based management in decisions within certain domains, usually in the areas of budget and personnel. The districts in the study still preserved control over the budgetary allocation for each school. One SBDM member complained, "What part of the budget do we see? Just the part that we can play around with, but we really haven't seen the entire thing."

The personnel policy in many districts that schools hire first from a district-wide pool of applicants is another example of district constraints on site-based management. This limits the flexibility of campus decision makers. It also can create tension between district and campus administrators. One principal complained that "since I am accountable for test scores, and since my job depends on test scores, I still have to take the person who is left in the pool whether I want to or not; that to me is a real problem."

In this respect, site-based management had not produced full decentralization at any of the schools in the study. One SBDM member stated that central office involvement "has affected some of the decisions we have made. They have slowed us down." Another noted, "There is a tendency sometimes for upper administration not to want to let go." One SBDM member suggested that the relationship between central office and campus decision makers was akin to the relationship between a parent and a child; she stated, "We are fledglings . . . we want to fly and they don't think we are ready."

Together with the idea of empowerment was the belief that involvement in decision making facilitated ownership in group decisions. One principal stated, "If you make people believe that it is their idea, it is going to be done better than if it was my idea being imposed on somebody." Another believed that "if you bring your staff into the major decisions and they buy into it . . . if they are a part of the decision-making [process], the system is successful."

Another principal suggested that "the more people that are involved in decision making, it makes the whole school feel as [if] they're a part of the whole and more apt to work together. It's like ownership. The more informed you are, the better decisions you make. If you create the environment that you're willing to listen and to take suggestions, people want to be part of the environment. If they don't think you want to, then people will just withdraw." One principal stated, "We try to use a lot of 'we' here;

it is not my school or my department." A teacher on the SBDM committee said, "The teachers feel that they are buying into it [decisions made under SBDM], that it is our school."

Teachers and staff were active participants in the personnel decisions of each school. One principal actively involved all the assistant principals in hiring a colleague. In most schools, members of the SBDM committee participated in hiring campus personnel. In many of these schools, the principal usually had final authority for selecting a candidate. In one school, the principal presented three possible candidates and the committee chose among the three. A teacher on the committee remarked, "I think we should have a voice [in personnel decisions]."

The empowerment of students was another theme emerging from the data. Administrators and staff at effective schools recognized the importance of involving students in the decision-making processes of the school, although that involvement usually was limited to consultation. "We hear them [students] out on certain issues," one SBDM member explained. "We allow them to be a part of decision making." A principal stated, "I treat students the same way I treat adults."

Importance of Professional Development

The continued professional development of staff was a recurrent theme in the interviews. One principal stated, "You aren't gonna learn a new idea by being here . . . because the work keeps you busy all day long. . . . I have been allowed by the district to visit other campuses and to go to state conferences and learn" new ideas, methods, and approaches. The sharing of ideas was an important element to continued school improvement. Teachers and staff visited other campuses to engage in the sharing of ideas. In many of the schools we visited, teachers were encouraged to make presentations at professional conferences.

The emphasis on staying current with the research literature was found throughout the study but was particularly prevalent in the most effective schools. One SBDM member related, "A lot of what we do is derived from the research." Another proudly noted that "we are very up-to-date when it comes to the research literature." Teachers and staff collaborated and shared materials and ideas for student success.

Many administrators voiced a preference for the trainer-of-trainers model of professional development as opposed to having staff attend one-day workshops where the presenter comes in, makes a presentation, and then leaves. The trainer model ensured that trained consultants remained on campus. As one principal mentioned, this method places "the responsibility on us."

Continued professional development was identified as a key ingredient of continuous school improvement. "The whole staff has been through a lot of training the last 4 or 5 years and that has made a big difference," said one SBDM member. One principal noted that "we have a good staff development program. There is a lot of flexibility" in terms of how much and what types of staff development are offered in the school. Most of the districts offered district-wide training in site-based management, but one district left it up to the individual campuses. One of the districts in the study paid a stipend to those training in site-based management.

An Ethic of Care

Effective schools consistently exhibited an ethic of care in their culture. One principal reflected, "We found out early on that we had to become a caring institution." Another remarked that "we care about our kids and we want to help them as much as we can. We will do whatever it takes because we care." Another stated, "Children's needs determine what we do." Yet another responded, "We truly care . . . [and] will go that extra mile." This produced a change in the atmosphere of many of the schools and led to a reduction in gang and discipline problems. Parents were involved extensively in creating an atmosphere of community in the schools.

This ethic of care applied not only to students and the community, but to the teaching staff as well. One teacher noted, "The administration cares so much about us and they believe in us. We are always being told that we are the best." This positive reinforcement flowed from the administration to the staff, parents, students, and the community.

Success for All

Related to the ethic of care found in the effective schools we studied was the belief among administrators and teachers that students who traditionally had been labeled as disadvantaged were just as bright and capable as those who are more advantaged. These schools explicitly denied (and, more important, internally rejected) the cultural deprivation argument prevalent in much of the literature on effective schools. One principal made this very clear when she stated, "We have proved that living in an economically disadvantaged [area], that we can run with the best and our kids are just as smart; they just have not had the experiences that perhaps your kids and my kids have had." Another stated, "We have to make them [the students] believe in themselves because we believe in them. These kids are just as smart. All children can learn but at a different pace."

One particularly outstanding school was moving toward implementing the accelerated school's philosophy of trying to give all students access to enriched instructional materials, which previously had been limited to only a few, labeled as gifted. This campus was in the process of getting all the teachers trained in Gifted and Talented (GT) methods so they could implement this philosophy throughout the school. The GT teachers were doing presentations for all students using GT strategies.

An Emphasis on Accountability

Administrators and staff accepted responsibility for school performance and analyzed student data to improve school effectiveness. Texas Assessment of Academic Skills (TAAS) data were used to determine areas of weakness. Scores were presented and discussed among the entire professional staff. Site-based decision making made staff more accountable to the schools. The school board could no longer hire friends or family for jobs. One principal stated that "we found out that by selecting our own people . . . they are more accountable to us."

Each school held itself accountable to its campus improvement plan and was willing to take whatever steps were necessary to achieve the goals set by the committee. This included offering TAAS tutoring after school as well as on Saturdays.

Rather than viewing shared decision making as a threat to their authority, many principals viewed it as a way to hold more people accountable for school performance. One principal took many decisions to the SBDM committee, even those for which council approval was not needed. By involving as many people as possible in decision making, she was able to make decisions everyone's property, not just hers. She stated, "It's not me anymore; it's the campus council. It's hard to attack the council. It is not difficult to attack one person." This principal saw site-based management as a way to gain collective ownership of decisions and thereby diffuse accountability through the school system.

A Culture of Innovation

Administrators in effective schools were willing to try almost anything to improve their schools. As a result, these schools had a dynamic quality frequently absent from the traditional bureaucratic model of schooling. One principal stated, "The campus is on the move. There is no new program that we haven't tried or applied for." Administrators in these schools encouraged innovation in the quest for continual improvement. One principal stated, "If something doesn't work, we will try something else." One SBDM member said, "We try to incorporate everything possible that is out there so that we can see what works and what does not."

One teacher said, "She [the principal] allows us the flexibility to try new ideas or try new things and . . . implement all these new ideas for the benefit of our students and for the success of our school." A principal at another school agreed, stating that "it is an atmosphere where you can experiment and you can flop and nobody is going to get upset with you. Nobody is going to yell at you. You are free to give your ideas and expand on them."

BARRIERS TO INVOLVEMENT

Despite the effectiveness of the schools in the study, they were not without problems. The single largest barrier to full community involvement was the unfamiliarity of most parents and community members with the somewhat complex operation of the schools. This problem was particularly acute in the area of site-based management. One SBDM member stated:

> What I see as one of the biggest obstacles to it—we're sitting there discussing things these people [parents and community members] don't know anything about. I can see where it can be awfully frustrating for them. It's unfortunate but we have so many things to get through that to take the time to make all these explanations is a little difficult to do.

The unfamiliarity with the detailed operation of the school and the somewhat arcane educational lingo posed significant barriers to the full, active involvement of parents and the community.

A few parents and members of the community who were serving on the SBDM committees at some campuses complained that some of the training manuals were incomprehensible and written by someone "with a 600 I.Q." One parent summed up the feelings for many when she complained, "Sometimes it is hard to get the idea. Sometimes you wonder what you just read."

The lack of training affected the degree to which parents and the community became involved in site-based management at most schools, although lack of training was identified as a barrier to teacher and staff involvement as well. It also limited the extent to which the campus and district-wide SBDM committees participated in decision making. One SBDM member noted that "the state told us to do SBDM but made no plans to really train us for it." Another stated, "We have not gotten training on that [making personnel decisions], not specifically to hire people. That can bring about lawsuits if you are not careful about what you do." The most frequently voiced complaint among teachers, parents, and members of the community was the lack of training in site-based management.

Another barrier was the perception that some superintendents, teachers, and staff were not involved enough in the community. One board member questioned the commitment of a superintendent to a community because he did not live there. "We need to get a superintendent who is going to live in this community and be committed to this community," the board member said. Another board member in the same district did not feel that some of the principals, teachers, and staff were involved enough in the community. "That is one area that I think would lead to substantial improvement . . . to see the kids in a different light. There is very little involvement in the community. It would be a different world" if they were more involved in the community, the board member suggested.

It is important to note that the most effective school in the study went to great lengths to ensure that staff understood the community from which their students came. Teachers at this school made home visits at the beginning of each year to get to know parents better. Every teacher also rode student buses during the first week of school to get to know where the students lived and the problems and issues they faced and had to solve. Administrators at this school encouraged teachers to write at least one positive note to parents regarding their children's progress in school. Faculty took every opportunity to send parents information they could use to help their children be successful in school. Teachers kept a log of how many times they contacted parents. Finally, instead of sending report cards home, parents went with students to pick up the report cards at the school. At this time, the student led a parent–teacher conference in which the student explained what he or she had done the past 6 weeks at school.

FACILITATING COLLABORATIVE GOVERNANCE
AND LEADERSHIP: KEY FINDINGS

The findings of the study are consistent with much of the earlier research on effective schools. Raywid (1992) notes that in successful schools, both teachers and students have a significant amount of autonomy and responsibility, are encouraged to cooperate with their peers, are treated as important and valued contributors to the school, and are controlled more by a shared set of common values and guiding principles than by rigid rules and regulations. Bergman (1992) found that effective principals learn to let go and provide the means for staff to solve their own problems. This includes learning to listen, establishing open and known patterns of communication, investing time and effort to understand individual styles, promoting open communication, building trust, and promoting autonomy. Effective teachers place a high value on professional autonomy and look to administrators to provide needed resources to help them achieve their goals (Mathews, 1988).

Schools with effective governance arrangements have higher levels of teacher collegiality and maintain positive school–community relations (Bennett et al., 1992; Cummins, 1986). The findings of this study are consistent with that research. Collegial relations in the school appear to have a strong impact on effectiveness (Funkhouser, 1992). Principals in effective schools solve problems through collaboration (Funkhouser, 1992). They promote collaborative planning, collegial work, and an atmosphere conducive to experimentation and evaluation (Purkey & Smith, 1983).

There was variation in the decision-making structures of the schools in the study. All the schools practiced site-based management, although the degree of shared decision making varied from school to school. This finding is consistent with previous research on site-based management (Wagstaff & Reyes, 1992). The value of site-based management seems to lie in its function as an enabler of structural and process change through involvement, open communication, and collaborative decision making in schools. The fact that some principals retained final decision-making authority (i.e., veto power) did not seem to hinder the degree of open communication and collaboration among school administrators, teachers, and parents.

There was near unanimous agreement that site-based management contributed significantly to the creation of an open, collaborative environment in the schools. This is consistent with research by Riley (1984), who found that teachers are satisfied if they influence or make recommendations on building-level matters, without actually making the final decision. Being part of the process appears to be more important than having the last word in the decision itself (Bair, 1992). Staff participation in planning and policy committees or task forces encourages interaction on school practices and professional concerns (Stevenson, 1987). Such meetings allow for the exploration of solutions to school problems, permit staff to influence the development of school policies, and promote feelings of ownership and efficacy in the implementation of policies (David & Peterson, 1984).

Research suggests that an important function of administrative leadership for improving school effectiveness is the maintenance of a school climate conducive to learning. Wayson (1988) emphasized that excellent schools are run by staff who are committed to creating a positive climate that communicates to students that they are wanted, are valued, and can succeed. Staff create ways to involve students in the life of the school. This may

involve approaches that value linguistic and cultural diversity and that promote cultural pluralism (Stedman, 1987). All school leaders in the study
were vocal proponents of the virtues of linguistic diversity and cultural
pluralism. Such traits were looked upon as strengths rather than weaknesses,
unfortunately a view not prevalent in many schools throughout the nation.

Effective principals are confident in the ability of their children to learn,
are committed to seeing that all of their students receive the tools necessary
for success, and have compassion for and understanding of their students
and the communities from which they come (Lomotey, 1989). In a study
of effective high schools with large numbers of Latino language-minority
students, Lucas, Henze, and Donato (1990) found that school leaders make
the education of language-minority students a priority. These leaders hold
high expectations for language-minority students, are knowledgeable of
instructional and curricular approaches to teaching language-minority students and communicate this knowledge to staff, and take a strong leadership
role in strengthening curriculum and instruction for all students, including
language-minority students. The findings of this study strongly support this
approach. School leaders explicitly rejected cultural deprivation arguments
and other deficit models of schooling, seeking instead a rigorous curriculum
for all students, a curriculum not limited to or reserved for a select few.

RECOMMENDATIONS FOR PROFESSIONAL DEVELOPMENT

It is well known that improving low-performing and underperforming
schools, particularly those with large numbers of limited English proficient
students, is not an easy task; nor is it one whose solutions can be found in
a recipe from a cookbook. It is important to point out that there is no
single formula or prescription for success; no single combination of dazzling
procedures will produce an effective school (Lucas, Henze, & Donato, 1990).
As Pink (1992) notes, in school reform efforts, some school districts have
applied a prepackaged program for an effective school in all their schools,
without allowing each school to tailor the program to its particular needs.
Clearly, such strategies rarely have improved student achievement. However,
schools can begin to work toward success by following the lead of effective
schools in ways that are appropriate and realistic for their particular school
settings (Lucas, Henze, & Donato, 1990).

There are several recommendations for practitioners desiring to assist
administrators in creating more effective schools. These include:

- *Stressing the importance of creating a collaborative work environment and a leadership style that emphasizes modeling behavior, administrator as facilitator, dedication, hard work, high visibility, building trust, learn-*

ing to listen, understanding individual styles, and providing teachers with the resources they need. Administrators who are self-centered and who rule with an iron fist are not effective. It is important that administrators recognize the talent of faculty and staff and collaborate with them to create the conditions necessary for student success. Teachers and staff respond well to administrators who are willing to work with them to solve the complex problems of effectively educating students along the border. Accordingly, we recommend that a model of professional development for administrators be created to help them become more open, communicative, and collaborative with faculty, staff, students, and the community.

• *Encouraging open communication among staff and the community.* In an organization as complex as a school, open communication among administrators, staff, teachers, parents, students, and the community is essential for success. A system of open communication allows more people to become involved and participate in schools. It also forges links between schools and communities. Accordingly, we recommend a model of professional development for administrators be created to enhance understanding of and skill in such communication. There should be two dimensions to this professional development program—interpersonal and organizational communication, understanding, and skill.

• *Creating a clear vision and mission of what is to be accomplished.* It is essential that administrators, staff, teachers, parents, students, and the community share a common vision for success and have a detailed plan for achieving that success. Schools cannot function effectively if staff operate at cross-purposes. It is essential that a common vision and plan for school improvement be developed to which all participants agree and are committed. Accordingly, we recommend a model of professional development for administrators be created that emphasizes such goals.

• *Respecting the professional judgment of teachers and staff and giving them the autonomy to do their jobs.* Administrators need to recognize that they don't have all the answers to improving education and must be willing to respect the judgment of the professional teaching staff. This includes learning to let go, get out of the way, and provide the means for staff to solve their own problems. Administrators should serve as resource people for the faculty. Accordingly, we recommend a model of professional development for administrators be created to promote development of such habits.

• *Providing extensive professional development for administrators, faculty, staff, and parents.* Schools cannot fulfill their mission if administrators, faculty, staff, and parents are not properly trained. This includes training in effective methods of curriculum development, instructional delivery, and site-based management. Accordingly, we recommend a model of professional development be created to train these groups in effective instructional and governance strategies.

• *Fostering a strong belief in and commitment to the potential of all children to achieve at high levels and an explicit denial of the cultural deprivation argument. This should include access for all children to gifted and talented curriculum and instruction.* The best schools actively promote the belief that all students, whatever their background, can learn and they demonstrate that commitment by providing access to high-content materials and instruction for all students. An explicit refusal to accept failure pervades such schools. Accordingly, we recommend a model of professional development be created that fosters these beliefs and provides the knowledge and skill to work toward achieving them.

• *Emphasizing results through accountability and a willingness to try innovative techniques and strategies to improve student achievement.* Administrators and staff in the most effective schools along the border refuse to lay blame for failure on students and insist on accepting responsibility for student performance. They work collaboratively and aggressively to seek improvement in student performance. They are willing to take whatever measures are necessary to achieve success. The result is an environment that fosters a culture of success and innovation. By accepting primary responsibility for student success and being willing to be judged on that basis, administrators and staff become active forces for change in schools. Accordingly, we recommend a model of professional development be created that fosters such beliefs and provides the knowledge and skills to build such a culture.

REFERENCES

Bair, L. H. (1992). What research has to say about school-based management. *Catalyst for Change, 21*(2), 17–19.

Bennett, A. L. et al. (1992). *Charting reform: The principals' perspective. Report on a survey of Chicago public school principals.* Chicago: Consortium on Chicago School Research.

Bergman, A. B. (1992). Lessons for principals from site-based management. *Educational Leadership, 50*(1), 48–51.

Cummins, J. (1986). Empowering minority students: A framework for intervention. *Harvard Educational Review, 56*(1), 18–35.

David, J. L., & Peterson, S. M. (1984). *Can schools improve themselves? A study of school-based improvement programs*. Palo Alto, CA: Bay Area Research Group.

Funkhouser, C. W. (1992). *Education in Texas: Policies, practices, and perspectives*. Scottsdale, AZ: Gorsuch Scarisbrick.

Lomotey, K. (1989). *African-American principals' school leadership and success*. Westport, CT: Greenwood Press.

Lucas, T., Henze, R., & Donato, R. (1990). Promoting the success of Latino language minority students: An exploratory study of six high schools. *Harvard Educational Review, 60*(3), 315–340.

Mathews, J. (1988). *Escalante: The best teacher in America*. New York: Henry Holt.

Pink, W. T. (1992). The politics of reforming urban schools. *Education and Urban Society, 25*(1), 96–113.

Purkey, S. C., & Smith, M. S. (1983). Effective schools: A review. *Elementary School Journal, 83*(4), 427–452.

Raywid, M. A. (1992). Why do these kids love school? *Phi Delta Kappan, 73*(8), 631–633.

Riley, D. (1984). Teacher utilization of avenues for participatory decision-making. *Journal of Educational Administration, 22*(1), 35–46.

Stedman, L. C. (1987). It's time we changed the effective schools formula. *Phi Delta Kappan, 69*(3), 215–224.

Stevenson, R. B. (1987). Autonomy and support: The dual needs of urban high schools. *Urban Education, 22*(3), 366–386.

Wagstaff, L., & Reyes, P. (1992, November). *Report on school site-based management*. Presentation to the State of Texas Educational Economic Policy Center, The University of Texas at Austin.

Wayson, W. W. (1988). *Up from excellence: The impact of the excellence movement on schools*. Bloomington, IN: Phi Delta Kappa.

CHAPTER 3

Building Collaborative Relationships with Parents

Jay D. Scribner, Michelle D. Young, and Anna Pedroza

Parent involvement encompasses a multitude of complex phenomena. Differences in the family structure, culture, ethnic background, social class, age, and gender represent only a few of the factors affecting interpretations of or generalizations about the nature of parent involvement. Notwithstanding the limitations these factors place on our findings, the "what" of parent involvement in the high-performing Hispanic schools we studied appears to depend on whom you ask: professional staff or family members. Opinions differed on what activities parents ought to be involved in, on who should be responsible for initiating these activities, and on what roles professionals and parents should play in facilitating the parent involvement responsibility. Thus, a determination of what parent involvement is, belies simple description. Our findings revealed the following themes: parents participating in formal and informal parental involvement activities, parents and school staff creating collaborative relationships, and school staff developing a people-oriented, professional atmosphere.

WHAT IS PARENT INVOLVEMENT?

Participating in Formal and Informal Activities

Clearly, the degree of formality or informality of parent involvement can vary immensely from activity to activity; however, for school staff and parents, descriptions fell more often into one of the two extremes. For example, the majority of professional school staff interviewed said that parental involvement means participating in activities such as school events, meetings, workshops, and governance activities, and working as teacher aides, tutors, and school advocates within the larger school community. For parents, informal activities at home were identified as the most important parent contributions to children's success in school. Checking homework assignments, reading and listening to children read, obtaining tutorial assistance, providing nurturance, instilling cultural values, talking with children, and sending them to school well fed, clean, and rested were among the informal activities parents saw as involvement with the educational process.

For the most part, teachers defined parent involvement as a way of supporting the academic achievement of students, whereas parents conceptualized involvement as a means of supporting the total well-being of children. Parents' concerns were not only with how well children performed academically, but also with nurturing values of respect, honor, cooperation, good behavior, and responsibility of their children at school. Thus, parents' activities at home (e.g., monitoring children's progress, encouraging children to stay in school, getting tutorial help for their children, providing emotional support, and the like) and at the school (e.g., establishing a communication network with teachers, volunteering time, becoming familiar with the school curriculum, understanding the importance of standardized testing, and the like) were undertaken in an effort to nurture and support children's affective and social development as well as academic progress (Erickson, 1987; Petrovich & Parsons, 1989).

Thus, for many professional staff, the level of parent involvement at a school was defined in terms of the absence or presence of parents at formal, school-initiated functions like PTA meetings or parent–teacher conferences, or serving in school volunteer capacities as hall monitors, library support personnel, clerical assistants, or classroom assistants. In fact, one district-level parent involvement coordinator was planning to give "Campus of the Year" awards for the campus with the most parent involvement. Such involvement often was based on the number of clock hours parents volunteered to participate in formal activities. For instance, a teacher at Francisco Villa Middle School exclaimed, "It would be nice if parents would initiate involvement more often rather than the teachers always having to contact them."

While formal school activities were important to parents, so were informal activities at home. Parents' emphasis on home activities that support children's schooling makes sense given contextual limitations. For example, public transportation was nonexistent for many parents who wanted to participate in formal school activities. Limited-income families often relied on a single automobile, which was used primarily by the head of the household to drive to employment sites long distances from the home. Many of the mothers either walked or took taxicabs to the school. Therefore, participating in volunteer work at the school or enjoying visibility among teachers and other professional staff would require inordinate effort on the part of many parents.

Because many working mothers had difficulty attending meetings sponsored by the school, especially during the day, formal parent involvement, and thus on-site visibility, was limited. Mothers who had the time to serve and had some mode of transportation or lived close enough to walk to school constituted the majority of parent volunteers at the school. Home contextual conditions narrowed the pool of volunteers engaged in formal parent involvement activities, and recognition of these factors drew attention to reinforcing and enhancing informal, instructional-related involvement in learning activities at home (Delgado-Gaitan, 1991; Southwest Educational Development Laboratory, 1994).

On the formal–informal continuum, high-performing Hispanic schools emphasize activities near the end of the continuum that focuses on facilitating more direct involvement of family members in their children's education within the home environment. This appears to be a key factor in facilitating parent contributions to children's increased academic achievement and social and psychological development (Epstein, 1992; Simich-Dudgeon, 1993) in the borderland schools along the Texas–Mexico border.

Creating Collaborative Relationships

What parent involvement means depends on whether the relationship between parents and school staff is top-down (school-centered), bottom-up (parent-centered), or collaborative. To bring about a change, someone or some group must advocate for it (Fullan, 1991). The professional staff of the border schools offered mixed responses on how to bring about meaningful parent involvement. Some staff members tended to think of parent involvement as a parent responsibility to be initiated by parents, rather than as a collaborative responsibility of the entire school community. In other words, parents must advocate for involvement in school. Others felt that school staff should advocate for parent involvement by providing parents with opportunities to advise on certain aspects of the educational process and to express their opinions to professionals who listen and respond by taking appropriate action. In either case, school-centered parent activities tended to include activities that focused on broadly conceived school issues, remotely related to classroom instruction and student achievement (Bermudez, 1994).

Although parents often were faced with certain barriers, such as inadequate transportation, lack of interpreters, and an unwelcome school environment, many still found ways to participate formally. These parents were adamant about understanding what was going on at the school and in the classroom, as well as finding out how well their children were performing academically. An example of advocacy was provided by a mother from Porfirio Diaz High School.

> I could tell at home he was having a hard time with his homework and I requested an ARD [Admission, Review, and Dismissal] meeting to have him tested. Years back, I met with a brick wall . . . I kept fighting and fighting and finally got it done. That is how I became involved. I knew that he needed all the help he could get, so it meant I had to be really involved.

Many of the parents mentioned that it was their responsibility to ensure that school personnel did everything possible for their children. Some parents who had children with disabilities or whose children were experiencing academic or disciplinary problems were concerned about transitions to higher grade levels.

Parent involvement also was defined in terms of different forms of collaboration, which included collaborative communication, two-way communication, and relationship-based communication (Villanueva & Hubbard, 1994). School-centered advocacy and parent-centered advocacy focused on either or both the school staff and parents. Collaborative relationships were characterized by the sharing of information, expertise, and power.

Collaboratively oriented teachers, for example, viewed parent involvement as a way to inform parents about school functions, meetings, classroom events, testing schedules, and individual student information. Similarly, for mothers in this study, parent involvement meant having access to information they otherwise might not be privileged to know. They communicated a desire to know what was going on in school, how their children were doing, and what teachers needed. This was especially true among parents of children in middle and high schools. A parent said, "I want to know why she [my daughter] is not doing well so I get acquainted with the teachers."

In an open, two-way communication form of collaboration, parents and teachers forged personal relationships that created a more durable structure for exchanging information. For example, sending notices to parents through students was not always a reliable method of communication. Consequently, some parents established personal relationships with teachers and other school staff. Parents who attended meetings or participated on committees were able to strengthen their collaboration with the school community. In this form of collaboration, parents were receptive to and, indeed, invited phone calls and other opportunities for personal contact. A parent from Porfirio Diaz High School said, "I want them to call me up and let me know—don't be afraid to call me at home, don't be afraid to call me at work."

Communication also was facilitated by the development of relationships among parents. Information networks among parents had the advantage of providing Spanish-speaking parents access to bilingual persons who could translate and not just relay information to them (Garcia, 1994). The more effective strategies found in the high-performing Hispanic schools involved parents working both with other parents and with the school staff to advocate for increased parental involvement in school activities and their children's education.

Developing a People-Oriented/Professional Atmosphere

A third area of collaboration involved the development and support of a school environment that facilitated personal contact, communication, and collaboration. Schools with collaborative environments were perceived as places where the individual, as a person, took precedence over a professional role, places where each person worked for the good of all. For example, a group of parents at Carranza Elementary School believed that being involved meant supporting all the children at the school. They described the students as being *todos son nuestros hijos* (all our children) and explained that "the good of one was the good of all."

One parent described how good it felt to walk into the school and be acknowledged and welcomed. The openness of the school's environment, caring attitudes of school staff, and positive interpersonal relationships empowered parents to participate in a shared power relationship, a collegial relationship for the betterment of the children. A simple smile, a friendly gesture, and an acknowledgment of respect allowed parents to become allies in the difficult task of educating their children. A high school parent said, "They make time to greet you and it makes you feel so much better."

Participating in environments where the individual is valued and respected sustained the involvement of many parents (Power, 1985). Many parents believed participation involved more than being concerned for their own child's education. In an environment where people come first, they felt empowered to be responsible for all the children in the school. One parent explained, "The truth is we should feel for all children. It would be selfish not to feel for all our children." Collaborative schools are places where people join together to serve the needs of all children, unencumbered by role differentiation. These are places that are neither top-down nor bottom-up; they are places where power is shared (Cummins, 1984; Johnson, 1993).

Perceptions of what parent involvement means in high-performing Hispanic schools selected for this study vary among school staff and those who are either parents or others who advocate for parents. Activities and relationships between school staff and parents span from the more formal school-centered activities to the more informal parent-centered activities. Activities that combine top-down, bottom-up, and reciprocating partnerships appear to enhance the school's climate, classroom instruction, and student achievement. Thus, the meaning of parent involvement is defined through the eyes of the beholder, especially in terms of differing perceptions of activities, relationships, and roles. In the next section, the question of "why" parent involvement is valued underscores the need for creating a balance of collaboration, sharing, and mutual respect.

WHY DO PARENTS AND SCHOOL STAFF VALUE PARENT INVOLVEMENT?

In general, school staff, including teachers, administrators, and parent specialists in the high-performing Hispanic schools, considered parent involvement an important way to serve the needs of both the school and the children. While parents valued similar considerations, their primary concerns were to assist their children academically and socially and to strengthen the relationship between the home and school. A secondary concern for parents was to be available as volunteers and fund raisers. Areas in which parents and school staff considered parent involvement to be of value were as follows:

Parents
Enhancing the school environment
Building and strengthening relationships
Showing concern for the development of the child
Providing role models for the child
Accruing benefits for oneself

School Staff
Increasing student achievement
Building and strengthening relationships
Creating a community environment
Garnering support and assistance
Providing parent education

What Parents Value

Enhancing the School Environment. Parents stressed the positive effects they could have on the school environment by becoming involved. By providing "extra eyes" for teachers, a group of middle school volunteers considered their involvement at the school a contribution to creating safer learning environments. Likewise, by solving problems overlooked by school staff, as in the case of one elementary school parent who volunteered her time to simply keep a door, too heavy for the children, open at a specified time each day of the week. Moreover, in those schools where parents' contributions were welcomed and where staff relationships with parents were well developed, English- and non-English-speaking parents had supportive communication networks to exchange information and develop social relationships. In these settings parents spoke positively of schools and described how they felt they were part of the staff. They felt they were needed, empowered, and an integral part of the school's community. This collaborative relationship allowed parents to build and strengthen relationships with all participants in the school's leadership.

Building and Strengthening Relationships. Parents often acknowledged the importance of establishing a strong working relationship with the school. They took the initiative to become informed about what went on in the school. They inquired about what their children were learning and what they were experiencing in school. In short, it was important to demonstrate how much they valued education by taking the initiative to be better informed about what went on in the school.

An example of how one mother developed a strong relationship with school staff resulted from a traumatic incident experienced by her daughter. The daughter suffered from depression and anxiety attacks. Since keeping the child out of school would be in noncompliance with school policy, the mother sought out a collaborative arrangement with school officials to remedy the situation. Ultimately, the mother took the initiative to become a daily volunteer at the school, placing herself in an easily accessible position for the daughter whenever feelings of anxiety surfaced. While this represents one of the more extreme examples of how parents and school staff worked collaboratively to build and strengthen relationships between the home and the school, this parent personified a common characteristic of parents working in the collaboratively caring environment of the high-performing Hispanic schools.

Showing Concern for the Development of the Child. Parents generally described their motivation for involvement as expressions of their concern and love for their children, and desire to be supportive of their children's educational and social development in the school setting. With the support of a caring parent specialist and a receptive school environment and school staff, parents transcended their fear of the school and the teachers for the benefit of their children.

In the best interest of her son, one parent at Francisco Villa Middle School became involved because she wanted to be made aware of all the challenges he faced. She described herself as follows: "They call me the Watchdog of Francisco Villa. If my child is having problems the first day, I want to know right away." Moreover, with the help and guidance of teachers, parents showing concern for their children's progress were empowered to assist their children at home with homework and related activities. Often this was simply a matter of sharing expectations and information necessary to monitor the children's progress at home. Although parent involvement often began because of a concern for the development of the child, the parents also recognized that their activities at school provided positive role models for students.

Providing Role Models for the Child. Many parents thought volunteer participation in school organizations, committees, and extracurricular activities was an important way to stress the value of school to their children. For example, parents who did not fully understand English, yet worked in the school, demonstrated the importance of overcoming barriers. Students often admired their parents' courage in participating in school functions that were conducted in English. Parents felt their involvement encouraged their children, by example, to continue to strive for excellence in their coursework in spite of the odds. Lastly, while parent involvement tends to be much lower at the high school level because children actually discourage parent involvement because of peer-related social pressures and the need for independence, there was evidence of the importance of providing good role models even at the high school level. In the high-performing Hispanic schools, many parents continued providing good role models in the face of teen resistance, transportation problems, and uncertainty about who to contact about their children's educational problems in the larger, subject-oriented setting.

Accruing Benefits to Oneself. Parent involvement benefited the children, the school, and the parents themselves. Parents met new friends, established neighborhood networks, acquired new skills, and became better informed in a variety of areas benefiting them. This was especially true for the parents of older children who frequently forgot to relay information to them. Spanish-speaking parents experienced personal growth, as a result of improving English and overall communication and interpersonal skills. They engaged in adult education activities, acquired typing skills, learned how to use the library, improved their relations with their children, and developed self-confidence. Newly acquired skills often were used to enhance their children's educational experience. For example, knowing the library and being able to type were skills these parents could use to assist their children in preparing better reports. Parents also discussed learning to recognize that children develop at different rates, and that they needed to be more realistic with their expectations for children. Knowledge about children's behavior and discipline management transferred to the home, and communication between parents and students increased. As one parent put it, "When you're involved, teachers know you care." The bottom line is that in the high-performing Hispanic schools, involvement provides personal benefits for many parents.

What School Staff Value

Increasing Student Achievement. Of primary concern to school staff was student achievement. To facilitate this goal at the elementary level, teachers designed assignments that engaged parents in the learning process, such as spelling lists and math tables, class projects, or other home learning activities. Teachers also provided opportunities at school that would enable parents to help children improve academic performance.

For example, a teacher at Francisco Villa Middle School indicated that parents who volunteered in her classroom helped monitor on-task behavior, learning about subject matter, teacher expectations, and teaching techniques transferable to the home environment. One middle school sponsored Saturday academies in which family members participated in teaching activities in the academic subjects with trained teachers. Similarly, the South Texas Engineering and Mathematics (STEMS) program at Francisco Villa Middle School involved parents in learning projects with children. Lastly, parent involvement had an indirect positive impact on student achievement. Several teachers made comments regarding the motivational effect that the parents' presence at the school had on children, often keeping students in school.

Building and Strengthening Relationships. Opportunities for building and strengthening relationships between school staff and parents appeared to increase in the lower grade levels. Informal encounters at all grade levels provided opportunities to communicate expectations and information to parents about their children. Informal encounters allowed teachers to communicate in more relaxed settings. An indicator of how much school staff actually participated in building relationships directly with individual parents appeared to be how much they valued parent involvement and its purpose.

One teacher explained that informal encounters at the upper grade levels became more difficult because each teacher has responsibility for so many children. Additionally, as students got older, they often discouraged their parents from having any contact with the school. According to another teacher, when parents were alienated from the school, or having infrequent contact, students tended to manipulate the situation. A Porfirio Diaz High School parent further explained, "The thing is that they (students) don't want their parents to, in my opinion, come in until it's something that they don't like. Then they want the parents to come in and confront the teacher." Relationships between school staff and parents at the secondary level often served a policing function concerning student achievement and behavior. Thus, building and maintaining strong, positive informal relationships were critical for effective two-way communication and ultimately for overall school effectiveness.

Creating a Community Environment. In the high-performing Hispanic schools, parent specialists often attempted to work with parents who seemed most distanced from the school culture. These parents typically were over-whelmed by the school's bureaucracy, intimidated by the unfamiliar language, and insecure about what was required of them. Interviews with parent specialists indicated that some parents had negative past experiences with the schools and many, at the secondary level, were discouraged from visiting school by their adolescent children. These factors could have detracted from establishing a sense of community within the school. However, many of the school staffs in this study who valued the concept of community devised ways to overcome such barriers. They actively sought to establish more effective relationships with parents. Parent specialists were employed who knew the communities, knew the families, and were perceived by parents as their advocates.

Establishing a sense of community at the secondary level was problem-atic, but, as discussed later in this chapter, where teaming or schools within schools existed, promising attempts were made to make these schools centers of learning for all. "Very few parents just drop in at this level (secondary). We need to try to do more to make parents feel less intimidated," said an administrator from Francisco Villa Middle School. Clearly, establishing a sense of community within the school setting was a high priority for many of the key personnel interviewed in this study.

Garnering Support and Assistance. Differences were found in the kind of support and assistance valued by school staff at the high-performing Hispanic elementary and secondary schools. At the elementary level, for example, school staff valued parent assistance in many of the mundane but important activities teachers rarely had time to do, such as duplicating, laminating, making photocopies, assisting in lunch rooms, on playgrounds, and in classrooms. At the secondary level, teachers tended to rely more on parents to serve as chaperones, sponsors of extracurricular activities, and fund raisers. Parents often donated time, money, and other resources to assist the school or to support an activity in which their children were involved (e.g., senior graduation celebrations, Folklorico dances, career days, etc.).

While participation in traditional PTA varied greatly among the high-performing Hispanic schools, where it was highest teachers regarded it as symbolic of the parents' support of the school. Likewise, because counselors, coaches, administrators, cafeteria workers, and other noninstructional staff interviewed in this study benefited greatly from the many services and actual jobs performed by parents, understandably school staff placed more value on this kind of support, as compared with the more informal support valued by parents. Thus, while the kinds of support and assistance valued by school staff do vary, formal involvement activities, such as participating in fund raising, chaperoning, sponsoring events, and assisting in a range of class-room, school, and extracurricular activities, were a high priority at both levels.

Providing Parent Education. School staff valued the importance of having parents involved in parent education programs. Several teachers described the importance of having parents understand the school's curriculum, the importance of and reasons for standardized testing, and the changes in standards for the different content areas. For example, a mathematics teacher at Francisco Villa Middle School suggested:

> It might be good to have inservice for parents to look at curriculum so that they know that we are teaching. Parental involvement lets parents know what we do in math. Some parents are afraid of math and this rubs off. We want them to understand.

Parent specialists designed parent education programs and worked closely with parents in developing the parents' skills and building their self-confidence (important aspects of involving parents). School administrators, particularly assistant principals, argued for parent education designed to assist parents in supporting school expectations for student learning, home-work, behavior, dress, and attitudes toward school, as well as for how to be school advocates within the neighborhood and the larger community. Teachers described the importance of having parents understand the school's curriculum, the rationale for and limits of standardized testing, and issues concerning child development and pedagogy.

Finally, school staff valued adult education classes offered at their schools. Organized by borderland school districts, these classes included keyboarding, sewing, and arts and crafts, as well as Graduate Equivalency Diploma (GED) and English as a Second Language courses. Overall, staff members viewed parent and adult education favorably. School staff members and parents at secondary and elementary schools volunteered their time to teach adult education classes at the school. Provision for child care was organized for instructors and students involved in these classes.

Parents, teachers, administrators, and parent specialists valued parent involvement for a variety of reasons. Educational staff considered parent involvement an important way to serve the needs of both children and the school. While parents valued similar considerations, their primary concerns were to assist their children academically and socially and to strengthen the relationship between the home and school. A secondary concern for parents was to be available as volunteers and fund raisers. Although major distinctions existed between what school staff valued and what parents valued, in most instances these differences were complementary and reinforced each other in the high-performing Hispanic schools. Fostering mutual awareness of what parents and school staff value was seen as a major enhancement of student success in school.

HOW DOES PARENT INVOLVEMENT DIFFER BETWEEN ELEMENTARY AND SECONDARY SCHOOLS?

Differences in the nature of parent involvement between high-performing Hispanic elementary and secondary schools had much to do with variations in the schools' relative structures, teaching and learning processes, human development, and other relevant factors. Many of the differences identified in the subsequent discussion of elementary and secondary schools could be a result of structural differences, such as span of control, size, and degree of subject matter specialization and departmentalization. Other considerations undoubtedly relate to student age levels, degree of child dependency on parents, and number of years parents are associated with a particular school (e.g., relationships with particular schools could cover grade spans of 8, 6, 4, and 3 years, depending on the level). Differences between elementary and secondary levels are explored in greater detail in the following discussions of (1) the nature of involvement at the elementary school and (2) the nature of involvement at the secondary school.

Parent Involvement at the Elementary School

In this study of high-performing Hispanic schools, parents, parent specialists, and teachers at the elementary level were engaged in both formal and informal activities. These activities included volunteerism, serving on school committees, and attending school functions. Participating in such activities enhanced the school environment, demonstrated the importance of education for children, and provided increased opportunities for personalized communications.

Volunteering. Parents provided valuable assistance to teachers, allowing the elementary teachers time to plan and to teach. Volunteer activities in which elementary school parents participated included tutoring children, helping with bulletin boards, and laminating materials for the teachers. Parents also monitored hallways, opened doors for children, and assisted in the library. English language proficiency of parents had no significant impact on participation in these volunteer activities. Other formal activities included participating in school-sponsored field trips, assisting in the office, typing, answering the phone, and fund raising.

Establishing a Nurturing Environment. In reciprocation for parents' volunteer efforts, schools' staffs and teachers worked to create a caring, nurturing environment. The school climate at the elementary school level can be described as inviting and welcoming. Parent specialists made phone calls, assisted parents with family concerns, such as health information, and networked to arrange transportation when possible. Seeing parents in the halls, cafeteria, and office was perceived as a significant way of enhancing the school climate. Parents and school staff agreed that having parents at school contributed to a more nurturing environment.

Participating in Committee Work. Many parents at the elementary level are involved in committee work. Formal activities for parents included participation in Parent Advisory Councils (PACs) and the Language Proficiency Advisory Council (LPAC)—two programs that typically were better established at the elementary level than at the secondary level. PACs that were organized at the school campus appeared to be better developed and more active than those organized at the district level. Spanish-speaking parents conducted meetings in Spanish and appeared to have a sense of ownership of the goals and projects established by the PAC.

Unlike in less formal volunteer activities, English language proficiency appeared to make a difference to those who participated in decision-making committees, such as PTA/PTO or site-based, decision-making teams. The primary participants in these groups or organizations tended to be either English-speaking or bilingual parents.

Reinforcing Education at Home. Other informal activities included parents monitoring children's homework assignments, reading or having children read to them, watching educational television programs or monitoring television time, and engaging children in learning activities around the home. Parents sought guidance from school officials on how to help children perform academically. Parents wanted to know what was going on at school so that they would know what to reinforce at home. Parents relied on teachers to help them learn better ways to reinforce those skills at home.

The attitude of "you can achieve whatever you want" seemed to represent the mothers' motivation for their self-growth as well as for their children's growth. These mothers were committed to doing whatever they could to help their children. Their show of commitment to education provided positive role models, demonstrating to their children what acquiring an education could mean to them. Parents wanted their children to value the education provided them by their schools and reinforced in their homes, and to realize the importance an education could have for their futures.

Providing Opportunities for Personal Contact. Parents and teachers, particularly at the elementary level, tended to create opportunities for close personal relationships. Personal contact and communication were highly valued by parents. It appeared that staff at the elementary schools recognized the importance of personal communication more than did secondary school staff. Elementary teachers made phone calls to parents to chat with them and share students' progress reports. Leaders of "teacher teams" were provided telephones in their classrooms that they could use to contact parents immediately about the positive achievements of their students, as well as about concerns. Many elementary teachers had an open door policy and interacted with parents informally and frequently. Emphasis was placed on building trust between the teachers and parents.

Parent Involvement at the Secondary School

Levels of commitment to parent involvement at the secondary level were somewhat less than those observed at the elementary level (Villanueva & Hubbard, 1994). Some school officials recognized the need for such involvement and included it as a component of site-based management plans. Many secondary school parents admitted that their children would rather have them stay home, but this appeared to be more prevalent among families that had been less involved at the elementary level. Also, this appeared to be more of a problem for adolescent boys than girls. Moreover, opportunities for personal contact between teachers and parents decreased markedly at the secondary level, and often were left to rare informal contacts at school events or even at more formal school meetings. As suggested below, involvement tended to be facilitated through specialists, networking among parents, becoming visible at school functions, and focusing on student behavior.

Facilitating Parent Involvement Through Specialists. As the number of teachers per child increases at the secondary level, parents are less likely to be able to monitor classrooms and keep in close personal contact with their children's teachers. Teachers also find it difficult to bond with the parents of more than a hundred students with whom they work on a daily basis. Thus, it is the nonteaching staff, such as parent specialists, librarians, custodians, and cafeteria workers, and professionals, such as the counselors, school psychologists, diagnosticians, and special education teachers, that share in the responsibility for creating a caring, open environment for the secondary school.

Comparatively speaking, at the secondary level much needs to be done in this area. As one parent from Madero Middle School put it, "It is like you don't exist. . . . I understand that teachers don't have time to call and say your kids are doing great. All these extra activities that teachers are involved in takes away from the time they should be spending with me and my children." Coupled with the commitment of many of the professional and nonprofessional staff, parent specialists were used most effectively to facilitate involvement.

Networking with Other Parents. Interaction with other parents is one of the factors that impels them to spend time at school. Those parents whose children participate in school functions have opportunities to exchange information, seek advice, and enjoy each other's company. Moreover, parents whose children were engaged in various programs, whether scholastic, artistic, musical, or athletic, seemed to have higher levels of involvement than parents whose children were not involved in extracurricular activities (Melnik & Fine, 1990). Higher levels of involvement not only increased the probability of increased informal contact with school staff, but expanded parents' opportunities to network and mobilize support and make demands on the school.

Becoming Visible at School Functions. Becoming visible at school-related activities, supporting their children's activities at home, and, regardless of the common barriers at the secondary level, taking the initiative to keep in contact with their children's teachers and other school personnel was a common practice among the more involved secondary parents. Several interviewees at various secondary schools indicated that the way to get parents to attend PTA meetings was to have their children engaged in some form of performance (e.g., a play, choir, etc.). Parents of student-athletes often were involved in booster clubs and attended their children's games and awards ceremonies. Nonetheless, involvement at school functions where children performed appeared to be the primary avenue for parent participation at the secondary level.

Focusing on Student Behavior. Formal involvement at the secondary level often involved procedural or behavioral elements. For example, parents attended admission, review, and dismissal meetings; parent conferences with team members; and conferences with counselors to discuss issues dealing with their children's behavior. One school installed a new Communities in Schools program targeted for "at-risk" students and focused mainly on involving parents in the lives of their children. Some of the instructional teams at Madero Middle School required parents to accompany their students at school when the child had been misbehaving. At Benito Juarez Middle School, parents monitored the hallways, reducing behavior problems and providing a break for teachers.

In the high-performing Hispanic schools, a significant number of parents and school staff expressed concern about the diminished involvement in the upper grades where they felt involvement was most needed. They agreed that students who were supported by their family were much better able to cope during this difficult stage of their lives. They shared a concern for the multitude of adversities faced by adolescents. They reasoned that parent involvement improved the behavior of secondary students.

WHAT CAN BE DONE TO BUILD COLLABORATIVE RELATIONSHIPS BETWEEN PARENTS AND SCHOOLS?

Five broad categories of best practices were derived from the qualitative data gathered in this study. Any application of these findings should be undertaken with caution. Best practices, from whatever source, should be applied differently depending on the unique characteristics of the school setting where they are to be incorporated. As Huberman and Miles (1984) and others (e.g., Clark & Astuto, 1994; Firestone & Corbett, 1987; Fullan, 1991) suggest, "best practices" are useful as guidelines in helping practitioners make sense of their unique situation, for it is the uniqueness of the individual setting that is the critical factor.

Each campus in this study represents a distinctly different historical, political, economic, and educational context, responding to localized needs, interacting with unique cultures, operating under different sets of assumptions, and responding to environmental and organizational changes differentially. Nonetheless, many practices already mentioned throughout this chapter contributed to building collaborative relationships among school staff and Hispanic parents at both the elementary and secondary levels. The five best practices mentioned below represent a combination of various strategies used by school staff and parents to build collaborative relationships.

Thus, in our study we found that *the high-performing Hispanic schools*

1. build on cultural values of Hispanic parents;
2. stress personal contact with parents;
3. foster communication with parents;
4. create a warm environment for parents; and
5. facilitate structural accommodations for parent involvement.

Building on the Cultural Values of Hispanic Parents

Cultural values emanate from various sources. As suggested earlier, culture is dynamic, complex, and the result of a myriad of factors, such as birthplace, regional differences, acculturation stages, class, gender, formal educational opportunities, and personal experiences in the mainstream culture. Beyond an understanding of the Hispanic cultural context, Garcia (1994) argues that personal commitment, knowledge of what makes a difference in teaching and learning, and educational leadership are requisites to effective teaching and learning. Our research findings corroborate Garcia's assertion and suggest four main themes that characterize high-performing Hispanic schools.

Understanding Cultural Values. Effective principals, teachers, and other school staff understand key cultural values of parents and recognize the diversity of Hispanic parents' experiences in their interactions with mainstream culture, particularly as reflected in school settings. This was an important determining factor in any attempt to foster collaborative relationships between schools and parents (Garcia, 1994; Montecel, 1993).

Building on the Strength of the Extended Family. Effective principals, teachers, and other school staff recognize that Hispanic mothers tend to view all children with whom they interact, regardless of whether they are the children of relatives, friends, or neighbors, as their children. Teachers whom parents trusted often were invited to family celebrations, as part of the extended family; likewise, parents reported being treated as part of the school family. In short, these schools built on this basic cultural value of the extended family, familial interdependence, family loyalty, and family-oriented interactions (Epstein, 1992; Garcia, 1994).

Making a Personal Commitment to Learn About the Hispanic Culture. School leaders, including administrators, teachers, and other school staff, make a concerted effort to encourage parents to become involved, by learning about their cultures, learning their language, hiring bilingual school staff, extending personal invitations to them in their language, and providing rooms where parents can find support from other parents in an informal, nonthreatening setting. Parents are encouraged to take part in their children's education within a cultural context that transcends home and school.

Stressing Personal Contact with Parents

According to data collected in this study of high-performing Hispanic schools, one of the most effective ways to communicate information, nurture a caring environment, and gain parents' trust and support incorporates personalized communication and direct contact with individual parents. Calling parents, visiting them, or speaking to them individually in a nonpatronizing, noncondescending way are representative of practices used by principals, teachers, parent specialists, and other school staff. Creating opportunities for positive interaction on a regular basis, engaging in small talk with parents, calling parents by phone, and making home visits were primary strategies used by school staff to make personal contact with parents in high-performing Hispanic schools.

Creating Opportunities for Positive Interaction. In these schools parents are inclined to overcome fears related to limited English proficiency or formal education because the school staff communicate respect, warmth, and caring when they greet parents. Whenever teachers or administrators meet parents in the classroom, at the school, or at school functions, they acknowledge the children's accomplishments. In high-performing Hispanic schools every student and every parent plays a significant role in the school's community and, whenever the occasion arises, receives appropriate acknowledgment for doing so. Teachers and administrators go out of their way to find opportunities to provide positive, constructive reinforcement to students and parents.

Engaging in Small Talk. Simple, authentic greetings to parents when they arrive at school or attend school functions actually increase parent involvement. For the borderland parents, a personal note, phone call, or personal invitation was used strategically to develop and sustain parent involvement. Small talk is important in the Mexican American culture. It is used as a way of building relationships. Therefore, when parents engage in small talk with teachers and other school staff, it is time well spent. Interestingly, workshops, rather than parent–teacher organizations, are considered a more viable vehicle for small talk. Workshops concentrated on topics that met parents' needs and were considered events where they could engage in meaningful communication.

Calling Parents by Phone. Another frequently used technique for making personal contacts with parents was the simple use of the telephone. Several staff members indicated that talking to parents individually on the phone was the best way to gain parental support. A teacher from Francisco Villa Middle School commented, "Personal contact is important. Phone calls take extra time, but are worth it." Team leaders at this school had phones in their classrooms, making it easy to engage in an impromptu call congratulating a parent on a student's accomplishment or providing important information that the parent could use to facilitate a child's learning. Personal contact in the high-performing Hispanic schools, regardless of whether it is person-to-person or by telephone, always includes something positive about the child.

Making Home Visits. Parents and parent specialists identified home visits as a helpful way of fostering positive home–school relationships. Conducting home visits was identified as a best practice for six reasons: (1) parents perceived home visits to be an extension of courtesy by the school; (2) parents who had children attending school often had younger children at home; (3) most of the sites were located in communities that had no public transportation; (4) home visits were conducted by staff members who knew and often were from the community; (5) home visits conducted by teachers were viewed by parents as a form of caring; (6) home visits were a form of personal contact, which was highly valued by the borderland families.

Fostering Communication with Parents

Fostering communication is regarded as critical to building collaborative relationships between parents and teachers, between parents and children, and between children and teachers (Bermudez, 1994). The schools in the study reported here engaged in a variety of communication strategies to initiate communication with, make information accessible to, and create shared experiences for parents. Typically, knowledge about the processes involved in communicating ideas takes precedence over understanding the feelings that people are communicating. But this was not the case in the high-performing Hispanic schools. The "feeling message" permeated verbal and nonverbal communications. Let us turn now to three major processes found within the high-performing Hispanic schools that show how good "vibrations" in the communication process can facilitate collaborative relationships.

Initiating Communication. Clearly, initiating meaningful, timely communication is one of the keys to increased parental involvement, both formally and informally. In the schools studied, several strategies are used to initiate effective, clear, and honest communication with parents. They include traditional methods, such as providing handbooks containing teachers' names, their teams (secondary), schedules, and the like; organizing open houses at which student work is displayed, report cards are issued, and attendance is required of all teachers and parents; mailing communiqués to parents to improve the likelihood of their arrival at the home; informing parents of upcoming events through television announcements; and issuing newsletters. Although school staff use these more formal strategies quite effectively to inform parents, information that is communicated directly and personally to parents, by a familiar school staff member, is valued more highly by parents. The important point here is that school staff engage in a planned process in which a variety of mechanisms for initiating communication are employed to ensure that important information is transmitted to each student's family.

Making Information Accessible. At all school sites, staff make extensive efforts to make information accessible to all parents and to the surrounding community. Information is communicated in English and Spanish. Non-English-speaking parents find that teachers who communicate with them in Spanish are more approachable than those who speak only English or use interpreters. Making information accessible, understandable, and useful encourages positive perceptions of the school staff.

Moreover, access to information is vital in forging collaborative relationships with Hispanic parents. Many of the parents are experiencing socialization into a new culture, learning a second language, and becoming familiar with a new educational system. Access to information can facilitate the transition of parents unfamiliar with our educational system to becoming full participants in their school's community. When school staff make information accessible to parents, levels of trust increase and parents become more effective participants in their children's education.

Creating Opportunities for Shared Experiences. In addition to providing access to information, school staff in the high-performing schools we studied believe it is necessary to provide opportunities for parents and school staff members to communicate regularly. When situations exist where teachers can inform parents about the importance of their involvement in their children's education at the school and at home and what this means to the school, the teacher, students, and parents recognize the importance of sharing their involvement in school. Moreover, in these schools it is important for teachers to know what parents perceive their responsibilities to be with respect to their informal involvement with children's education. Two-way positive and proactive communication is necessary for the development of effective parent involvement programs.

Activities that create shared experiences for parents and their children strengthen family communication. Activities such as computer laboratory sessions, school-wide academic projects, and field trips are an important part of fostering strong relationships between parents and teachers, as well as among parents and their children. For families living along the Texas–Mexico border, strong parent–child communication is an asset in the acculturation process. Often, parents and children struggle to find common ground in the painful process of acculturation and childhood maturation. Rather than allowing the school experience to be a catalyst for irreversible separation from cultural mores and values found in the home, the school setting becomes a place for parents and children to engage in meaningful, learning interactions that provide a basis for continued dialogue at home.

Creating a Warm Environment for Parents

In high-performing Hispanic schools warmth, caring, a sense of belonging, respect, and positive reinforcement supersede notions about efficiency. Teachers, administrators, and parents in these schools refuse to adhere to rigid, lockstep curricula and to place minimal state standards over the notion that every student can meet his or her optimal level of achievement. These schools encourage democratic participation and positive interaction by providing a welcoming school environment, showing empathy and understanding toward parents, students, and staff, and by engaging students and parents in meaningful activities at school.

Welcoming Parents. At several schools, it is readily apparent that school staff embrace a welcoming environment, just by noting exterior appearances while approaching the school's entrance. School grounds are immaculately clean; parking areas and directions to the entrance and principal's office are well marked and visible. Inside the building hallways are orderly; wall posters and displays are attractive and reveal current student activities and individual work. Students, custodial staff, teachers, and other adults are smiling and friendly, offering assistance and welcoming parents entering into a place that shows the considerable pride of school staff. Most important, students emit positive attitudes and indicate their happiness to see and meet a visitor.

For many parents, the initial contact with the school is their child's teacher and the office staff. Schools that foster a warm and caring environment have climates in which collaborative relationships between the school and the parent are demonstrated through basic interpersonal skills. In such circumstances, parents serve as student advocates and parent efficacy is high. As one parent suggests:

> I would like to feel welcome. When we arrive in the morning and sign in, parents and teachers greet one another. As a result, friendships evolve that have been built by working together on a day-to-day basis. They make time to greet you and it makes you feel so much better.

Showing Empathy. Empathy with parents is identified as another important and valued skill that teachers, counselors, and other staff of caring schools possess. Respect that results from the ability to be empathetic becomes important when professionals attempt to establish positive working relationships with parents who may feel marginalized in the larger social arena because of classism, racism, and language differences. The high-performing Hispanic schools have staff members with well-developed interpersonal skills who are able to distinguish between their professional and personal roles, enjoy warm and friendly relations with all members of the school's community and individually, and as a group forge strong personal relationships with borderland families (Erickson, 1987; Garcia, 1994). Showing empathy and understanding to parents involves a deep commitment to respecting the individual parent as one who has a unique contribution to make to his or her children's education and to the school.

Engaging Students and Parents. When students are engaged in extracurricular activities, their parents usually are more involved both formally and informally. However, it is difficult to ascertain which phenomenon precedes the other, student engagement or parent involvement. Does engagement of students send a message to parents that the school staff have taken an interest in their child? Do students become interested in school activities because of their parents' involvement? Or does it work both ways? While these remain unanswered questions in this research, it appears that when students are involved, parents have a reason to become involved with their children's social and academic activities.

Activities sponsored by secondary schools, which engage students in academic activities with their parents, appear to be another useful practice for increasing parent involvement. Francisco Villa's Saturday Academy exemplifies such a program. In this particular program, parents interact with teachers and their children while working on math and science projects. At several schools, whenever a meeting is held in which parents are the invited participants, school personnel organize a student performance to precede it. One-act plays, choral or band performances, a science fair, art, and other displays are among the attractions. These activities allow students to showcase their talents for their peers and parents. A mother at Francisco Villa Middle School said, "The way to get more parents involved at Open House or other school functions is to have the band play, the choir sing, or the cheerleaders cheer, and then you will get a larger turnout because parents will come to see their kids."

Facilitating Structural Accommodations for Parent Involvement

Finally, the schools studied use various structural accommodations to facilitate the building of collaborative relationships between parents and the school. The most effective, at both elementary and secondary schools, is the use of the parent specialist and the creation of parenting centers. Teaming with parents is also a very useful structural adaptation adopted by the larger secondary schools. And lastly, the use of organized parent advisory committees is known to be an effective avenue for parent participation in school governance.

Creating Parent Centers. Parent centers are places where space is provided for volunteers and visitors on the school campus. The centers are used for a variety of purposes to assist the parents and the school staff. More important, however, parent centers provide opportunities for meeting new friends, networking, and interacting with other parents. Parents find the school environment to be intimidating, particularly at the secondary level. The parent centers provided an informal atmosphere for parents to discuss their children, their successes, and problems; to work on projects; to assist teachers; and to meet with others who shared their interests (Johnson, 1993).

Teaming with Parents. Academic teaming offers several advantages. Teams of teachers are responsible for a defined group of students. Teachers are able to share information about a common group of children among themselves, with psychological and social service personnel, and above all with parents of individual students. Academic teaming also allows parents a cross-disciplinary overview of their child's academic progress and personal development (McAfee, 1987). In addition, teaming makes an important contribution to an effective home–school relationship. Teaming allows teachers to make contact with and become knowledgeable about many more parents than they would otherwise. For parents, teaming means fewer and more productive parent–teacher conferences, as well as acquisition of more useful and comprehensive information about their child's academic, cognitive, social, and emotional development. At the secondary level team teachers schedule annual meetings with each parent. When a parent needs to discuss concerns about a child's progress immediately, other meetings are held.

Teaming fosters less formal contact with parents. After getting to know a parent in a group setting, individual teachers often call to arrange a one-on-one parent–teacher conference. In short, large secondary schools provide a communal environment by consolidating their resources through academic teams.

Organizing Parent Advisory Committees. Organizing parent advisory council meetings at the school is identified by parents as a more effective structural accommodation for building collaborative relationships than is participation in PTA or site-base, decision-making meetings. Parent advisory committees are sometimes more permanent, other times temporary. They sometimes focus on special issues within the school and sometimes address school-wide concerns. They are arguably more effective than an "in-group" of parents who in the name of participatory governance advise on all the decisions made at the school. Their meetings provide non-English-speaking parents opportunities to network among other parents with similar linguistic skills and with children with similar academic needs. More important, such structural accommodations provide parents with opportunities to acquire leadership skills as parent advisory committee officers, chairs, and committee members. Many of the federally mandated programs, such as those designed for at-risk students, special education, and early childhood education, offer more permanent opportunities for parent participation than those focusing on more temporary special issues within the school.

REFERENCES

Bermudez, A. B. (1994). *Doing our homework: How schools can engage Hispanic communities.* Charleston, WV: Appalachia Educational Laboratory.

Clark, D. L., & Astuto, T. A. (1994). Redirecting reform: Challenges to popular assumptions about teachers and students. *Phi Delta Kappan, 75*(7), 512–522.

Cummins, J. (1984). *Bilingualism and special education: Issues in assessment and pedagogy.* San Diego, CA: College Hill.

Delgado-Gaitan, C. (1991, November). Involving parents in schools: A process of empowerment. *American Journal of Education*, pp. 20–46.

Epstein, J. (1992). School and family partnerships. In M. Alkin (Ed.), *Encyclopedia of educational research* (pp. 1139–1151). New York: MacMillan.

Erickson, F. (1987). Transformation and school success: The politics and culture of educational achievement. *Anthropology and Education Quarterly, 18*(4), 335–356.

Firestone, W. A., & Corbett, H. D. (1987). *School context and school change: Implications for effective planning.* New York: Teachers College Press.

Fullan, M. (1991). *The new meaning of educational change.* New York: Teachers College Press.

Garcia, E. (1994). *Understanding and meeting the challenge of student cultural diversity.* Boston: Houghton Mifflin.

Huberman, M., & Miles, M. (1984). *Innovation up close: How school improvement works.* New York: Plenum Press.

Johnson, V. (1993). *Parent/family centers: Dimensions of functioning in 28 schools in 14 states* (Report No. 20). Baltimore, MD: Center on Families, Communities, Schools, and Children's Learning.

McAfee, O. (1987). Improving home–school relations: Implications for staff development. *Education and Urban Society, 19*(2), 185–199.

Melnik, S. A., & Fine, R. (1990, April). *Assessing parents' attitudes toward school effectiveness.* Paper presented at the annual meeting of the American Educational Research Association, Boston.

Montecel, M. (1993). *Hispanic families as valued partners: An educator's guide.* San Antonio, TX: Intercultural Development Research Institute.

Petrovich, J., & Parsons, L. (1989). *Focus on parents: ASPIRA five cities high school dropout study* (Report No. 027-162). Washington, DC: ASPIRA Association. (ERIC Document Reproduction Service No. 322-242)

Power, T. (1985). Perceptions of competence: How parents and teachers view each other. *Psychology in the Schools, 22*, 68–78.

Simich-Dudgeon, C. (1993). Increasing student achievement through teacher knowledge about parent involvement. In N. Chavkin (Ed.), *Families and schools in a pluralistic society* (pp. 189–204). Albany: State University of New York Press.

Southwest Educational Development Laboratory. (1994, January–April). Border issues (part 2). *SEDL Letter*, pp. 2–22.

Villanueva, I., & Hubbard, L. (1994, April). *Toward redefining parent involvement: Making parents' invisible strategies and cultural practices visible.* Paper presented at the annual meeting of the American Educational Research Association, New Orleans.

CHAPTER 4

Empowering the Surrounding Community

Ann K. Brooks and Paul C. Kavanaugh

The purpose of this project was to identify some of the best practices in developing and maintaining school–community relationships in selected schools in a large area of South Texas. Because the region is unique both culturally and economically, research members began this study with a conscious awareness that school–community relationships in the border region between the United States and Mexico might differ from what has previously been reported in the literature.

REFRAMING THE BORDER CONTEXT

The media typically portray the Texas border region as a homogeneous region, populated largely by people of Mexican heritage, and overwhelmingly impoverished. However, the researchers on this study perceived this region as characterized by far more diversity among communities demographically and historically than usually is reported. Historically, communities in this region ranged from those in which families could trace their residence back generations to communities with a predominantly new immigrant population. Demographically, community populations ranged from highly stable to highly transient. Community populations ranged from consisting of entirely Mexican Americans who had owned land in the community for generations, to individuals who had European American and Mexican American ancestry, with varying lengths of longevity in the communities, to predominantly new immigrants. Similarly, although a significant proportion of the population of some communities lived in "colonias," the colonias themselves ranged from extremely impoverished and undeveloped to neighborhoods with paved streets that virtually were indistinguishable from many working-class neighborhoods in the nearby towns. Economically, all the schools the research team visited were of lower socioeconomic status and were situated in communities where job opportunities were extremely limited.

REFRAMING SCHOOL–COMMUNITY RELATIONSHIP

Because of the distinct sociocultural and economic characteristics of the border region, researchers decided it was important not only to document the ways in which schools enacted relationships with communities, but also to pay special attention to how school personnel conceptualized their relationship to their community. Did these schools and communities along the border interact in the same ways as schools and communities that are predominantly European American?

Through this analysis, the research team identified three ways in which these schools' staff conceptualized their relationships with their communities. Each of these ways was formulated into a model to describe the relationship and its characteristic context. These models are ideal types in that although schools tended toward one model or another, no single model could be characterized as completely one type.

The Community as Resource Model

Most of the schools the researchers visited fit this model. These schools were part of communities characterized by a high level of transcience and a culturally diverse population consisting of European Americans and Mexican Americans, both groups including long-term border residents and new immigrants. The schools had limited relationships with surrounding communities, and the relationships that existed were predicated on a view that the community was a resource for funds, services, and volunteers. This model was the one evident in most of the existing descriptive literature on school–community relationships. It derived from a view of the world as economically driven. School personnel tended to look outward toward business and government for help in solving their school's problems.

The Traditional Community Model

Communities and schools within this model were comparatively culturally homogeneous. Two schools seemed to fit this model, and in both cases the communities claimed strongly Mexican American cultural identifica-

tions. The communities and schools formed apparently seamless relationships, with the schools serving as a center of activity for the surrounding
community. In one case, the community was isolated from other communities, either on the U.S. or the Mexican side of the border, with few families
either leaving or entering the district. In the other case, the school served
almost entirely new Mexican immigrants and in many ways the tight relationship between the school and community echoed that found between
many schools and communities in Mexico. It derived from a view of the
world as community-based. School personnel were closely tied to and integrated with their community. They tended to look to themselves as members
of that community for help in solving their school's problems and saw the
school as a participant in helping to build and strengthen the community.

The Learning Community Model

In this model, the school viewed itself as the center of a larger community
of learning. The school staff assumed a proactive stance toward its relationships with the community, driven by the assumption that in order for children
to learn, the entire community must learn. School leadership asked teachers
and staff to engage in ongoing learning rather than to just teach or fulfill
a staff function, or to give time and money to the school. The school's
leadership motivated and coordinated these learning activities. Researchers
identified one school that fit this model. This school was situated in a
community that was entirely Hispanic, highly transient, and fragmented in
that the population came from diverse regions in Mexico and from various
backgrounds. School personnel saw themselves as the source of solutions
to the school's problems. In particular, they seemed to see the development
of the surrounding community as an important way of strengthening the
school and to see themselves as a catalyst for empowering the surrounding
community.

REFRAMING THE RESEARCH LITERATURE

The research literature reflected the assumption that the term "community" referred primarily to the business and civic community within which
a school is situated (Carter & Chatfield, 1986; Purkey & Smith, 1983;
Stedman, 1987). Based on researchers' interviews and observations with
these Region I borderland schools, that understanding of community should
be broadened to include the multiple layers of community with which the
schools interact. These layers are represented by the concentric circles in
Figure 4.1.

The research literature also assumed that school–community relation-

FIGURE 4.1. Multiple Layers of Community

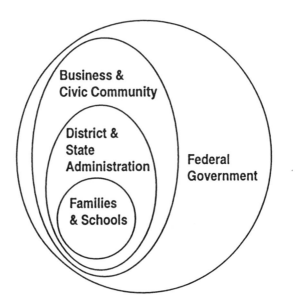

ship referred to a relationship in which the community was a resource for the school and that the community mainly contributed financial support (Leaky, 1994). Studies along the border helped research members to formulate two additional models: the traditional community model and the school as the center of a learning community model.

The researchers are presenting the findings of the study according to the particular model of school–community relationship they represent. This is because each school's administrators and personnel enacted the school's relationship to the community according to their particular understanding of the relationship. Similarly, what was a best practice for one school was not a best practice in a different school, because the beliefs about how a school should interact with its community were different. For example, school staffs that viewed their communities as financial resources enhanced the school's success by networking broadly with key people in the community. Therefore, when opportunities arose to secure resources, the staff members were well positioned to take advantage of these resources. However, the school that fit the model of a center of community learning was not active in pursuing financial resources from the community because of the time it took away from teaching students and community members.

The researchers also made an attempt to discuss and include relevant sociocultural contextual material in the descriptions because the border region constitutes a diverse yet unique geographical area, and the best practices make more sense within the context of respective sociocultural settings.

Communities as Resource Model: Schools Using Community Resources

Most of the literature on school–community relationships reported on efforts in which the communities served as a potential fund of resources, primarily financial, that could be donated to or solicited by school personnel (Leaky, 1994). Five of the schools in this study conceptualized school relationships with the community in this way. These schools included Calles Elementary, Huerta Junior High, Madero Middle School, and Benito Juarez High School. Francisco Villa Middle School shared the same orientation, but some of its more recently developed strategies focused on expanding the scope of its relationships and on building a learning community.

Schools conforming to the model of community as resource were located in highly fragmented communities with high transience and low socioeconomic status. All but one of the schools were located in urban settings and were experiencing moderate to high growth. The schools interacted with the community for the purpose of garnering financial and material resources for programs the schools' administrators wanted to implement. In addition, school personnel requested assistance from community members to enhance the curriculum to which the school had given priority. The school's administration established the goals and purpose of the initiatives, and the success of the programs, events, or activities was dependent on the generosity and support of the community.

The best practices of these schools capitalized on the resources the community had to offer. These practices reflected the establishment of relationships between school and community similar to those typically described in the school–community relations literature. "Adopt-a-school" or similar collaborations were the most common mode of school–business collaboration for schools in this model. Relationships were forged between schools and community groups or businesses in order to access materials or resources. Ways that businesses contributed to schools are illustrated by the following. A principal stated: "Businesses contribute door prizes at PTA meetings and . . . every month McDonalds treats our most improved classes to happy meals. Wendy's is another one that does that."

When researchers asked school personnel at Calles how collaborations with business contributed to the academic achievement of students, one counselor replied:

Collaborative efforts with businesses and other agencies contribute to student achievement through purchasing incentives to promote attendance, honor roll, and academic excellence. Funds are provided to defray expenses for educational field trips. Students' work is displayed at the businesses. This raises their [students'] self-esteem and confidence in themselves.

A Calles Elementary School counselor attributed the success of these types of collaboration to the principal of the school, who solicited businesses. Consequently, the school was "adopted" by almost 20 businesses in the community.

School personnel in the middle schools seemed much more skeptical about adopt-a-school relationships with businesses. Whereas one school's personnel "contacts businesses to display students' work and they are cooperative," establishing meaningful adopt-a-school relationships involved significantly more from both the school and the "adopting" organization. In one instance researchers observed, a successful adopt-a-school relationship involved a middle school and a local organization that provided judges for school science projects. A school official explained, "A member of the organization served on the site-based management team, and the organization provided a lot of support for a technology project that the school is working on."

The nature of this community relationship building placed the responsibility on school personnel who sought out the support of business. In this type of arrangement, school personnel often relied on the tenuous relationship between the contact persons and on the match between the interests of the school program objective or need and that of the entity whose aid was being solicited. Thus, adopt-a-school practices were viewed cautiously not only by the business but also by the school, as noted by a middle school principal.

Many times it's sporadic. Stores like HEB [supermarket chain] might have programs, but if we're not aware of them we won't be able to participate in any of them. They'll adopt a campus with funds or donations, but the campus, in turn, doesn't give anything back to the store, and after a while of not seeing any benefits from what they are doing, they have second thoughts about adopting another school. That's my view.

Therefore, it is not surprising that the best practices often reflected ways of nurturing and matching interests and needs. The following best practices emerged in those schools that focused on community as resources.

Staff went to the community to learn about its needs and interests. The staffs at all five schools sponsored projects that involved the school in the community, and in that way sought to rally the community and parents' support and engage them in the educational process. One parent coordinator explained, "Parents are more likely to get involved if they see that issues they are interested in are being addressed."

Focusing on meeting the interests of the community coupled with teachers' commitment to making the relationship work were key to these types of successful initiatives. It was evident that teachers had a very important effect on whether and to what degree parents would become involved in a school. One teacher at Francisco Villa Middle School observed, "If parents see us giving extra time, they will want to give extra time. If parents see good things going on, they will feel good about participating."

A school counselor at the same school believed that "when staff goes out [into the community], it is more likely that parents will come in [to the school]. Teachers also need to be exposed to the [students'] home environment. That makes a difference."

Staff sought ways of establishing relationships by going out into the community. For example, vocational education teachers went to people in the business community in order to find out what skills they required in their places of work. A vocational education teacher at Francisco Villa Middle School said, "I used to have an advisory council to find out what the community needed from workers. Originally, the program was informed by business people in the community." However, that level of involvement was no longer in place at the time of the visit. The practice of selecting program goals, curriculum foci, and workshop topics, or establishing a schedule of events that were sensitive to the interests and convenience of the community and included opportunities for community input, seemed to significantly enhance community contributions to the schools.

Staff increased community contributions by maintaining a network of relationships with key community members. Schools with the most innovative collaborative programs were those in which the school staff knew where to get extra resources for the school. The most effective way for school personnel to acquire information about programs and resources was to establish collaborative relationships outside the school, including those with other educators in the region. One counselor was especially efficient in finding out about programs that benefited his school. Having been a graduate student of a local university, he had established relationships with several professors. The federal government had granted the professors money to develop innovative projects in science and math at the middle school level. Because of the counselor's personal contact with these professors and his interest in innovative program development, he was able to get his school involved in the grant.

In addition, the counselor established relationships with a number of schools and the district's central office because of the position he held before his current job. His personal relationships with school administrators throughout the district allowed him to stay in touch with what was going on in the school district's central offices in ways not available to most other counselors or teachers. In other words, personal contacts, outside information, and relationships enabled schools to establish collaborations with business as well as special programs that brought additional resources to the school.

Vocational education appeared to be another area that actively solicited extra resources from the community. The schools established advisory committees to provide an avenue of input from the business community. At Benito Juarez High School, for example, the advisory committees solicited the involvement of the business community to enhance vocational education programs. A teacher noted:

> We have an advisory committee from the community. In my case,
> that would be members of the community knowledgeable of the auto
> industry. They introduce us to what is new in the industry, new tech-
> nology. We meet about twice a year.

The advisory committees also informed the business community of what the vocational programs needed. The auto technology teacher at Benito Juarez High School provided an example of how the business community had helped.

> Dealerships give us parts, and people from the dealership come in
> and talk to our students about the automotive industry. I got a truck
> from GM. It was donated to our school because it was damaged. It
> was the same colors [as those] of the school.

The business community also can provide students with motivation to achieve academically. The vocational education teacher who taught marketing at Benito Juarez spoke positively about how influential employers can be.

> Lots of kids don't think math is important until they see what it is
> used for. Businesses tell us in what areas students may need extra
> help. Bad kids are good in co-op classes. I get all the kids involved in

the marketing club. Pushing a kid in the right direction can help them.

Some employers will tell me that students need help with math or writing skills. I will get help for them with the English teacher. If we have a discipline problem with student absenteeism, etc., employers will tell them to straighten out or they won't keep them.

Money talks! When they see their future depends on their ability, they are willing to work on their English and math. They look up to employers. If employers tell them they need to improve in a certain area, they will try to improve.

Teachers can learn something from employers about student potential. Maybe we have been in the classroom too long. We forget to show them [the students] the relevancy of what they are learning to their life after high school.

Given the economic reality of the borderland communities and the need for developing academic and job skills for students, the creation and maintenance of healthy network relationships with key members of the community were considered relevant and necessary for accessing additional resources, especially to augment vocational programs and initiate innovative programs. However, these relationships were tenuous, and consequently the success and continuation of certain educational programs became highly contingent on the generosity of the community.

School staff provided education to the caretaking adults of the students. Elementary school personnel worked to educate not only the students in their charge, but also the adults in the students' families. This adult education took place under the sponsorship of a variety of entities in the schools. Even the PTA in one school demonstrated commitment to the education of parents and families. In the words of one parent:

During PTA meetings we have speakers. We have DARE and drug officers and nurses talk. We are trying to relay the message to parents. We're trying to inform parents of what's going on. We have had a speaker on sexual abuse. And the school facilitator and the principal have spoken on discipline.

School personnel at the middle and high schools also placed an important emphasis on the education of parents. Two of the middle schools in this study provided opportunities for parents to learn computer skills along with their children on the weekend and during the evening. Computer training was of interest to parents and other adults in the community, and activities of this type were very popular. Besides computer training, adult literacy programs were also popular. Some middle school personnel expressed deep concern about how to address the high levels of adult illiteracy in their community: "We see a need for helping parents who are illiterate to get a stronger hold on the lessons that kids are working on in school, so that they can in turn help them at home."

A group of counselors interviewed in this study thought that parents may be alienated from the schools because of inadequate understanding of what schools are trying to teach: "Parents do not understand the concept of special education. We explain to them that their child has a learning problem and that things need to be done."

This was especially true in the area of special education and other special programs. It is important to consider that Mexico did not offer special education programs comparable to the ones administered in Texas. Therefore, in these quickly growing communities with high numbers of people moving back and forth across the United States–Mexican border, the distribution of information and educational opportunities for parents regarding special education programming had become even more pronounced and necessary.

Counselors in several of the schools believed that more efforts were needed to educate parents. One middle school counselor explained: "Parents are becoming more involved in school. They want to know what programs are being offered and what teachers are doing to meet their children's needs. They are becoming more aware of their child's education."

Because the structure of the middle schools was different from that of the elementary schools, middle school staff assumed the role of educating parents to the new and different demands of secondary school. Parent orientations were very beneficial for facilitating the transition from elementary to middle school. One teacher explained, "We have orientations for parents of incoming sixth graders and let them know what electives are being offered. Before they [the students] chose anything [they wanted]. They need to choose courses in consultation with their parents."

Some counselors saw the need to link parents to resources in the community. One counselor noted:

> There's more that we can do with them [parents] like providing them with educational skills and making them aware of the resources in the community for the family, such as the Head Start Program. This gives advantages to younger children and gives parents time to work in older children's schools.

By increasing the scope and strength of their relationships with their students' families through relevant adult education opportunities, school personnel increased the likelihood that adults in the students' families would feel comfortable in the schools. Thus, the adults would help with their children's education and volunteer their time and talents to help in the schools and to raise money.

A coordinator in the vocational department at Benito Juarez High School explained that the demand for adult education classes was substantial: "There are computer classes for adults in the evening. . . . Learning computers is a way to get a promotion or a pay raise. These classes are free for the adults. Job Training Partnership Act (JTPA) is helping to subsidize the classes. There are more opportunities for those who know computers. The vocation education department spends a lot of money getting the best computers we can get."

School personnel within the community as resource model recognized the contribution they were making to their community by providing learning opportunities to families. For communities struggling with pressing social issues, schools provided information and education. School personnel from this model provided skill opportunities to the parents and guardians of the students they taught. However, they often overlooked the fact that adults in these highly transient communities did not know much about public education. They did not understand curriculum requirements, the school infrastructure, their rights as parents of special education students, and graduation requirements.

Schools solicited resources from hospitals, the police, and churches. Schools typically engaged in collaboratives with businesses that contributed materials and resources, which were used as incentives or awards for students, teachers, and parents. However, school personnel also solicited health services or materials. Given the poverty in the region and the accompanying lack of access to medical care for many of the families, acquiring these resources and services was very important.

School staff were resourceful in finding ways to involve the community in the health care of its students. For example, local doctors, optometrists, and community organizations such as the Lions' Club donated resources for students in need. One nurse described how a health laboratory contributed to her school: "We have a company that comes in that does lab work for students, faculty, and staff at reduced fees. They do cholesterol screenings and they give us coupons so that we can go to their labs at reduced fees all year."

School nurses and teachers found health fairs to be as successful at both the middle and elementary school level. These activities served to promote health and to foster health education—something that most of the nurses found woefully lacking at the schools in which they had worked:

"Our school had a health fair and about 50 different groups were here. They set up in the gym and provided all kinds of services and information."

One school district realized that the lack of coordinated services, access to health services, and available information about those services were problems that affected the health of students. The district identified resources available in the community and produced a guidebook for its staff to use to help link people to services.

When school personnel needed to refer students and their families for social services and counseling, they often turned to the Texas Department of Human Services and Texas Mental Health and Mental Retardation Department (MHMR). Occasionally, for-profit health organizations donated time or resources to assist the school.

School nurses and counselors reported spending a significant amount of their working day utilizing personal contacts to obtain services for students with insufficient financial resources. One nurse described how she was able to arrange for doctors to donate time to one of her students by working through a friend at a local hospital. Another school nurse appealed to the two physicians and the pharmacist on the local school board. She said, "If I have a medical need, I talk directly to them and they work with me." Yet another example was a school nurse who obtained supplies for the science and health classes. This nurse, whose husband was a nurse-anesthetist, said, "We have friends who are physicians who will donate things for science projects."

School personnel also forged relationships with local law enforcement departments and attempted to find ways to include them in the curriculum. Law enforcement officials sponsored bicycle registration and safety workshops. However, such issues as gangs, drugs, sexually transmitted diseases, and teenage pregnancy concerned parents at the middle and high school levels. Thus, school staffs tried to meet the growing and complex needs of the community by providing information and creating alliances with groups in the community with expertise in these areas.

Lastly, schools in the study forged important relationships with churches. Several counselors and nurses worked closely with Catholic churches to find help with health care, food, and clothing.

School personnel found meaningful ways for community members to contribute skills and knowledge to the schools. Although many school–community collaborations centered on the contribution of financial resources, a more meaningful relationship was developed when individuals and organizations contributed time and talents. Academic teaming seemed to have been very helpful in this regard. The principal of Francisco Villa Middle School said, "Academic teaming is saving us."

Another administrator at the same school said, "Instead of regular PTA, they are having academic team meetings of between 140 and 150 kids. [As a result] we are getting 100 to 150 parents out for open houses."

Academic teaming was helpful when local universities assigned preservice teachers to the schools for their practicum. Because of the open nature of academic teams, outsiders such as novice teachers and their professors could engage as members of the team. One school administrator explained how this worked in one case: "[One of the university professors] does his teaching right there on the [middle school] campus. Every year a new group goes in. What I'm after is by bringing those young people in, they can push learning levels of teams, by bringing new ideas, etc."

Parents also reported that academic teams in both the middle and high schools helped them get more relevant information, allowed them to meet with more than one teacher at a time, and facilitated getting to know each other. Academic teams seemed to build strong community relationships for some schools.

Another kind of activity gave students a chance to learn about the world of work. One middle school administrator reported:

We send 150 to 200 invitations to members of the community. We get a real good response. They see what's going on at school. Ninety to 110 people from the community will be here. It's a part of the instructional day [of the students].

Another middle school in the study devoted effort to developing a career education curriculum that would motivate students to achieve academically. Administrators described how these courses work.

Kids discover areas of interest, jobs and earnings, and educational requirements for jobs. We have this opportunity for middle school kids. They don't have to wait to get into high school to get involved in this sort of thing. Kids will do research on a job cluster, do company tours, and do self-assessment. Guest speakers will be part of the curriculum.

In the process of learning about careers from guest speakers, tours, and research, students worked on improving their writing skills. They also got lots of positive encouragement about pursuing higher education.

In addition to regular teacher education programs, local universities were involved in the schools in innovative ways. Researchers found, for example, one middle school's staff providing a program under the auspices of a university talent search.

Ten kids are identified at the sixth-, seventh-, and eighth-grade level who have the potential for college but not the financial resources. Someone from [the local university] comes to talk to them about career choices once a month. They go on field trips to Kingsville, Austin. When they are seniors they can go to any university in the nation to visit. There are also parent orientations. At the first meeting they had over 100 parents. It is funded through a Department of Education grant.

Another local university-sponsored program was Tex Prep. This program, open to any student who had an interest in engineering, mathematics, or computers, was conducted during the summer and taught by instructors who assisted students in research and math.

One school administrator explained:

Job Training Partnership Act and Private Industry Council [PIC] also provide enrichment programs at San Marcos, Texas, through [a local university], for at-risk students. Students can pick up some extra credits, earn extra money, and experience the college life because they are housed at the universities.

Local universities seemed to be collaborating with the schools of Region One, and specifically with the middle and high schools, in novel ways. The universities were working at the grass-roots level not only to train teachers, but also to improve the academic experiences of the students of the region.

Traditional Community Model: Schools Integrated with Their Communities

Two of the schools reflected strong integrated relationships with their communities. The researchers characterized these schools as exemplifying a traditional model of school–community relationship. In addition, they reflected traditional Mexican culture and community relationships. These schools seemed to have well-integrated relationships among teachers, parents, and the community at large. In these communities, a long personal history existed among community members. Teachers knew the families of their students, and administrators knew families and the community leaders. For example, Porfirio Diaz High School was located in a rural area in which community members claimed that "everyone is related." In this community, the Mexican concept of family truly extended to the broader community and schools.

In the case of Carranza Elementary, a school located in a long established border city, the close-knit community included recent immigrant families as well as more established families. The experienced Mexican American principal and staff respected Mexican culture and values and used their understanding to build strong rapport with the community. The principals at both schools viewed themselves as community members rather than as outsiders.

Relationship building began long before children ever arrived on the campus. At the elementary school, relationship building began before children even reached kindergarten. Carranza Elementary offered a home-based educational program administered by the central district staff for parents of 3-year-old migrant children. Parent specialists visited homes and conducted developmentally appropriate instructional lessons with children and parents. The purpose of the program was to provide cognitive, affective, social, and psychomotor skill development opportunities to children and have these reinforced at home by parents. The principal explained:

> The purpose of the home-based program is to get the little ones ready for the transition from home to school. Children are more relaxed when they can visit the school campus once a month. There are no more children crying in school. They feel more comfortable.

The community aides (paraprofessionals with a high school diploma or its equivalent and experience working with prekindergarten children) went to the neighborhoods of this Chapter 1 school looking for parents of 3-year-olds in order to assist them in preparing the children to attend school. According to the principal, "When these children come in, their attention span is greater; their time on task is greater. They're coming to a place where they have already achieved success. They're more comfortable."

Reaching out to the parents of these children is not easy, but school personnel eventually gain the support of the community. The parent coordinator explained:

> The first visit is difficult. They're defensive. What helps us is that we try to assign ladies that live within the neighborhood, so parents already know the aides. After 2 or 3 years, the community aides have been seen in the neighborhood and are known. The parents support the aides because they want to help their children.

The community believes in providing a safe learning environment for children, as evidenced by the state-of-the-art early childhood centers located throughout the district. Even though this district and community had a poorly developed tax base, it committed itself to providing safe learning environments and involving parents early in their children's education. In this community, schools supported and addressed parents' concerns that school be safe, that day care be high quality, and that adults have opportunities to develop parenting skills.

The school also demonstrated commitment to preparing students for middle school. One school counselor explained:

> We introduce the children to middle school so that they keep a sense of belonging. We show them how fun it can be. Even after our graduates go to middle school, we have open house and report card night for our middle scholars. That way there's more parent participation.

Elementary school personnel also tried to ease a child's transition from day care to the school setting and life beyond high school. For example, the staff at Porfirio Diaz recognized that limited employment opportunities existed in the community. Therefore, the community supported the school's focus on not only vocational training, but academic programs for college preparation as well.

> We dare them to dream. We plant the seed. Eighty-five to 90% [of the students at Porfirio Diaz] start at some kind of institution of higher education. Lots of our kids enroll in vocational programs. We're trying to push them to realize they need to get out to get training. Our kids recognize that the job market is bad here.

Community members contributed their time and talent to students' success. School personnel recognized the value of community talent and what was possible through a healthy interchange of information between the community and the school. For example, the parent specialist saw the monthly visits to campus as one of the most important strategies of the home-based education program.

> They see how their children are doing relative to the other children. Parents ask questions about their children's development and how they can contribute to it.
>
> They have children look at books and have them make up stories. Parents have the opportunity to meet one another so they can support and help one another.

A side benefit of some of these programs was the opportunity for community members to learn. The curriculum for parents who participated in the home instruction of 3-year-old children was an example of this.

Children come at different stages because parents do different things. We give parents [of 3-year-old children] a monthly calendar of activities. We provide readers for the parents. We work very closely with the community.

One teacher made the following observation, "In the past, schools would solve all the problems. We've come full circle. Schools can't do everything by themselves."

Another noted: "There are people who are resources in the community who can do things some teachers can't. The superintendent in one of the school districts . . . gets people who are musicians to perform for the schools."

At Porfirio Diaz High School, a focus in the curriculum on community concerns made the interdependence of skills and information obvious to the students. The citizens of the county were extremely concerned about the poor quality of the water in the Rio Grande, their primary source of water. The school infused water quality issues throughout the curriculum, and the students became involved in water-related projects. In order to facilitate this program, school personnel brought in speakers from the community to educate students about water pollution and its effects, and how to improve water quality.

At Carranza, one of the most important ways the community became involved with the school occurred through a reading program. A school administrator described this collaboration:

Children write stories and people from the community come in and read the stories. The children have an autograph book, and after someone reads the story they make comments about the stories in the autograph book.

Clearly, community members did not have to be highly skilled in order to play an important role in the schools.

Community values were integrated into and supported by the schools. The curriculum emphasized the celebration of holidays unique to Mexican American culture, the value of bilingualism in the communities, and the community's hopes for the children. The Carranza Elementary School administrator pointed to the district's involvement in purchasing and restoring dilapidated buildings in the community's historic center and transforming them into functional structures used by the district. The schools' effort to preserve and restore pride in the culture and history of the community motivated the project. The success of this project required collaborative support from the community, city officials, the business community, and the school district.

Porfirio Diaz teachers spoke of the values of respect and extended families. One teacher, who made very little distinction between the high school community and the town, offered this description.

> This is a unique area. We do not have a lot of big city problems here. The school is the center of a lot of activity. We take a lot of pride in our school and in our community. We want to keep the old values like respect. Everything comes from the school. Being a small town, everybody knows everybody and everybody is related to everybody.

In the community, students were known by name and watched over by all members of the community. A parent coordinator described her interpretation of the community as an extended family.

> We are sheltered. We have maintained a small town environment. Teachers are concerned about teaching everyone. Students complain that "You can't do a thing here because the teachers will call home. The teachers are always bugging your parents. They notice if you're absent." We still have the situation where if somebody is skipping and they go to Dairy Queen, they'll [employees] look at the kid and ask them what they are doing. Extended family is still important here.

Traditional schools also forged very close relationships with central office personnel. School staff perceived central office personnel as collaborative supporters. The rural nature of the communities, the traditional value of community, and the reliance on established personal relationships nurtured over time were factors that seemed to enhance the campus–central office relationship. School personnel understood power structures and interpersonal behaviors, maintained open communication, interacted sensitively in an environment where "everyone knew everyone," and worked to build community consensus on the contributions that school personnel were making to better the entire community. In turn, the community committed itself to sustaining early childhood centers, preserving bilingual ability, fostering citizenship skills in students, and emphasizing academic excellence.

School as Centers of a Learning Community Model: A School Serving as a Center of a Learning Community

One of the eight schools researchers visited had a distinctly different philosophy and approach to relating to the community. This school served as a center of learning for a community that was poor, fragmented, and highly transient. Obregón Elementary staff members struggled with multiple issues such as gangs, unemployment, poverty, health needs, and drugs. However, through various strategies, the staff created a close-knit community committed to educational activities that enhanced the development of both children and adults. Their philosophy emphasized that it is never too late to learn and that everyone in the community is responsible for developing learning opportunities. Staff members emphasized building community, not just networking with the community. Everyone in the community, including school personnel, took responsibility for developing the school and finding solutions to the school's and the community's problems. The staff at Obregón seemed to value the concept of empowerment for students, staff, and community. They believed they should provide information to the community so that the community members could interact effectively in a culture that was new and unfamiliar for many of them.

On the surface, the best practices at Obregón Elementary School resemble those of the schools that thought of their communities as resources and, to a lesser extent, the traditional community model. Many of the best practices found in this school have been described in Chapter 3. Among all the high-performing Hispanic schools, however, Obregón was the most conscious, explicit, and articulate about its values. Obregón's best practices were a direct reflection of the values it held.

Proactive approaches are used to forge relationships with the community. The administrative and professional staff at Obregón Elementary School nurtured supportive, personal relationships that reinforced the feeling of belonging to a large family of parents, school, and community. They maintained direct personal contact with parents and, in fact, viewed personal contact and familiarity to be the foundation of a collaborative relationship among school, home, and community.

The words of one teacher suggest the beneficial outcomes of using personal contact between parents and teachers.

> You get as personal as you can. When parents see us working for the kids and actively seeking their ideas, they will offer their suggestions and be enthusiastic about participating. Parents want you to come and tell them how their children are doing.

The practice was significant in that it is congruent with the Mexican American parents' concept of "platica," which literally translates as "conversation." Thus, the community meetings mirrored the idea of the community conversation. Also, this practice was important given the fragmented, discontinuous social context of the school community. Because no intact neighborhoods really existed in the rural colonias (areas populated mostly by people from various regions of Mexico), the efforts of school personnel to establish and facilitate various interactions with parents appeared to be effective as well as culturally appropriate. Their personalized efforts facilitated successful exchanges of parents to parents, teachers to parents, administrators to parents, and community to community. The effectiveness of these efforts in the fragmented and transient communities that have become increasingly common across Texas and other parts of the United States must be noted.

Obregón Elementary leadership gave staff members explicit responsibility for drawing up a personal plan of action stating what each person would do during the school year to engage families and the community at large in learning events at the school. A staff member noted, "The principal makes it explicit that each one of us on the staff needs to do what we can in order to reach out to the community. [She] really wants to get the parents involved."

Forging relationships with parents was not solely the responsibility of parent specialists and teachers. School nurses, counselors, administrators, teachers, and others assumed the responsibility for establishing links with parents and the community at large.

Two key assumptions were central to this broader conception of what constitutes the school community: (1) all members of the community want to learn, and (2) everyone benefits from learning. The broader conception of community is congruent with Mexican Americans' broadening of their family to include "comadres," "compadres," and friends in need.

Empowering the surrounding community necessitated the use of school buses to transport teachers to homes within large rural areas and among the several "colonias." This made it possible for all parents, those with and without transportation, to become active members of the school's community and to engage in their children's learning.

Proactive approaches are used to empower community members. Fund raising traditionally has been the purpose of forging collaborative relationships between school and community. Typically, the school administration set fund-raising goals, parents raised the money, and the school staff decided how to spend the money. However, Obregón administrators and staff made it clear that the funds parents raised would be used on projects the parents valued. One of the counselors at this school recognized the necessity of providing parents with the autonomy to set project goals, decide how to reach them, and create a sense of ownership regarding their projects. The counselor observed: "Parents are more likely to get involved if they see that issues they are interested in are being addressed."

Granting autonomy to parents and other groups seemed to engender their participation in more activities and discussions. School officials treated parents as intelligent adults and respected them as decision makers and contributing members of the community. Giving autonomy to parents was a way of proactively empowering them and according them respect. Respect is highly valued by the Mexican American community.

Obregón Elementary School served a community populated mostly by families who had limited experience in the dominant culture. Therefore, school counselors, teachers, and the parent specialists played an active role as culture informants and forged links to information exchange networks. A staff member described what he thought parents wanted: "English language. Work. . . . They want job training. They want training on how to better communicate with their kids, discipline. They want to understand the system, how it works."

Extensive efforts were made to provide parents access to information. The philosophy of the school was to provide information that empowers people. Moreover, school personnel at most of the schools in this study seemed clear that many of the families in their district did not understand the social service system. Schools then took responsibility for educating parents and heads of households about how to work with the social service bureaucracy. A staff member from one school explained:

I do a lot of social work. Lots of families are recent immigrants. They are not oriented to services from the county such as the Health Department and the legal system. Basically, what I do is orient them to what is available.

Obregón's approach to this problem, like that of the other schools in this study, was to establish links with the limited social services in the area. However, more important, Obregón took a proactive stance by engaging in educational activities that empowered parents to understand the dominant culture's institutions, including the school system.

Finally, Obregón considered adult education to be not only a vehicle for empowering community members, but also an important contributor to students' academic success and supported it via several collaborative arrangements. All of the elementary schools in this study worked to educate not only the students in their charge, but the adults of those students as well. This adult education took place at all levels. As one administrator stressed, "Parents do want to learn. If they ask for [something], we need to do something to respond to them. We do math tutoring in the evening with students and a lot of parents have gotten involved." However, Obregón's staff sought to provide adult education programs that met the community's needs and made information accessible.

The school opened the computer lab to parents and students on Saturday mornings. Opening the lab on Saturdays contributed not only to honing the skills of students, but also to the development of parents' skills so they could help the students. It also brought parents and students together to learn within the school context. The parents proved to be hungry for education, as one administrator described: "Two teachers volunteered for a couple of hours one Saturday a semester. Parents would come to help their children. Then the parents themselves began to ask for computer training and then for ESL classes."

A school nurse informed interviewers that the greatest need regarding the health of the students in her school was education for parents. For example, laws on immunizations have changed. "They need to be informed about these things. Families don't realize all the ways that we can help them regarding health."

Similarly, a school counselor informed researchers that the way she went about administering adult education had changed dramatically. She explained:

> In the past, I have done some training with parents on how to keep kids off drugs and out of gangs. Now, however, I'm looking to parents for ideas on what kinds of educational programs they would like. Parents ask about discipline and they have asked for presentations on AIDS and women's issues. Parents are looking for things for them personally and for their children.

Parent coordinators also worked with adult education at school campuses. One parent coordinator described functioning more as a community organizer than as a coordinator of parent volunteers. As a former migrant student herself, she knew from personal experience the situation of the families with whom she worked. She was an extremely strong proponent of adult education as a way to motivate parents to get involved in their children's education.

> I tell the parents, "If I can do it, you can do it." I have to convince them that it is not too late for them. Adult education is a whole new concept for them. Those who change their mind-sets—it will be a transformative experience for them.

In order to do her job, this parent coordinator/community aide went into the community to talk to parents personally and to conduct neighborhood meetings. She saw herself as an advocate for parents within the school: "I've gone door to door to get my name known and I am trying to get GED classes and a PTO on our campus." This parent coordinator was quite adamant about what she believed parents wanted.

> They want to understand the school system and how it works. . . . If parents can understand how the school district is governed, they will come to realize how much they can influence things in the school. . . . We've just started going out to the colonias.
> Parents do want to learn English. The problem is that there is no rural transportation system out here and it is difficult for them to get to school. Some of them will walk to school and participate, but it is hard for them to do that on a daily basis; but the interest is there.

Rural areas such as the one served by Obregón usually presented special problems to parents who wanted to improve their lives through education and participation in their children's schools. Obregón addressed these issues.

Proactive approaches are used to meet family needs through collaboration with available social services and health agencies. Given the low socio-economic level, the high unemployment rate, and the resulting impoverished community conditions, social services were important to the well-being and survival of many of the families served by Region One schools. Many lived in conditions of severe poverty. As one school counselor pointed out: "Lots of families receive food stamps. Lots of our families receive Medicaid. There is lots of domestic violence in the homes and a lack of basic needs. We have to ask if the child's hygiene needs are being met."

Because of the tremendous need for social services along the border and the lack of such services, school personnel often fulfilled a number of social service roles in the schools where they worked. One school counselor summarized the situation.

> We are the social worker, crisis counselor, academic counselor. . . . We get lots of training in crisis prevention, abuse cases, conflict resolution, and suicide prevention. Many times we are the ones who end up talking to parents about what is going on in their families. Sometimes you can't refer or you can't wait to refer.

A parent coordinator informed researchers that

> If they have family problems, I will work as a go-between for the people of the family who are not getting along. People also contact

me if they get eviction notices and they don't have a place to live. I work with the Health Department and the Welfare Department also.

One counselor shared the following:

Many times the children's basic needs are not being addressed. We try not to be . . . contacted. Instead we try to empower the parents to make the contacts with the public agencies and [make] the appropriate appointments.

These last two comments again demonstrate the proactive, but developmental, manner in which schools integrated adult education into their relationships with the communities they served.

Staff sponsored and organized school initiatives that met family and community needs. Because of the large numbers of migrant and immigrant students in Region One schools as well as the large rural population, school personnel shared a deep concern regarding the immunization of the children who attended those schools. Child immunization definitely was not taken for granted along the border. School nurses consistently told us of the efforts that they made to ensure that all children were immunized. At Obregón, the school administrator promoted student attendance at school in order to take advantage of school immunization clinics. A school nurse said, "We have different clinics during the year that we provide for the students. There are two immunization clinics where nurses come in to give shots."

A way to improve attendance was to make it convenient for children to get required immunizations before attending school. If school personnel required students to have immunizations, but did not provide the service, then most likely some children would miss school while waiting to get immunized. By sponsoring immunization clinics at school, school personnel supported community wellness and increased the likelihood of attendance.

School personnel realized that children could not achieve academically if they and their families did not have good health. Acute problems (such as cuts and bruises received on the playground) did not concern school personnel as much as preventive public health measures. In order to promote good health, a number of schools instituted health fairs. A school nurse at Obregón described its school health fairs.

We have a health fair in January and bring in people to check vision and hearing, and someone from Child Protection Services comes. The Police Department comes for drug education and the Fire Department comes for fire safety instruction.

> Three hundred families came to the health fair. . . . It was . . . open to the public. We offered glucose screening, blood pressure checks, weight, and we also do cholesterol.

When asked to what she attributed the success of the health clinic, one nurse responded:

> I called the agencies and they volunteered to come. It was all volunteer. I was surprised how easy it was to get volunteers. They just wanted to do something for the community. We just stressed that we wanted to get the community involved.

Obregón extended the invitation to the health fair not only to its own students and parents, but to the community at large and parents whose children were enrolled in other schools.

Obregón responded to community health issues by initiating several practices that were helpful to the community. For example, it promoted health at parent–teacher conferences. Typically, parent–teacher conferences do not include school nurses. However, at Obregón the school nurse played an important role during school-wide parent–teacher conferences. The nurse explained, "During parent–teacher conferences, I open my office to do blood pressure checks and heights and weights. I'm trying new things every year."

Thus, the school nurse at Obregón linked the community and parents and provided some helpful services that otherwise would not have been available to them.

Researchers identified several interesting elements from conversations with Obregón school personnel regarding their collaboration with outside agencies to improve the health of students. These elements include:

1. More nurses and doctors are needed to ensure and maintain students' health.
2. A significant amount of health education is necessary for students, parents, and the community at large.
3. The most important health concerns in Region One are public health concerns (i.e., immunizations, sanitation, alcoholism, drug abuse, infectious disease, and child abuse). Consequently, the health of the students often is affected by the health of the community in which they reside.
4. The most effective way to improve the health of the school community is to emphasize prevention.
5. The best schools have staff members who reach out to the community and provide the community with avenues to pursue better health.

As school officials find themselves interacting with the complexity brought on by the growing diversity of cultures, transience, permeable national borders, interdependent economies, limited health options, and a growing population that is economically limited in opportunities for personal improvement, officials will have to reconceptualize the role of the school. Obregón has begun to explore and initiate practices intended to place the school as a center of learning for the entire community. Obregón saw the promotion of new collaborations and cooperation among school, parent, and community groups as everyone's responsibility. Obregón saw itself as the leader in this effort. The school's purpose was personal growth for everyone. A school staff member explained:

> The principal is really into empowering both kids and adults. She says, "I know you're going to do your best for the kids." She lets kids take responsibilities. She is never satisfied. She's always asking what we can do to make things better. She's looking for ideas and she's good at working with problem solving and decision making with the staff. If we need time and training, she wants us to tell her what we need. She's always looking to see if new ideas fit our philosophy. She models well with regard to motivating people.

Obregón demonstrates a perspective on schools and their communities that extends far beyond the dependency relationship that typically develops within the institutional model. As traditional communities break down and individuals and families are left increasingly isolated, Obregón models a way in which schools can lead their communities in learning and in so doing strengthen the education of children, even those who find themselves in the most difficult and impoverished of circumstances.

DISCUSSION OF MODELS

The findings fell into three major categories. The first category focused on findings that reframed previous literature regarding school and community relationships and previous depictions of the border context. The second category focused on those findings related to best practices found within the proposed models of school–community relationships that emerged from the study. The third category related to community issues identified to be of concern to school and community members. Often, the practices and activities initiated by the school or community were responses to one of these identified concerns.

REFRAMING THE BORDER CONTEXT AND SCHOOL–COMMUNITY LITERATURE

Researchers perceived this region as far more diverse demographically and historically than usually is reported. This diversity among community members and the transience in the communities, the rural or urban location of the communities, the historical relationship among groups of community members, economic conditions, and future job prospect potentials all affect the nature of the relationship forged between schools and communities. Additionally, each community's concept of what constitutes community influenced the relationships among school personnel, parents, business, and community organizations.

The research literature reflects the assumption that the term "community" refers to the business and civic community within which the school is situated (Allen, 1989; Heaviside & Farris, 1989; Leaky, 1994; McMullen, 1990; Silver, 1990). Based on researchers' interviews and observations of borderland schools, that understanding of community needs to be broadened to include the multiple layers of community with which the schools interact. These relationships include central office staff, the school board, and Region One Educational Service Center staff. These relationships typically are not considered or described in the literature. However, borderland educators fostered them as critical.

Research literature reflected the assumption that school–community relationship referred to a relationship in which the community was a resource for the school (Chilton & Warren, 1989). These resource relationships traditionally function as avenues for schools to gain access to financial support from business and community organizations. This study of border schools resulted in the formulation of two additional models, each reflecting a different context and a distinct set of values and beliefs: the traditional community model and the school as the center of a learning community model. Best practices emerged within these three distinct interaction methods.

The researchers formulated each of these interaction methods into a model to describe the relationship and its characteristic context. For example, Francisco Villa Middle School was described as a school that made overtures to establish a resource relationship with its community, but it also had begun to initiate programs and activities that reflected an orientation toward that of school as the center of learning.

THREE TYPES OF SCHOOL–COMMUNITY RELATIONSHIPS
AND SCHOOL PRACTICES

Community as Resource

The best practices, in schools where the personnel conceptualized their communities as resources, involved capitalizing on community resources. These practices reflected the establishment of relationships between school and community similar to those typically described in the school–community relations literature. "Adopt-a-school" or similar collaborations were the most common mode of school–business collaboration for schools in this model. Relationships were forged between schools and community groups or businesses in order to access materials or resources.

The nature of this community relationship placed the onus of relationship building on school personnel who sought the support of business. In this type of arrangement, school personnel often relied on the tenuous relationship between the contact persons and on the match between the interests of the school program objective or need and that of the entity whose aid was being solicited. Thus, adopt-a-school practices sometimes were viewed cautiously not only by the business, but also by the school.

School personnel within the community as resource model recognized the contributions they made to the community by providing access to learning opportunities to the families they served. For borderland communities struggling with the realities of pressing social issues, schools became important sources of information and education.

School personnel from this model focused their efforts primarily on providing skill opportunities to the parents and guardians of the students they taught. One of the distinguishing characteristics between the community as resource and the school-led learning community model was that in the latter the school made a more intense effort to meet informational needs and bridge cultural gaps between the parent community and the dominant culture. The community as resource schools often overlooked the fact that many adults in these highly transient communities were not knowledgeable about basic educational considerations, such as curriculum requirements, the school infrastructure, parental rights regarding special education, and graduation requirements. Staff members limited their attention to activities that enhanced skills, but did not necessarily increase knowledge, broaden understanding of the school structure and the school's relationship with the wider community, or move the community toward greater empowerment in the political process.

Traditional School–Community Relationships

Two of the schools reflected a strong integrated relationship with their communities. They reflected a strong traditional Mexican culture and community relationship and infused these into the school culture. They demonstrated well-integrated relationships among teachers, parents, and the community at large. Community members had long personal histories with each other, teachers knew the families of their students, and administrators knew families and the community leaders. The boundaries of the school community were often indistinguishable from those of the wider community.

The interdependent relationship between the school and the community often meant that the community became involved with the school in a variety of roles. School personnel recognized the value of community talent and the range of possibilities that capitalized on the exchange of community–school information.

Schools reflecting the traditional model also forged very close relationships with central office personnel. School staff perceived central office personnel as collaborative supporters. The rural nature of the communities, the traditional value of "community," and the reliance on established personal relationships nurtured over time were factors that contributed to the quality of community relationships. Additionally, the school integrated into its culture Mexican American values such as respect, extended family, small talk, and the value of personal contact. The schools and communities considered these values and customs to be strengths to be nurtured and maintained, rather than deficiencies to be ameliorated.

School-Led Learning Community

One of the eight schools researchers visited was distinct. It had a uniquely effective philosophy and approach to forging relationships in the community. This school served as a center of learning for a community that was poor, fragmented, and highly transient—a school and community that typically are viewed as producing a disproportionate number of "at-risk" students. This school lived by the belief that children cannot learn if parents, community members, teachers, and staff are not learning. Therefore, personal contact with members of the community was very important to this school. The school's best practices usually aimed to build a sense of community and purpose within the school and community. This kind of relationship building is important for schools such as those on the U.S.–Mexican border, given the fragmented and discontinuous social context of the school community. Because no intact neighborhoods exist in the rural communities of colonias, the efforts of school personnel to facilitate interaction with parents was effective as well as culturally appropriate. Personalized efforts built successful exchanges between parents and parents, teachers and parents, administrators and parents, and school community and the larger community. The effectiveness of these efforts on such fragmented and transient communities must be noted, given the changing nature of community across the United States.

Families with limited experience of the dominant U.S. culture constituted the community served by the school. Therefore, school counselors, teachers, and the parent specialists often played the role of cultural informants and helped families build links to information exchange networks.

As school officials find themselves interacting with the complexity brought on by the growing diversity of cultures, transience, permeable national borders, interdependent economies, few health options, and a growing population that is economically limited in opportunities for personal or professional/vocational improvement, officials will have to reconceptualize the role of the school and previous relationships. Obregón Elementary explored and expanded a broad concept of school–community relationship. The development and nurturing of relationships were not perceived as the responsibility of any one person at the school level or left to the chance of community-initiated efforts, but were thought of as a dynamic interaction and the responsibility of all those living in that community.

Borderland Community Concerns Emerging from the Study

Three areas of critical importance emerged from this study. School personnel, parents, and key persons in the community repeatedly brought up their concern over health, safety, and economic problems. Health issues mentioned included children's immunizations, high blood pressure, borderland water quality, diabetes, and nutrition. Safety issues mentioned were gang activities, drugs within the school community, violence at school, and the provision of safe places for children to play. Economic concerns included job preparation of students, funding needed for educational programs, financial support for fast-growing school districts, and the creation of employment opportunities. These issues echo the problems faced by communities across the nation, if not the world. Often, the activities, initiatives, and visions for future programs in the border schools and communities were responses to these areas of concern.

In many of these communities, the largest employers were limited to a major Texas grocery chain, the school district, or a nearby university. These jobs often provided limited insurance and benefits. The international economic relationship with Mexican sister cities or towns also affected the economic situation of these border communities. Consequently, the job opportunities for many adults and graduating students were limited and low-paying, had minimal health benefits, and were subject to international fluctuations in both Mexican and U.S. economic markets.

The borderland community schools visited by the researchers were attempting to respond to the needs of their diverse populations and community situations. School programs such as health fairs and partnerships with community health organizations, the provision of school personnel to work with the community, the infusion into the school curriculum of school-wide projects such as the Rio Grande water quality project, the increasing emphasis on vocational education, and the accessibility of school computer laboratories and other facilities were ways the schools tried to meet the emerging needs and challenges faced by borderland communities at the close of the twentieth century.

CONCLUSION

This final section presents three recommendations regarding school–community relations for the development of school personnel working in border schools. First, professional development intended to enhance school–community relationships should consider the cultural and economic characteristics of the communities. This research suggests that the cultural values embedded in the communities and the Mexican and Mexican American families make the borderland schools and communities unique from the dominant, traditional Anglocentric schools and communities. The inclusion and honoring of culturally relevant values and norms such as respect, informal small talk, and personal contact are important to building relationships among parents, community members, and school staff.

Second, professional development must recognize the dynamic and changing nature of the communities themselves. The borderland communities are not static and neither is the relationship between schools and their communities. Socioeconomic status, the historical relationships among community members, the school's urban or rural setting, and the length of time members have lived in the community are factors that interact to influence the diversity and fluidity of existing relationships. Thus, any professional development program designed for the borderland region should include an understanding of how economic, class, racial, and political factors interact in the community and the school. This sociopolitical dimension seldom is considered in the traditional professional development programming.

Third, professional development initiatives focused on school–community relations should empower not only the school staff, but the entire community if it is to move the schools away from dependency and toward leadership. The challenges of what has come to be called a postmodern society, such as a high degree of mobility, permeable national boundaries, and social fragmentation, greatly affect borderland communities. School officials must deal with the negative effects of community alienation arising from transiency and social fragmentation, anxieties and stress arising from a clash between prior cultural expectations and socialization into the dominant culture, limited access to health care and education, limited job possibilities, international market consequences for local economies, and the increasing effects of violence and drugs. The traditional dependency relationship between schools and their communities creates a tenuous dependence on the uncertain generosity of business partnerships and on an ongoing source of government funds. Funding and other support are susceptible to unpredictable cutoffs because school officials do not control the funding nor does a continuous agreement exist between the school and the funders on the goals of particular programs.

Consequently, in this study of borderland schools, the best practices for collaboration between schools and their communities aimed to develop the skills of adult caretakers, provide information, and extend learning opportunities to the broader community. Teachers, counselors, staff, and administrators made efforts to proactively learn about their communities' needs, hopes, and fears and then to initiate opportunities for learning that extended beyond school walls. This study illustrates how a school's assumptions about its role in the community structure the relationship it ultimately builds with that community. The study illustrates the changing nature of community on the border between Mexico and the United States. Many of these changes are echoed throughout the United States. Finally, the study provides specific suggestions for schools that wish to take a leadership position in transforming the kinds of fragmented communities that are becoming increasingly common in a postmodern world into communities of learning.

REFERENCES

Allen, J., (1989). What is the role of business in education? In K. Chilton & M. Warren (Eds.), *It's education's turn to restructure* (pp. 11–16). St. Louis: Center for the Study of American Business, Washington University.

Carter, T. P., & Chatfield, M. L. (1986). Effective bilingual schools: Implications for policy and practice. *American Journal of Education, 5*(1), 200–234.

Chilton, K., & Warren, M. (Eds.). (1989). *It's education's turn to restructure.* St. Louis: Washington University, Center for the Study of American Business.

Heaviside, S., & Farris, E. (1989). *Education partnerships in public elementary and secondary schools* (National Center for Education Statistics Survey Report). Washington, DC: U.S. Government Printing Office.

Leaky, S. B. (1994). One-on-one program: A school–business partnership. *Delta Kappa Gamma Bulletin, 60,* 56–60.

McMullen, T. L. (1990). *Private sector involvement in the school-to-work transition.* Unpublished master's thesis, University of Texas at Austin.

Purkey, S. C., & Smith, M. S. (1983). Effective schools: A review. *Elementary School Journal, 83*(4), 427–452.

Silver, M. B. (1990). The Compaq project: Bringing business and school together. *Educational Horizons, 68*(4), 172–178.

Stedman, L. C. (1987). It's time we changed the effective schools formula. *Phi Delta Kappan, 69*(3), 215–227.

CHAPTER 5

Creating Student-Centered Classroom Environments: The Case of Mathematics

Pedro Reyes and Barbara Pazey

In our study we found the high-performing Hispanic schools to be open, friendly, and culturally inviting. Instructional arrangements allowed students to interact with one another and use collaborative learning techniques. The chapter offers numerous examples of how mathematics instruction emphasized meaning and understanding, skills embedded in context, and connections between and among subject areas and school and life outside of school. Moreover, the most effective border schools encouraged student-initiated inquiry and experimentation, incorporated activity-based instruction, and structured a learning environment to support interactive and cooperative learning groups.

ELEMENTARY SCHOOLS

Mathematics Programs and Curriculum

Teachers organized or wrote their own curriculum. Rather than organizing by subject area, however, teachers aligned themselves more by grade level and worked together to write thematic units or design instructional materials, activities, and strategies geared to meet the essential elements of the curriculum and TAAS objectives. Teachers met over the summer to design lessons and develop time lines for the year. Time lines were determined by teachers and were based on their previous knowledge of specific mathematical skills and concepts with which students normally experienced difficulty or that they needed more time to master. Teachers also reviewed students' academic portfolios and test results to identify areas needing additional or more in-depth instruction or review.

Math Textbooks. Mathematics textbooks were acknowledged but, for the most part, elementary teachers made greater use of the mathematics curriculum they had developed within their grade, school, or district. Most teachers stressed that they rarely used the textbook for anything more than a resource for homework assignments.

Supplementary Materials. Most of the materials teachers used were written, by grade level, by teachers and, in some cases, by students in the school. Teachers felt that since they knew their student population better than anyone else did, they should create and design a curriculum with materials and activities tailored to their specific students' needs and interests. At all grade levels, teachers examined students' scores from the previous year, looked at student achievement for each objective, and determined a tentative time line for the TAAS objectives and the amount of time to be spent on each. They also wrote math modules that contained suggestions for instructional strategies; materials and handouts for skill building, higher-order thinking, problem solving, and enrichment activities; worksheets; and tests or quizzes. At the beginning of the year, each teacher was given a "skills box" that contained folders for each TAAS objective. Teachers also planned and developed thematic units to teach mathematics between and across the various core and extracurricular disciplines of science, language arts, social studies, music, art, and physical education.

Mathematics teachers at one of the elementary schools received training every 6 weeks through a consulting firm, which taught them strategies to teach math skills and objectives related to TAAS. As part of the training workshop, teachers were provided handouts—working copies and originals—that they could take back to school and use with their own students. Teachers also drew on past programs and training they had received such as "Mighty Math," a program offered through a grant from the regional university over the summer by the math coordinators at the district and university.

Numerous manipulatives were available that were provided by the district or school or were created by teachers and students. Other materials included: (1) *Dynamo*, a magazine that students could read at their own level containing articles and stories with real-life situations, applications, and strategies for mathematics skills and operations; (2) "Touch Math," a set of workbooks that provided students with visual representations for learning number concepts, counting, and mathematical operations and gave students the opportunity to learn through kinesthetic or tactile experiences;

and (3) a "daily maintenance program" that prepared students for TAAS by providing a form of assessment and record keeping that helped students, parents, and teachers focus on areas of weakness in math that needed to be retaught or reinforced.

Math Tutorials and Computer Programs. The elementary school sites offered computer-assisted instruction to students ranging from at least once a week to as much as every day. Computer programs included (1) computer games such as "Treasure Math Storm," which exposed students to mathematics operations, equations, and problem-solving skills; (2) TAAS-formatted test items with story problems and questions for each TAAS objective; (3) programs that worked with students at their mastery level and helped them attain mastery of the objectives for their grade level; and (4) networking abilities via the Internet where students experimented and linked math and technology to other subjects and information sources that were available on the computer network.

Montessori Programs for Prekindergarten. One school adopted the Montessori program and instructional philosophy for students in pre-K classes. Students were immersed in multisensory discovery learning throughout the year. Language proficiency in English or Spanish was not the focus of instruction. Instead, teachers concentrated on providing students with a wide variety of learning experiences by using manipulatives, creative experiences, or other types of events and activities. All pre-K teachers attended training seminars and workshops and used a Montessori curriculum.

Organizational Aspects of Instruction

Time Allotted for Mathematics Instruction. Although elementary teachers normally allotted 1 hour to mathematics instruction, some teachers stated that they went beyond that time frame and used extra time to take the students through the entire teaching cycle, for enrichment activities, or for opportunities to help students who needed one-on-one attention. Other teachers mentioned that they integrated mathematics into the other subjects and often extended the amount of time spent doing math activities to complement what students were learning in other classes or subjects. Average time spent on mathematics instruction per day, according to teachers, ranged from 45 to 90 minutes.

Team Planning. Teachers at all grade levels worked collaboratively in planning instruction. In many cases, teachers from each grade level integrated mathematics topics into other subjects and developed thematic units that exposed students to ways in which mathematics could be applied to other disciplines. Teachers from each grade level met from one to three times per week. In addition to weekly meetings, one of the schools staffed classrooms with assistants while teachers met twice every 6 weeks for several hours to accomplish the following: (1) share instructional procedures and strategies and ideas for enrichment, (2) ensure that their lesson plans covered the district's or school's designated math objectives for the next 3 weeks, and (3) develop or create materials and games for classroom use.

At the elementary schools, teachers were responsible for planning a particular subject area rather than preparing lesson plans or thematic units for every subject. They provided one another with copies of the lesson plans on Friday so that they had the weekend to preview and prepare for the following week. Teachers preferred organizing for instruction in teams because it minimized their work load, enabled them to focus their energy on students, and fostered a sense of camaraderie and community among themselves.

Classroom Instruction. When we asked elementary teachers to characterize a typical day of mathematics instruction, most teachers described a certain format or steps of a lesson cycle that they normally followed. Within each step, however, teachers were flexible and willing to deviate from the instructional process or lesson cycle to meet students' needs or to follow a line of student-initiated inquiry and experimentation. For example, if some students were unable to grasp fully a certain mathematical skill or concept, some teachers tutored students individually or in smaller groups while other teachers worked at different learning centers that targeted a specific skill or concept. After 10 or 15 minutes, students switched centers and focused on a different skill. Another similar approach involved dividing the class into three groups. The teacher worked with one group, the aide worked with another, and the third group worked independently or at skill centers. The groups rotated about every 20 minutes.

Although the lesson cycles described by teachers were similar, each teacher interpreted the steps and procedures in different ways and used a multifaceted array of instructional strategies to reach the same objective. A normal day of instruction involved the following: (1) start lesson with a focused activity or a game, or allow students to work with manipulatives; (2) follow up with whole group inquiry and instruction; (3) involve the students in guided practice and cooperative strategies with continued use of manipulatives and activities; (4) check for understanding through question and answer sessions or ask students to teach or perform a certain skill; (5) reteach if necessary and recheck for understanding; (6) give students group or independent practice; and (7) evaluate students' knowledge level through a project, worksheet, homework assignment, test, computerized program, or other type of formative assessment.

Cooperative Learning. All of the elementary teachers stressed that students benefit greatly by working in cooperative-learning groups or with partners. Thus, after teachers introduced a concept or skill through whole group instruction, they broke students into heterogeneous groups or pairs and allowed them to learn from one another. Through heterogeneous grouping, students who were limited in certain skills or abilities could gain from the expertise and explanations of other students who were more advanced in their understanding and application of a particular mathematical skill or concept. As students observed, practiced, and reflected on mathematical tasks to be completed (Brown, Collins, & Duguid, 1989; Daniels, 1993; Rojewski & Schell, 1994), teachers mediated their learning activity.

Every student performed a specific role or function, such as captain, reporter, timer, cutter, colorer, or paster, and worked with other members of the group to achieve a goal or complete a project. Through collaborative activity and by practicing skills with more experienced peers and adults, students were able to accomplish the following: (1) acquire a mastery of basic skills; (2) develop higher mental functions of logical memory, abstract thought, and categorical reasoning; and (3) internalize the problem-solving process for future activities and individual assessments (Rogoff & Wertsch, 1984).

Peer and Cross-age Tutoring. One of the elementary schools served as a site for students from the middle school to gain youth-service experience as tutors for the elementary students. The program, supported by the local Coca-Cola Bottling Company, identified potential youth dropouts and trained them as tutors. The program resulted in higher self-esteem, fewer disciplinary problems, and improved grades and attendance for both middle school and elementary school students.

Classes for Linguistically Diverse Students. One elementary school switched from homogeneously grouped LEP classes to heterogeneously grouped classes. Students who were language proficient in English were in the same classes with students who were dominant Spanish speakers and were in transition to English. Teachers stressed that students were able to transition faster because they were learning from students who were strong English speakers.

Another elementary school provided bilingual classes for recent immigrants, in which mathematics instruction was done in Spanish. Once students achieved a conceptual understanding of math in their primary language, they went to the ESL block, where the teacher relabeled the terms and concepts in English. Migrant students were in bilingual classes and were mainstreamed in regular classes according to their ability to speak and understand instruction in English.

Mathematics Instruction

Integration of Mathematics into Other Subject Areas. At all elementary schools, instruction of basic skills and academic content was organized around thematic units or integrated between and across subject areas.

Manipulatives. Without question, teachers believed that manipulatives and hands-on experiences were the key to student understanding in mathematics. Manipulatives were used: (1) to teach students basic skills in mathematics, (2) to introduce students to mathematical concepts and develop their understanding of such from the concrete to the abstract, (3) to involve students in critical-thinking and problem-solving activities, (4) to encourage students to ask questions and be active participants in the learning process, and (5) to foster continued interest and motivation for learning mathematics on a daily basis.

Selection of manipulatives, however, was not limited to commercially or teacher-made materials. Manipulatives made by students in art class or as a natural outcome of creative discovery and experimentation were prevalent. Examples of commercially made manipulatives are pattern blocks, fraction factory pieces, transparent chips, rainbow cubes, tangrams, compasses, geo-boards, units of measure for mass and weights, play money, electric boards, and flash cards. Examples of manipulatives made or provided by teachers and students include: collages and cut-and-paste materials made from newspapers and magazines; string, tape, straws, and chalk for counting and measuring distances or proportions or visualizing geometric shapes and sizes; students themselves acting as manipulatives, or everyday materials brought from home or used in the classroom, such as boxes, books, clocks, and desks; flannel boards, bulletin boards, the chalkboard, charts and graphs, posters, bingo math, or other math games; and Popsicle sticks or other manipulatives to signal "yes" or "no" for answering questions in guided practices and for checking student understanding.

Instructional Strategies for Linguistically Diverse Students. Effective elementary school classrooms were characterized by a highly interactive and supportive environment. Students developed thinking skills and learned to form, express, and exchange mathematical ideas and concepts through dialogue. By questioning and sharing ideas and knowledge through conversation, students learned new skills and concepts as they jointly participated in instructional conversations with the teacher or their peers (Tharp & Gallimore, 1991). Mathematics teachers integrated normal language use and interactive instructional approaches (Gersten & Woodward, 1994; Moll & Whitmore, 1993).

Students were empowered by their classroom experiences in the following ways: (1) the students' language and culture were regularly incorporated into the mathematics instruction and activities, (2) students were actively engaged in the generation of knowledge and the selection of appropriate topics for learning through genuine dialogue and meaningful language use (Cummins, 1993; Nuñes, 1992), and (3) interactional patterns of the classroom gave expression to multiple voices (Cummins, 1993). Through a multifaceted array of language experiences and interactions, a positive student self-identity was constantly being shaped.

Student-Initiated Learning and Brainstorming Through Interactive Classroom Cultures. When students broke into groups, they worked together to attain a goal. Within each group, they brainstormed possible solutions. Once the group attained its goal, one or more members presented their findings to the class. One teacher cut up overhead transparencies and distributed problems to different members of the class. Students worked individually, in pairs, or in a group to figure out problems and then taught the entire class, supporting their answer with argumentation and rationale. Students with other ways of solving the problem were invited to add to the discussion or try to offer alternative approaches. Students worked in a collaborative climate and learned to raise questions and formulate creative and critical analyses of problems and solutions.

Relating Mathematics to Work-Related or Practical Skills and Student Interests

Effective elementary teachers were able to connect mathematics with students' knowledge and cultural backgrounds. Students were invited to bring in their own stories or experiences and, as a class, they searched for ways in which mathematics and other subjects were applicable to the situation or story. A greater focus was placed on learning within a recognized context. Authentic or simulated contexts and environments (Bishop, 1985; Lo, Wheatley, & Smith, 1994) were used whenever possible. These provided naturally appropriate opportunities for students to interact and apply math to real life with teachers and peers.

Integrating Math with Other Subjects Through Field Trips. Teachers, students, and parents from one grade raised money through community activities to take students to the NASA space center in Houston. Students, staff, and parents were divided into small groups and were allowed to learn together. Prior to their field trip, teachers prepared students by exposing them to language experiences and simulated activities in all subject areas. By the time they got to the space center, students had a repertoire of experiences and understanding of the terminology and were able to make connections between math and science and what they were observing and experiencing.

Integrating Computer Technology with Students' Interests and Other Subjects. While students were talking about altitudes and the speed of rockets at NASA, they decided to contact NASA for further information via the Internet. After the students got the information and formulas for speed and velocity from NASA, teachers and students talked about the basic operations in the formula and what they meant. Students were excited because they were able to receive the information so quickly and searched for other ways to "surf the net" for information on topics of interest.

Assessment of Students' Skills and Needs

At all schools, teachers reported that they try to minimize the use of standardized tests to monitor progress. Nevertheless, they regularly assessed students with textbook or teacher-made tests at the end of each week.

Individualized Testing on Student Learning Styles. Kindergarten students were tested and a profile of their learning styles was prepared. Teachers had a full understanding of the ways and conditions under which each student learned best. They made every attempt to make the learning environment conducive to the strengths and preferences of every student. For example, students who were visual learners were taught with pictures, charts, or words. A general understanding of learning styles and implementation of various teaching styles and supports also helped increase student understanding in the classroom as a whole.

Informal Evaluation. Teachers at all elementary research sites stressed that they monitored student progress primarily through working with students one-on-one or by observing students in groups. Oral testing was performed frequently, particularly when students were still in the beginning stages of skill or concept formation. Many teachers felt that oral assessments removed pressure from students to perform well on written tests and helped them to: (1) focus more on understanding, (2) develop a mathematics vocabulary, (3) learn how to "think out loud" as they solved problems (Cobb, Wood, & Yackel, 1993), and (4) develop a firm foundation of language skills (in both English and Spanish) for later critical-thinking and problem-solving use.

Student Portfolios and Projects. After students completed work on a specific skill or objective, they frequently were assigned individual or group projects. Some projects required students to apply math to other subject areas or to gather information from contexts other than the classroom. Projects were not assigned unless students had already demonstrated a firm grasp of the relevant mathematical concepts or applications. For group projects, each student was held accountable for a certain phase of the project. Projects were due prior to formal assessment to ensure that students who were still struggling could be retaught if necessary.

To determine whether students were making progress in terms of skills and objectives, one school involved students in a daily maintenance program. Students were tested on one or more of the 13 TAAS objectives and, after receiving immediate feedback, graphed their progress in their folders. Students and teachers went over the profile together and determined the best approach for improving weak areas. Because students were involved in the assessment process, they were more willing and eager to receive special tutoring or assistance. During parent conferences, students were expected to explain their portfolios to their parents.

Computer Activities or Computer-Generated Profiles. Teachers involved students in computer-assisted activities in varying ways. They (1) assessed students' mastery of mathematics content or objectives, (2) retaught or strengthened certain mathematics skills, (3) diagnosed students' weaknesses and set up an individualized program of study and practice for each student, or (4) provided students and teachers with a profile of students' progress and helped teachers plan accordingly for subsequent lessons and activities.

Computer-Assisted Technology. The elementary schools provided students with computer-assisted instruction. One of the schools used a program that automatically placed students at their level. Students in pre-K, kindergarten, and first grade worked more with games, whereas students in the upper elementary grades focused more on TAAS skills. For example, math activities frequently were integrated into a story so students practiced reading and math skills at the same time. One elementary school was networking the computers in the classroom with the computer programs in the math lab so students could work independently on their math skills when they completed their classwork.

What Made These Elementary Schools Effective?

Strong Administrative Support and Communication. Strong leadership was cited by the schools as a major contributor to the overall effectiveness of each elementary school. Principals were always looking for ways to help teachers become better by one or more of the following: (1) offering teachers staff development time for planning together, (2) sending teachers to additional training seminars or workshops, (3) keeping teachers up-to-date with relevant research literature on teaching and learning, and (4) offering support to teachers through an open-door policy and ethic of care and justice.

Teacher Commitment. Teachers believed that teamwork helped invigorate them to try new ideas and seek alternative methods for instruction. Teamwork also contributed to a positive school climate and facilitated a more relaxed atmosphere because teachers were willing to carry the load and help one another with students and planning for instruction. In addition, teachers were willing to go the extra mile to help students in the classroom or help teachers with other students.

Strong Parental and Community Support. Elementary teachers felt that a major reason they were effective was parent involvement. The school held monthly parent meetings to educate parents about certain topics of interest to them or show them ways they could help their children learn. Parents also were asked to give input to teachers regarding their child's learning style and conditions they believed were most conducive for their child to study. Special speakers included individuals from Region One, community members, teachers, and administrators from the school. For example, parents were shown different strategies for helping their children with homework and were informed about possible reasons their children were having problems at school. Teachers also made home visits or sent communiques regularly to parents to update them on their children's progress.

Wide Variety of Programs and Activities for Students and Faculty. All school sites offered a wide variety of programs and instructional supports for both students and faculty. The school served as a hub of activity for students in and after school. One teacher noted that some type of event or activity was always occurring in the school that included and benefited students. Examples of student clubs included an acting club, a drug-free club, and a karate club. In addition, students were allowed to stay after school until they were picked up by their parents and were given access to the computer lab to get ahead in their lessons. A program (SNAP) also was created for students who needed an extra push or motivation to achieve.

Teachers acted as big sisters or big brothers to students and met regularly with them to see how they were doing, to encourage them, and to give positive reinforcement.

MIDDLE SCHOOLS

Mathematics Programs and Curriculum

In the middle schools, teachers were given a suggested curriculum framework based on the TAAS objectives and essential elements. The framework specified all the subjects and skill areas that should be taught within each academic school year. Although the school district provided teachers with a specific curriculum, teachers did not necessarily follow the time line that was dictated by the curriculum. As a mathematics department, teachers met to prioritize what students should be taught on the basis of what the teachers believed was most important for the students. Teachers also concentrated on the TAAS objectives and determined the order in which objectives should be presented. Thus, the math departments designed their own time lines according to the specific needs of the students they served.

In addition to a departmental time line, mathematics teachers for each grade level developed their own time lines and the specific skills and abilities to be mastered by each student in his or her specific grade. All the teachers started at the same grade level. They recognized, however, that some students may differ in their ability to comprehend specific mathematics concepts and skills. Thus, teachers realized classes might be at different places in the curriculum as they progressed through the year.

Mathematics Textbooks. Although teachers used the mathematics textbook, they found that the skills presented in the text did not correspond with the TAAS objectives as they are tested. Consequently, the math text was used primarily to introduce different concepts and skills prior to their application to the TAAS. Because the text was not the sole resource for instruction, teachers provided students with commercial and school-made materials that were based on the TAAS objectives and that simulated the format of the TAAS test.

Supplementary Materials. Other materials that teachers used to introduce and reinforce lessons included varying forms of manipulatives such as math grids and calculators. Manipulatives such as algebra tiles, fractionals, balance scales, and measurement instruments help students transfer and apply their concrete understanding of mathematical skills and concepts to the abstract characteristics and principles of mathematics. Teachers we interviewed stressed that manipulatives help students draw on previously learned information and knowledge to construct new knowledge and make sense of mathematical concepts and skills.

Math Tutorials and Computer Programs. Many of the programs were created by the math department within the school or district. Other programs focused on the development of mathematical or reading skills. TAAS math tutorials such as "Auto Skills" and "Step Up to TAAS" were used in the classroom and reinforced in the computer lab. Other resources included "TAAS Coach;" "TAAS Master;" "TAAS Moment," a program that involved students in practicing TAAS test items for 15 minutes, 2 to 3 days a week; and "Stick with the TAAS," a booklet that is provided by the state and gives sample problems from the TAAS test.

Saturday Academy. At one of the middle schools, students who were experiencing difficulty mastering the mathematics objectives were invited to participate in the Saturday Academy. The Saturday Academy originally was created to help students in mathematics and science. It provided hands-on activities where students worked with graphing calculators. Through manipulative activities, students were introduced to mathematics concepts and skills that are essential for pre-algebra and algebra. The Academy included a computer lab where students concentrated on developing math skills related to TAAS objectives. Such expanded learning opportunities nourished the strengths of individual students in mathematics and helped them overcome many of their weaknesses (Cummins, 1993).

In addition to providing specialized instruction, the Saturday Academy encouraged greater involvement of the home in learning activities. Students were asked to bring a learning partner, such as a parent or sibling, to help them both develop an understanding of mathematical concepts and hone their higher-level thinking skills. In this way, younger siblings and future students could be exposed to math before they entered the middle school. Moreover, parents were more aware of their youngster's skill level, strengths, and weaknesses and could provide the necessary support at home.

Informal Student Surveys. Some teachers developed their mathematics programs on the basis of the results of a personality or life-experiences survey they created. For example, at the beginning of the year, some teachers administered a survey to the students to learn about their cultural background and previous life experiences. In turn, they tried to equate what was being learned in the classroom to something that students knew, understood, or experienced so the learning was personally relevant to the students. Many of the teachers in the schools we visited had grown up in the community and were able to use their experiences and knowledge of the students' families and community to connect with the students.

Organizational Aspects of Instruction

Academic Teaming. The middle schools followed the academic teaming concept to strengthen their overall school program and instructional delivery system. Teachers of different subjects were brought together to teach the same students. Teachers were given common conference periods to allow them to integrate curricula across subjects and to work together to enhance students' intellectual development (National Council of Teachers of Mathematics, 1989). Teachers reported the following benefits from academic teaming: (1) teachers drew on one another's expertise and knowledge to create thematic units and implement innovative instructional strategies; (2) teachers got to know their students better; (3) students developed a stronger connection with their teachers, their peers, and the subject matter; and (4) opportunities for learning in real-life contexts occurred more frequently. The teaming concept also fostered camaraderie within each team and offered students a support group of teachers and peers.

Consistent expectations between teachers regarding student behavior also improved classroom discipline. When necessary, teams met with students and, in more severe cases, the parents, to discuss any problems that affected the student's schoolwork or relationships at school such as motivation, behavior problems, or personal problems. Most of the time, however, the problem was resolved through the initial team contact with the student. When a problem was serious, teachers referred the student to a school counselor or other support services.

TAAS Classes Via Block Scheduling. In one of the middle schools, TAAS team classes were offered to students whose TAAS scores were just below the passing score and who, with regular instructional support and coaching on specific skills, were likely to pass the TAAS test. These mathematics classes were scheduled in 90-minute blocks. Block scheduling enabled the teacher to focus on one skill or objective and go through the instructional stages (a warm-up, direct instruction, guided practice, question and answer, testing or informal evaluation, and reteaching, if needed). Students were able to concentrate on a specific mathematics skill and practice the procedural steps involved in achieving that skill from beginning to end.

As a result, students did not go home with much homework. Instead, they learned the work before they went home and could complete their assignment in class. Because teachers were able to explain the objective in one day's lesson, they spent less time reviewing work from the previous day. Students were able to spend more time on skill reinforcement, individual or group projects, and enrichment activities, and build a strong foundation for using higher-order thinking skills. In addition to 90-minute block scheduling, teachers also offered additional tutoring for students before and after school.

Cooperative Learning. In most cases, teachers stated that students eventually are divided into cooperative-learning groups and work together. In cooperative learning, students are placed in small, heterogeneous groups where they receive group rewards as well as individual grades (National Council of Teachers of Mathematics, 1989). Many teachers stressed that cooperative-learning strategies support students in the discovery learning process and strengthen student understanding of mathematical skills and concepts. They felt that cooperative learning is most effective when students are working on group activities or projects, or are learning certain skill or subject areas, as opposed to individual projects.

Peer and Cross-age Tutoring. In addition to cooperative learning, many teachers have students act as peer tutors by pairing students together within the class or have students draw on the strengths of other students in the school. In many cases, the peer tutor communicates to the student in his or her native language. Nearly every interviewed teacher observed that students often are able to explain problems more effectively than the teachers and in a way that other students understand so that they can make the necessary connection to what is being learned. Through cross-age tutoring, older tutors review basic skills and provide individual instruction to younger tutees (National Council of Teachers of Mathematics, 1989). Because of the noise level, however, teachers take certain precautions to make sure students have the necessary guidance regarding classroom rules for interaction and group or paired learning activities.

Mathematics Instruction

Thematic Units. To engage students in mathematical reasoning and critical-thinking activities, mathematics teachers worked with members of their academic teams to develop thematic, interdisciplinary units. The teachers promoted competency in specialized subject areas and encouraged students to reason critically and to integrate information from several disciplines (National Council of Teachers of Mathematics, 1989). Thematic units helped students make connections between and across the mathematics, reading, writing, science, social studies, and arts curricula by presenting information and discovery learning opportunities via a multisensory, multidisciplinary approach.

Manipulatives. Mathematics teachers reported frequent use of manipulatives. Nearly every interviewed teacher emphasized the need to involve students in hands-on experiences and provide students with visual representations of mathematical concepts and the procedural steps involved in problem solving and higher-level thinking skills. To introduce lessons and induce student interest and curiosity, teachers immersed students in discovery learning experiences through the use of manipulative activities, games, puzzles, or brain-teaser exercises. Manipulatives also were used to reinforce previously learned mathematics skills. Teachers incorporated everyday items that students brought from home or that they encountered in everyday life into the lessons. Thus, teachers related the mathematics content to students' lives and gave practical examples of how and why an understanding of mathematics was necessary for the future.

Measurements. Working in cooperative learning groups, students measured and charted the lengths, widths, and heights of various objects in the classroom and did the same with different objects in the school (cafeteria, administrative offices, hallway), in the parking lot, and on the school grounds. Students compared and contrasted measurements taken in the classroom to those taken outside the classroom.

To learn about weights, one teacher had students bring apples to class. Students weighed the apples at varying points in the project. For example, they peeled the apples, weighed them, and then cut them into quarters and slices, and weighed them each time, recording weights and describing the characteristics of the apples each time they were weighed. Students strung the apples across the classroom and 3 weeks later weighed them again. They discussed the differences in weight and described the ways in which the apples changed over time.

Instructional Strategies for the Linguistically Diverse Students. Students who experienced language difficulty in the classroom were given opportunities to learn in their primary language. Many teachers paired these students with other students who could translate for or communicate with the students in their native language. Some teachers permitted students to group naturally with one another. Teachers monitored the students and assisted them in their work and activities. When introducing a specific skill, many teachers reported acting as translators when necessary to ensure that students acquired a thorough understanding of the mathematical concepts and terms applied in the classroom.

Using Students as Experts in the Classroom. The teachers translated or used other students who had excellent Spanish skills. At the beginning of the year or semester, some teachers observed different classes and selected one or more students who demonstrated excellent Spanish-speaking skills to assist in the class. The student came to the lab, the teacher read in English, and the student translated in Spanish. Students were encouraged to try to answer questions in English as much as possible.

Modifications in the Classroom. Although linguistically diverse learners acquired mathematical skills quickly, some needed modifications, particularly with word problems. In such instances, teachers slowed down the instructional pace or asked students individual questions to assess their level of understanding. They focused on developing students' comprehension skills. The bottom line was, "Did the students understand the concept?" Because of the amount of vocabulary needed to understand math concepts, teachers focused heavily on teaching students the techniques for reading and understanding mathematics vocabulary.

Some teachers stated that if they placed students at the front of the room, students were more likely to ask questions about any material they did not understand. To help students experience success and develop self-confidence, teachers asked students questions they knew the students would be able to answer and gradually increased the level of difficulty of the questions. Most teachers tried to camouflage any instructional modifications they made for students. They wanted the students to experience success, but not at the expense of being singled out or identified as needing extra help or modified assignments.

Relating Mathematics to Work-Related or Practical Skills and Student Interests

In addition to the recommendations for developing skills in workplace literacy and critical thinking (National Council of Teachers of Mathematics, 1989) and providing a culturally responsive classroom learning environment, reports that target middle grades (Secada, 1992) stress the importance of teaching adolescents the following human qualities: (1) compassion, (2) regard for human worth and dignity, (3) tolerance and appreciation of human diversity, (4) a desire for social justice, (5) collaboration, (6) problem solving, and (7) conflict resolution. Middle school teachers noted that they link these qualities to various mathematics applications and activities that students participate in, both in and out of the classroom.

World of Work and Social Skills. Occasionally, students engaged in cooperative-learning activities experience conflicts with one another or have difficulty getting along with certain members of their group. In such instances, teachers pointed out the need for students to develop social skills to enable them to work with individuals that have different personalities. The class members discussed the world of work and future careers and the likelihood that they may encounter people who have different work habits or are more introverted or extroverted than others. Teachers served as facilitators and helped students solve problems. Students also learned to use one another's expertise and knowledge to reach a common goal.

Money and Percentages. To apply money problems and percentages to what the students knew, teachers converted or related story problems to situations that incorporated the students' way of life. For example, teachers related a problem that dealt with percentages to discount shopping at a department store, a car dealership, or their local food store. In addition, the teachers used newspaper advertisements and had the students visit a department store and calculate and compare the advertised sale percentage and reduced price with the actual amount in savings. Some teachers challenged their students to look for discrepancies between the two and emphasized that they should check to make sure they were being charged the correct amount. When the two amounts did not correspond with one another, the teachers and students discussed issues that were related to economics and consumers' rights. When students studied interest, they went through the process of buying a house and learned how much they would pay in interest on a home loan. They learned the importance of becoming wise consumers and making sure they "read the fine print" on a contract to determine the best deal on a house or car.

Home Construction and Geometry. Students were encouraged to talk about home improvements or construction such as painting, floor coverings, wallpapering, or carpentry that was being done by members of their family. Teachers used the students' parents and their home-improvement efforts as resources in teaching or supplementing student learnings. Students were able to connect mathematical principles with real-world activities when the teacher stressed the need to understand how to take accurate measurements of angles and find the perimeter, area, or volume of a room when working on the home.

Assessment of Students' Skills and Needs

Formal Evaluation. One of the middle schools used pretests and posttests. Students were given a pretest at the beginning of each semester and a posttest at the end of each semester. Teachers reported that the pretest exposed the students to what they would be learning each semester and helped teachers plan and tailor their instruction more effectively. The posttest helped teachers determine how much each student had improved. If the students had not mastered a specific skill, they were retaught and the skill was tested in a different format. Teachers also used their own teacher-made tests to assess students' understanding of specific math skills and concepts on a weekly basis and retaught and retested when necessary.

Informal Evaluation. Students were assessed regularly through a variety of methods. For example, students were required to complete a short quiz or asked to demonstrate and explain the procedures for working a problem or to find the answer to a specific problem. When students did not work the problem correctly or reached an incorrect solution, the teacher and students worked together to help the students solve the problem correctly and achieve success.

Use of Verbal and Nonverbal Cues. Teachers reported that they checked for student understanding throughout their classroom instruction. If students did not converse or did not participate, the teacher interpreted that as a possible sign that they did not understand, required further clarification, or needed to be taught differently.

Daily Work, Quizzes, or Homework. Many teachers used students' daily work and homework as informal assessments of student progress. Occasionally, they gave the students a four- or five-problem quiz. Teachers also engaged students in a lot of practice drills by involving them in question-and-answer recitation drills. On other occasions, students completed exercises or activities on an overhead transparency, or worked with manipulatives to reinforce their understanding of mathematics. In many cases, the students were not aware of the fact that their skill needs and abilities were being assessed.

Computer-Generated Profiles. In the computer lab, students were administered quizzes via the "Cinch It" computer program to check for mastery of each objective. Based on the students' quiz results, the Cinch It program created a profile for each student. Students who needed extra practice could receive computer-assisted instruction and advance at their own pace.

Collaborative Evaluation Techniques. Academic teaming helped teachers identify any academic, behavioral, social, or family-related problems that could be interfering with the students' schoolwork. By meeting as a team, students heard positive feedback from teachers of the classes in which they were excelling or doing satisfactory work as well as those classes where improvements were needed. Teachers were able to get to know the students better and work with other members of the team to identify any problems and make necessary corrections or suggestions for improvement. Teachers stressed the importance of using the team as a positive support and not as a threat to the student. If the student was doing well in a particular subject, that subject area teacher worked with the student's other teachers and offered assistance to both the student and teachers.

What Makes These Middle Schools Effective?

Strong Administrative Support and Communication. The teachers and administration were willing to try innovative ideas. Administrators strove to stay abreast of new programs and instructional programs that would help teachers improve instruction and enhance relationships between the school and the community. Administrators actively sought ways to support faculty through grants, funding for staff development, or searching for ways to buy new programs and materials.

Academic Teaming and Block Scheduling. Teachers felt that they could experiment and take more risks at innovative teaching because they had a support group through their team to discuss and brainstorm new ideas and topics to cover. Moreover, block scheduling enabled both students and faculty to benefit from a more comprehensive presentation of subject matter and provided ample time for guided practice, discovery and simulated learning activities, the development of critical thinking skills, and extra help when necessary.

Teacher Commitment. Overall, the faculty was willing to undertake new challenges, try new curricula, and implement change. The background of the faculty was diverse and reflected that of the student body. Teachers stressed their commitment to enriching the students' learning experiences and increasing student achievement. Many faculty were continuing their own education to gain additional skills to enhance their instructional practice.

In the end, teachers voiced a strong sense of unity and cohesiveness, both as a math department and a faculty as a whole. They continually shared ideas and worked together to strengthen faculty in other subject areas. Teachers did not believe they were just doing a job from 8 in the morning to 3 in the afternoon. Because of the pleasure many of them received from participating in efforts to increase student achievement, many considered their position to be a 24-hour job.

HIGH SCHOOLS

Mathematics Programs and Curriculum

Mathematics Textbooks. In both high schools, most of the mathematics teachers used the textbook as a primary curriculum resource. Instruction centered on the TAAS objectives, the essential elements, and specific objectives listed in the math texts. Selection of texts was based on what teachers felt would fit their needs as well as students' needs. Some teachers stressed the use of the textbook as a resource and were not driven by the math text in their instructional efforts. For example, students learned math definitions that were listed in the glossary or unit in the text. Most teachers sequenced their instruction in accord with the time line that was determined by the math department and, if necessary, tailored the text and presentation of topics and skills to the needs of their specific students.

Supplementary Materials. Despite a greater reliance on the text, teachers emphasized that they did not stick to any set curriculum but used whatever worked best for students. When teachers found materials or programs that made a connection with a certain type of learner or learning style, they shared those ideas with teachers who taught similar types of learners. Many made their own worksheets to strengthen or reinforce specific skills. Manipulatives and items such as newspapers and magazines were used with students who learned at a slower pace. Several teachers maintained an activity center with various materials that students could use for mathematics and school-related projects or activities. Manipulatives also were used to teach basic math skills and expose students to problem-solving skills and concepts. Other supplementary materials included posters, additional materials and workbooks related to TAAS, and real-life scenarios provided to students.

Math Tutorials and Computer Programs. Nearly every teacher incorporated some form of TAAS review into the regular structure of the course material. The questions and materials followed the TAAS format and were used at least once every week. Neither high school followed a set curriculum or set of programs and materials to prepare students for the TAAS. Some teachers drew from six or more TAAS-related publications and pieced them together to create their own curricula for TAAS. Examples of TAAS-related materials were "Step Up to TAAS," "TAAS Master," "TAAS Tutor," "Power TAAS," and "High on Mastery."

One high school used materials from the Office of Research and Development for Teacher Preparation. The materials focused on the development of critical-thinking skills. Problems required students to come up with new solutions that were entirely different from what they were accustomed to. Students had to develop alternative strategies or formats for answering each question.

Organizational Aspects of Instruction

The high schools placed a greater emphasis on content area and subjects than did the elementary and middle schools we visited. Consequently, instruction was organized more by specific subject areas and was much more compartmentalized. Students were tracked into different classes based on their ability and test scores.

Many courses were prerequisites for other courses, and some courses were designed to run over 2 years. Teachers maintained a greater level of independence in their approaches to teaching and rarely integrated mathematics across disciplines or with other subject areas.

The normal 45- to 55-minute period was in force at both schools. At one high school, however, classes were on a partial block schedule. Classes that met every day were 45 minutes. Classes that met every other day were 90 minutes.

Math Subjects and Scheduling of Classes. Algebra I introduces a variety of mathematical concepts and abstract ideas. For students who need additional time to learn the concepts and to practice and develop the skills inherent in algebra, the course spans 2 years. Teachers at one high school noted that the current geometry class requires students to use proofs. Many of the students, however, do not have the background for geometry. Therefore, the math department is restructuring the curriculum and hopes to introduce an informal geometry class that allows students to apply different aspects of geometry to real-life learning and naturally appropriate contexts.

Two-year classes contained students who had a difficult time with mathematics comprehension and language problems. The classes covered the same material at a slower pace. Teachers believed that, in many cases, 2-year classes were more intense since students spent more time completing the program. One teacher estimated that about 40 to 50% of the students in paced classes were not proficient in English.

Some classes consisted of students from freshman- to senior-class status. In such classes, teachers adjusted their teaching method to different levels of mathematical experience and expertise. Students generally took algebra I, geometry, and algebra II sequentially. Juniors and seniors who had not yet passed the TAAS were enrolled automatically in specific TAAS courses and given a large amount of TAAS-related instruction. In such classes, math instruction targeted the TAAS objectives. Teachers exposed students to as many word problems as possible. Combining classes from both high schools, the following courses were offered: TAAS prep., computer math, algebra I, geometry, algebra II, ACT-SAT prep., trigonometry, pre-calculus, and calculus.

Team Planning. Although teachers rarely met to plan thematic units or to integrate math into other subject areas, teacher representatives from each subject area worked together to ensure that students were prepared for subsequent courses. Lead teachers were also in the process of aligning the math curriculum between and across elementary school through high school. Although the curriculum was developed by the district, math departments at both high schools met monthly or weekly for one or more of the following reasons: (1) to discuss the overall curriculum, (2) to review the time line for teaching the TAAS objectives and essential elements, (3) to share teaching tips and materials with one another, and (4) to brainstorm ways in which they could incorporate TAAS objectives into their classes and help other subject area teachers with TAAS.

Classroom Instruction. Nearly every teacher followed a specific format or lesson cycle on a day-to-day basis. Teachers began their instruction with a focused activity and followed the activity with direct instruction or a question-and-answer session. After the presentation of new material and guided practice, students were divided into groups or pairs or asked to work independently on math assignments. In some cases, teachers described a traditional model of lesson delivery. For example, several teachers characterized a typical period of instruction in the following way: (1) teachers wrote the daily mathematics objectives on the board; (2) teachers reviewed previously learned material or asked students if they had any questions about the previous day's work; (3) students copied notes from the textbook; (4) teachers explained the meaning of new terms and went over examples from the book or created their own examples; (5) teachers and students engaged in guided practice and checking for understanding; (6) teachers assigned homework or independent practice; and (7) during independent study time, teachers monitored students and gave one-on-one help when needed.

On the other hand, many teachers described a highly interactive and group-oriented method of instruction. Focused activities varied from teacher to teacher. One teacher started his lessons with puzzles that required students to think critically. After students engaged in several puzzles, the teacher followed with a problem on the board that dealt with a TAAS objective or a new topic. These activities helped the students to settle down and focus within groups. Students were divided into five or six groups with four students per group. After a group worked together on assignments, a representative member from the group was asked to work a problem on the board and explain the problem-solving process to the class. If students were having difficulty, other members of the group were responsible for teaching those students.

Another teacher stressed that focus activities show students why the material is important to them. Prior to independent or group activity, he summarizes major concepts and invites questions. Students know they are free to ask questions throughout the remainder of the class. During independent study time, most teachers stated that they work one-on-one with students needing extra assistance.

Cooperative Learning and Peer Tutoring. The few teachers who deviated from the traditional model of instructional delivery involved their students in cooperative-learning activities on a regular basis. At the beginning of the year, some teachers allowed students to select the students with whom they wanted to work. Throughout the year, the teacher rearranged students into new groups. Students who were able to grasp specific skills and concepts were used as peer tutors or were given leadership roles to facilitate the efforts of other members of their group. In many situations, Spanish-speaking students were paired with bilingual students, and bilingual students helped explain the subject matter and problem-solving procedures in both Spanish and English.

Mathematics Instruction

Manipulatives. Teachers stressed that students grasp mathematical concepts more easily when manipulatives, visual aids, games, or activities are used in the instructional process. Nevertheless, teachers felt they needed more resources and materials for their classrooms. Many teachers made their own manipulatives or had students create visual aids and manipulatives to supplement lessons or as part of the lesson or activity involved in learning mathematical terms and concepts.

Instructional Strategies for Linguistically Diverse Students. Because high school students were scheduled into classes according to their test scores or based on a sequential ordering of course offerings, many teachers believed that some classes should follow the traditional model of instruction— teacher-centered delivery with students working independently in their seats or, on occasion, in pairs or groups of three. The most effective teachers of linguistically diverse students, however, structured their instruction more around a student-centered, collaborative model. These teachers believed their primary function was to create a caring classroom environment and help build students' self-confidence by empowering them with the necessary understanding of mathematical skills, concepts, and problem-solving abilities. For example, if students discovered an approach to solving a problem that differed from the teacher's, they were free to provide their strategies to the class or use procedures they felt more comfortable with. Focus was on student discovery and understanding, not rote learning or "one best way" of problem solving.

Teachers stressed math vocabulary for non-English students and quizzed them regularly to check for understanding. They spoke in Spanish to students when necessary. Throughout instruction, math concepts were related to the Mexican American culture and topics that interested the students. Reading and mathematics were integrated into the classroom, and teachers spent extra time with students in helping them understand and learn how to solve word problems.

Tapping into the Students' Culture. One teacher encouraged students to learn math vocabulary with a cultural poem or song. Students were also free to write their own poems and songs. To connect with many students' preferences for collaborative activity and to promote creativity, students were assigned both individual and group math projects. Occasionally, special speakers were invited to the class to discuss the importance of mathematics in the real world.

Teachers and students felt free to joke with one another within the boundaries set by the teacher and students. Respect and honesty were the guiding principles for all classroom activity. Students learned from each other. They were free to switch seats as long as they were working.

Many of the English math terms relate to the Spanish language. Because the terms are very similar, students can discover the similarities through language translation and visuals. In addition, when the problems are personally relevant to the students (such as adjusting the content of story problems to relate them more to where the students live; their culture, age group, and interests; and their environmental surroundings and personal experiences), students take a greater interest in learning mathematics.

Cooperative Learning and Student Experimentation. Students frequently were divided into five or six groups with four students per group. After students worked together on assignments, a representative member from a specific group was asked to work a problem on the board. Students were allowed to use whatever procedure or methods they found most useful or appropriate. Because one group often used a different strategy to work the problem, students were able to expand their repertoire of methods for working different kinds of problems. If students did an incorrect procedure to reach a solution, the entire class interacted and helped that group discover their mistake or make the necessary correction.

While students did their own work, they compared answers and checked to see how another peer approached the problem. Some argued or tried to convince the other person that their way was the correct way. When they both thought they were right, some students asked the teacher to intervene. The teacher did not help them but forced them to use their critical-thinking skills to draw on one another's strengths and to figure out the problem as a team. Although students became frustrated, they eventually worked the problem out. As a class, students got together and decided which solution they thought was better.

Relating Mathematics to Work-Related or Practical Skills and Student Interests

Everyday Interests. Most of the high school teachers we spoke with did not integrate math with other subject areas. However, many related students' everyday interests and activities to different aspects of mathematics. For example, one teacher used sports information and statistics to teach students how to read charts and understand percentages. Another teacher used cooking to teach fractions, and the different colors of candies to teach probability and to help students predict the number of candies that would be of a certain color.

Work-Related Skills and Applications to Practical Life in and out of School. Some teachers related geometry problems involving angles and slopes to carpentry and construction work. Regarding school subjects and future classes, teachers linked varying math topics to the TAAS objectives or linked geometry and trigonometry to algebra.

Making Connections Between Math and Real Life. Teachers stressed that they tried to instill in students the realization that there is no "one best way" for approaching or solving a problem. Instead, they helped students see different ways to solve the same problem. In turn, they suggested that the same principle applies to life. It doesn't matter how you got the answer, it just matters that you got the answer. As long as you can justify your rationale for finding the answer and stand behind your procedure or decision, there can be multiple perspectives and approaches to solving a problem in mathematics or life in general.

Critical-Thinking Skills for Careers. Teachers also tried to show students how they could use the same types of critical-thinking skills throughout their careers and as they aspired to achieve a career. For example, algebra gives students an appreciation for the need to develop accuracy and organization in their work. Students were taught to appreciate the need to develop the type of skills that would help them maintain or advance in their careers and respect the rights and safety of other workers. One teacher related the relationship between an incident in the news where a medical team amputated the wrong limb on a person and the importance of not being satisfied with getting an answer that is "close enough" (such as the difference between +1 and −1). Students were able to make the connection between real-life experiences, personal anecdotes, or current events and the importance of accuracy in thinking and following through to reach the proper solution. They learned not to settle for "second rate" work. The teacher also used students' stories or experiences to instill in students the need to develop self-discipline and apply personal-life situations to school-to-work applications.

Relating Math Subjects to Future Subjects and Skills Students Will Encounter in the Future. Students wanted to know the practical applications of algebra. The teacher explained that an understanding of algebra helps in developing logical, organized thinking. She tried to show students that algebra I and II served as the foundation for every other math class they would take as well as their future careers. Students were able to see the need for critical-thinking skills and the importance of developing the ability to work in groups, problem solve, and be flexible in their work habits and reasoning activities.

Assessment of Students' Skills and Needs

Formal Evaluation. Within the classroom, students normally were given tests every Friday that were based on the assignments from the week. Assessments were modified for students who were not able to understand English instruction. These students were expected to master the most basic concepts while increasing their language skills. Several teachers also exposed students to tests and exams that were similar to the SAT or ACT or to the types of tests they would encounter in college.

On a more global level, students were given a diagnostic test at the beginning of the year to determine their skill levels. When the test showed that the majority of students were having difficulty with a concept, students received additional instruction or were tutored by the teacher or cross-age peers. In addition, students taking algebra took an end-of-the-year algebra test at the end of the first or second year of algebra to determine their strengths and weaknesses and areas for improvement, both for teachers and students. Test results also were used to help determine the type of classes in which the students would be most likely to succeed during their junior and senior years.

Informal Evaluation. Teachers assessed students informally using a variety of methods. To determine students' mastery of lesson content or skills, teachers used question-and-answer techniques. During independent work, teachers monitored students as they worked in groups or independently. By listening to how the students explained the problems and interacted with one another, teachers were able to identify weak areas that needed clarification. Depending on the number of students who were not grasping the material, teachers retaught them as a group or through one-on-one instruction.

When going over homework—which consisted of several problems per skill area—students were asked to explain what they did, demonstrate their work on the board, or tell the next step in the problem-solving sequence. Other types of evaluation included (1) daily or weekly quizzes after every lesson, (2) homework assignments and tests, and (3) exams designed to determine the level of comprehension as correlated with the essential elements and TAAS objectives. Before- and after-school tutoring was offered to students who did not master the content. Students also were permitted to retest.

What Makes an Effective School?

Strong Administrative Support and Communication. Faculty and administration at both schools operated with an ethic of care and considered students their first priority. Teachers believed they had an open-door policy with the administration. The administrative staff encouraged new methods of teaching and tried to bring in new programs to help the student body. At one school, the principal, assistant principals, counselors, and members of the math department met monthly to discuss successes and problems in math classrooms.

Faculty Camaraderie and Teacher Commitment. Teachers at both high schools emphasized that members of their math department worked as a team. Teachers met and shared teaching tips. They were also willing to make changes, experiment with new programs, or try new teaching techniques as a department. Because of the camaraderie among the math department faculty, teachers felt free to argue and disagree but were also willing to stick together and work through their differences toward a common goal. They respected one another's opinions and did not put each other down because of different ideas.

Many of the teachers in the department went to college together, took math classes together, and started teaching at the same time. Math teachers got together on their own time and socialized. For example, teachers were involved in a campus-wide wellness program and aerobics classes for teachers and students and, as a department, went on a retreat to the state park. Overall, the math teachers worked together professionally and personally. Because the teachers and students valued a sense of community, they were able to work together effectively.

Willingness to Take Risks. Because of the close-knit ties that math teachers felt with one another, they were not afraid of failure. They considered risk taking and innovation as a normal part of the teaching and learning process. Even though they did not have a strong technological component in the schools, teachers considered themselves to be pro-technology, advocated the use of computer programs, attended staff development workshops, or visited other schools to get ideas for their own schools. Teachers also challenged students with a variety of math activities, projects, and events, and encouraged students to go on to college. Many emphasized the importance of math at the college level and instilled in students the desire to take advanced math classes.

Strong Parental and Community Support. In addition to strong administrative and faculty support, interviewees at both schools noted that parental and community support contributed to the overall effectiveness of their school. Members of the school and school community were close-knit and caring. Many teachers were from the community or had graduated from the high school in which they taught. They took pride in building their community through teaching and working with students. In turn, they felt that the community appreciated and supported their efforts to increase student achievement.

Students. Lastly, and most important, teachers at one high school stressed that they had few student discipline problems. They felt that students were interested in helping out around the school. As a result, students were united and supported one another as family.

CONCLUSIONS

Mathematics Programs and Curriculum

Students who are empowered by their school experiences are more likely to experience enhanced academic performance and positive social and emotional identity (Cummins, 1993). In the research sites, mathematics programs and curricula were selected or developed to empower students through their classroom experiences. The students' language and culture were incorporated into the mathematics program. In fact, students were encouraged to participate actively in generating knowledge and in selecting appropriate topics for learning.

Academically rich mathematics programs enhanced student learning and overall performance. The following curricular considerations were prevalent: (1) common belief that learning is a holistic endeavor; (2) respect for ethnic diversity; (3) use of students' language, culture, and strengths to plan and implement lessons around individual learning styles; (4) creative problem solving integrated throughout lessons and activities; and (5) involvement of parents and the community (Cummins, 1993; Garcia, 1991, 1993; Sosa, 1993).

Organizational Aspects of Instruction

In the elementary schools we visited, linguistically and culturally diverse mathematics classrooms served as learning environments that were open, friendly, and culturally inviting. In such classrooms, instructional arrangements allowed students to interact with one another and use collaborative-learning techniques. Parents were encouraged to participate in school activities and were involved in their children's learning.

Teachers modeled appropriate mathematical behavior, provided examples that would facilitate students' conceptions and communication about mathematics, and guided student activities (Baroody, 1991; Scheid, 1993, 1994). Depending on the students' needs, teachers used direct instruction, set up simulated practice sessions, or created situations that were conducive to discovery learning, divergent thinking, and open-ended problem solving (Noddings, 1990).

In the most effective classrooms and schools we visited, students received personal attention. Academic teaming in the elementary and middle schools helped lower the student–teacher ratio and gave teachers more time to interact with the students and monitor their progress in mathematics (Stedman, 1985, 1987). Although high school mathematics classes were organized more around a specific content area and 50- to 55-minute instructional periods, many teachers organized their teaching in a way that allowed students to work independently, in pairs, or in groups of three or four students.

Mathematics Instruction

The most effective mathematics classrooms incorporated student-centered instructional practices. Teachers drew on students' backgrounds, expertise, and knowledge throughout the instructional cycle. They incorporated resources from the students' cultural environments to make mathematics more relevant to the students' lives (Moll & Whitmore, 1993). Moreover, students were allowed to use Spanish as a tool for inquiry, communication, and thinking (Moll, 1992). An informal, family-like atmosphere fostered student learning.

Moreover, instruction was aimed at preventing rather than remediating academic problems. For example, students were permitted to progress from native language usage to English without feeling pressured to do so by the teacher. Teachers provided opportunities for students to learn through oral as well as written activities (Garcia, 1991, 1993; Sosa, 1993; Tharp & Gallimore, 1991). If a student experienced difficulty grasping a mathematical concept, the teacher instructed the student in his or her native language, allowed the student to work with a more knowledgeable peer, or both.

Across all grade levels, the most enthusiastic teachers used instructional strategies that required students to formulate and test hypotheses, execute specific mathematical operations, communicate and defend their answers, and reflect on the procedures they used and results they generated (Davis, Maher, & Noddings, 1990). Students were encouraged to construct their own mathematical concepts and relationships (Noddings, 1990). Throughout the instructional process, teachers and students offered alternative problem-solving strategies and assisted or questioned one another about their thinking as they attempted to solve mathematical problems. As students observed, practiced, and reflected (Brown, Collins, & Duguid, 1989; Daniels, 1993; Rojewski & Schell, 1994), teachers or other students mediated their learning.

Relating Mathematics to Work-Related or Practical Skills and Student Interests

Students want to know how what they are learning is going to apply to their future and how it is going to fit into their world. Mathematics classrooms must support the culture of students' lives (Cobb, Yackel, & Wood, 1992; Resnick, 1987; Sinclair, 1990). Before they can be motivated to achieve, students first must see the relevance of achieving in their lives (Moll & Whitmore, 1993). For example, the Secretary's Commission on Achieving Necessary Skills report (1992) indicates both skills and personal qualities essential for the workplace.

Teachers in the most effective schools stress the importance of mastering basic skills in mathematics; thinking, decision-making, problem-solving, and reasoning skills; and personal qualities such as personal responsibility, self-management, and integrity. In addition to relating the mathematics learning to students' futures and career-related interests, instructional programs that incorporated the culture of linguistically diverse students were also effective. For example, students were recognized as possessing certain skills and understanding, or "funds of knowledge" (Moll, 1992), acquired through their everyday social events and activities and exchanges, both in and out of the classroom. The most effective teachers took advantage of the social and cultural aspects of their students' lives and used students' social relations as a motive and context for acquiring and applying knowledge in the classroom. Students, then, had a vast reservoir of knowledge and skills that, when given the opportunity, could be used as a powerful curricular resource. Much of the teaching and learning was initiated by students' interests and their questions rather than imposed by adult teachers (Moll & Whitmore, 1993).

Assessment of Students' Skills and Needs

At all sites, especially elementary and middle schools, student progress was measured and monitored systematically. Nevertheless, teachers and administrators placed a greater emphasis on student development and the acquisition of a well-rounded academic curriculum than on test scores (Stedman, 1985, 1987). In addition, formal evaluations were used sparingly and only after students had shown consistently they understood the material to be tested. Formative assessments were frequent and involved a combination of informal evaluations, computer-based assessments, projects, and activities. Most teachers continued to review mathematical principles throughout the year. As they exposed students to new mathematical skills and concepts, teachers built upon previously learned student understanding. Thus, formative assessments played a major role in generating best instructional practices and effective mathematics classrooms. Student results, strengths, and needs for improvement were individualized, maintained as portfolios, and discussed frequently with both the student and his or her parents.

Integration of Educational Technology

Numerous reports have suggested that technology holds great potential for revolutionizing education (Mathematical Sciences Education Board, 1990; National Council of Teachers of Mathematics, 1989; National Research Council, 1989). Nevertheless, technology purchases and uses have been driven more by efforts to improve the effectiveness of what schools are already doing than by efforts to transform what schools do. Choices about instructional software frequently have been based on whether the system was likely to increase standardized test scores. Many of the available systems are aligned with existing curricula and tests, are individualized and self-paced, and require little, if any, teacher involvement (Cummins, 1993).

Although many of the schools we visited used similar types of programs, the most effective teachers supplemented computerized programs with instructional approaches that had three principal features in common.

1. *Emphasis was placed on meaning and understanding.* Students were taught how to "read between the lines" when working with story problems. Teachers provided alternative problem-solving approaches and focused on helping students to understand what mathematical procedures were most appropriate for a given situation and how they could be used with unfamiliar problems.

2. *Mathematical skills were embedded in context.* A conceptual understanding of mathematics was emphasized and discrete mathematical skills were de-emphasized. Whenever possible, a range of mathematical topics other than arithmetic were included in the curriculum. Materials related to geometry, measurement, problem solving, logical reasoning, statistics and probability, and patterns and sequence also were used.

3. *Connections were made between subject areas and between school and life outside of school.* Instructional approaches stressed the correlation between subjects and connected what students were learning in school to their culture and relationships with friends, family, and the real world (Cummins, 1993; Heath, 1983).

While students were exposed to computerized programs that were geared primarily to the TAAS, effective teachers acted as facilitators and encouraged student inquiry and the construction of knowledge. Classroom and computerized activities were learner-centered and interactive. Teachers and students collaborated and interchanged roles from learner to expert and vice versa. Student assessment included criterion-referenced data, portfolios, and performances. In short, technology was used as a catalyst for change and as a tool for creating, implementing, managing, and communicating a new conception of teaching and learning mathematics and a system that supports it (Heuston, 1994). In the process, basic skills in mathematics were learned as well or better through these alternative instructional approaches.

What Makes an Effective School?

At the end of the interview, we asked teachers to tell us what they most believed made their school effective. Across the board, teachers communicated the belief that strong administrative support and a faculty commitment to students and their academic achievement and well-being were the major contributors to their success. In other words, a strong and cohesive school climate that fostered a community for learning was viewed by all teachers as more important than programmatic and instructional efforts. Nevertheless, teachers also targeted specific best practices that were shared by all grade levels or were specific to their particular grade level.

To varying degrees, each school site established a school and classroom climate that was conducive to learning and matched the culture of the individual school as well as its members (i.e., administrators, teachers, students, and staff). At the same time, it is imperative that borderland school districts and their individual schools note that the success of any mathematics program within a school is dependent on

> a set of common values, beliefs, and norms of behavior that form a shared organizational culture. . . . Effective schools depend on such things as allocation of resources, community leadership, local policy-making, distribution of authority, district support, and freedom to be different. There is no model that can be duplicated and mass produced according to some blueprint. (Duttweiler, 1990, p. 74)

We stress Duttweiler's statement that "there is no model that can be duplicated and mass produced according to some blueprint" (p. 74). Each school must be given the freedom to look at its own culture and devise the best procedure for instruction that will meet the needs of their specific student population. In some cases, the school's organization and culture may need to be changed (Secada, 1991).

Although our interview protocol did not target school climate specifically, we found that a positive school climate was pervasive at all sites we visited. Mathematics teachers' and administrators' conceptions of how academic content should be taught, how and what students should learn, and what constituted evidence of student understanding shaped and determined the level of achievement and success students experienced. These positive attitudes were communicated to students through mathematics programs and instructional practices.

TEACHER BELIEFS ABOUT LEARNING AND
PERCEPTIONS OF STUDENT ABILITY

Throughout the schools, teachers communicated the belief, either explicitly or implicitly, that all students can learn. They never mentioned that their students were difficult to teach or were deficient in any manner. For example, teachers viewed the use of Spanish and bilingualism as a positive student attribute. Instructional models were based on a constructivist view of the learner as an active participant in the teaching and learning process. Constructivist ways of knowing are based on three principles of learning.

1. Learning is a process of knowledge construction, not absorbing and recording pieces of separate information.
2. Learning depends on previous knowledge as the principal means of constructing new knowledge.
3. Learning is closely related to the situation or context in which it takes
   place. (Resnick & Klopfer, 1989)

Teachers did not view themselves as the sole purveyors of knowledge. Instead, students were encouraged to select relevant information from their environment, interpret it through existing knowledge, and construct mean-ing in a given situation. Together, teachers and students developed a concep-tual understanding of mathematics and created new knowledge through goal-directed activities (Saxe, 1991). Instructional goals concentrated on helping students develop learning and thinking strategies that are appro-priate for working within a variety of settings and subject areas (Mayer, 1992).

Although much of the mathematics curriculum was based on the TAAS objectives and essential elements, teachers did not reduce their instruction to the automated practice of basic skills. Students were encouraged to inter-act with their social and physical classroom and school community. Thus, for each student, new knowledge and skills emerged and continued to develop throughout the teaching and learning process. Students were encouraged to use manipulatives to discover new facts and mathematical concepts. Knowledge construction was an ongoing process of discovery, experimenta-tion and hypothesis testing, and reconstruction (Wittrock, 1991).

STUDENT PERCEPTIONS REGARDING ABILITY TO LEARN

The most effective schools encouraged student-initiated inquiry and experimentation, incorporated activity-based instruction, and structured a learning environment to support interactive and cooperative-learning groups. To increase the participation of minority and female students in mathematics, intervention programs and activities—designed to cultivate personal relationships between teachers and students—had been initiated or were already in place (Clewell, Anderson, & Thorpe, 1992; Damarin, 1990; Garcia, 1991).

Because students were treated as active and able participants in the teaching and learning process, many students were involved in the day-to-day activities of the school and took responsibility for school affairs (Stedman, 1985, 1987). Consequently, they developed a strong belief in themselves and in their ability to learn. They also possessed a heightened view of other students' abilities, regardless of gender, class, ethnicity, or disability. Because students encountered positive social and academic events and consequences, their cognitive-processing abilities, goals and behaviors, and academic performance continued to develop and grow. Furthermore, students expected to succeed in the future. As a result, student learning, motivation, and self-esteem increased.

REFERENCES

Baroody, A. (1991). Teaching mathematics developmentally to children classified as learning disabled. In D. Reid, W. Hresko, & H. Swanson (Eds.), *A cognitive approach to learning disabilities* (pp. 375–429). Austin, TX: Pro-Ed.

Bishop, A. (1985). The social construction of meaning: A significant development for mathematics education? *For the Learning of Mathematics, 5*(1), 24–28.

Brown, J. S., Collins, A., & Duguid, P. (1989). Situated cognition and the culture of learning. *Educational Researcher, 18*(1), 32–42.

Clewell, B. C., Anderson, B. T., & Thorpe, M. E. (1992). *Breaking the barriers: Helping female and minority students succeed in mathematics and science.* San Francisco: Jossey-Bass.

Cobb, P., Wood, T., & Yackel, E. (1993). Discourse, mathematical thinking, and classroom practice. In E. A. Forman, N. Minick, & C. A. Stone (Eds.), *Contexts for learning: Sociocultural dynamics in children's development* (pp. 91–119). New York: Oxford University Press.

Cobb, P., Yackel, E., & Wood, T. (1992). A constructivist alternative to the representational view of mind in mathematics education. *Journal for Research in Mathematics Education, 23*(1), 2–33.

Cummins, J. (1993). Empowering minority students: A framework for intervention. In L. Weis & M. Fine (Eds.), *Beyond silenced voices: Class, race, and gender in United States schools* (pp. 101–117). New York: State University of New York Press.

Damarin, S. K. (1990). Teaching mathematics: A feminist perspective. In T. J. Cooney & C. R. Hirsch (Eds.), *Teaching and learning mathematics in the 1990's: 1990 Yearbook* (pp. 144–151). Reston, VA: National Council of Teachers of Mathematics.

Daniels, H. (1993). Coping with mathematics in the national curriculum: Pupil strategies and teacher responses. *Support for Learning, 8*(2), 65–69.

Davis, R. B., Maher, C. A, & Noddings, N. (1990). Introduction: Constructivist views on the teaching and learning of mathematics. In R. B. Davis, C. A. Maher, & N. Noddings (Eds.), *Constructivist views on the teaching and learning of mathematics* (pp. 1–3). Reston, VA: National Council of Teachers of Mathematics.

Duttweiler, P. C. (1990). A broader definition of effective schools: Implications from research and practice. In T. Sergiovanni & J. E. Moore (Eds.), *Target 2000: A compact for excellence in Texas's schools* (pp. 65–74). San Antonio, TX: Watercress Press.

Garcia, E. E. (1991). *The education of linguistically and culturally diverse students: Effective instructional practices.* Santa Cruz, CA: National Center for Research on Cultural Diversity and Second Language Learning.

Garcia, E. E. (1993). Language, culture, and education. In L. Darling-Hammond (Ed.), *Review of research in education* (pp. 51–98). Washington, DC: American Educational Research Association.

Gersten, R., & Woodward, J. (1994). The language-minority student and special education: Issues, trends, and paradoxes. *Exceptional Children, 60,* 310–322.

Heath, S. B. (1983). *Ways with words: Language, life, and work in communities and classrooms.* New York: Cambridge University Press.

Heuston, D. H. (1994). Technology in school improvement. In C. E. Finn & H. J. Walberg (Eds.), *Radical school reform* (pp. 193–221). Berkeley: McCutchan.

Lo, J., Wheatley, G. H., & Smith, A. C. (1994). The participation, beliefs, and development of arithmetic meaning of a third-grade student in mathematics class discussions. *Journal for Research in Mathematics Education, 25*(1), 30–49.

Mathematical Sciences Education Board. (1990). *Reshaping school mathematics.* Washington, DC: National Academy Press.

Mayer, R. E. (1992). Cognition and instruction: Their historic meeting within educational psychology. *Journal of Educational Psychology, 84,* 405–412.

Moll, L. C. (1992). Bilingual classroom studies and community analysis: Some recent trends. *Educational Researcher, 21,* 20–24.

Moll, L. C., & Whitmore, K. F. (1993). Vygotsky in classroom practice: Moving from individual transmission to social interaction. In E. A. Forman, N. Minick, & C. A. Stone (Eds.), *Contexts for learning: Sociocultural dynamics in children's development* (pp. 19–42). New York: Oxford University Press.

National Council of Teachers of Mathematics. (1989). *Curriculum and evaluation standards for school mathematics.* Reston, VA: Author.

National Research Council. (1989). *Everybody counts: A report on the future of mathematics education.* Washington, DC: National Academy Press.

Noddings, N. (1990). Constructivism in mathematics education. In R. B. Davis, C. A. Maher, & N. Noddings (Eds.), *Constructivist views on the teaching and learning of mathematics* (pp. 7–18). Reston, VA: National Council of Teachers of Mathematics.

Nuñes, T. (1992). Ethromathematics and everyday cognition. In D. A. Grouws (Ed.), *Handbook of research on mathematics teaching and learning* (pp. 557–574). New York: Macmillan.

Resnick, L. (1987). *Education and learning to think.* Washington, DC: National Academy Press.

Resnick, L., & Klopfer, L. (1989). Toward the thinking curriculum: An overview. In L. Resnick & L. Klopfer (Eds.), *Toward the thinking curriculum: Current cognitive research* (pp. 40–58). Alexandria, VA: Association for Supervision and Curriculum Development.

Rogoff, B., & Wertsch, J. V. (Eds.). (1984). *Children's learning in the "zone of proximal development."* San Francisco: Jossey-Bass.

Rojewski, J. W., & Schell, J. W. (1994). Cognitive apprenticeship for learners with special needs: An alternate framework for teaching and learning. *Remedial and Special Education, 15*(4), 234–243.

Saxe, G. B. (1991). *Culture and cognitive development: Studies in mathematical understanding.* Hillsdale, NJ: Erlbaum.

Scheid, K. (1993). *Helping students become strategic learners: Guidelines for teaching.* Cambridge, MA: Brookline.

Scheid, K. (1994). Cognitive-based methods for teaching mathematics. *Teaching Exceptional Children, 26*(3), 6–10.

Secada, W. (1991). Agenda setting, enlighted self-interest, and equity in mathematics education. *Peabody Journal of Education, 66*(2), 22–56.

Secada, W. (1992). Race, ethnicity, social class, language, and achievement in mathematics. In D. A. Grouws (Ed.), *Handbook of research on mathematics teaching and learning* (pp. 623–660). New York: Macmillan.

Secretary's Commission on Achieving Necessary Skills. (1992). *Report for America 2000.* Washington, DC: U.S. Department of Labor.

Sinclair, H. (1990). Learning: The interactive recreation of knowledge. In L. P. Steffe & T. Wook (Eds.), *Transforming children's mathematics education: International perspectives* (pp. 19–29). Hillsdale, NJ: Erlbaum.

Sosa, A. (1993). *Thorough and fair: Creating routes to success for Mexican-American students.* Charleston, WV: ERIC Clearinghouse on Rural Education and Small Schools.

Stedman, L. C. (1985). A new look at the effective schools' literature. *Urban Education, 20,* 295–326.

Stedman, L. C. (1987). It's time we changed the effective schools formula. *Phi Delta Kappan, 69*(3), 215–227.

Tharp, R. G., & Gallimore, R. (1991). *The instructional conversation: Teaching and learning in social activity.* Santa Cruz, CA: National Center for Research on Cultural Diversity and Second Language Learning.

Wittrock, M. C. (1991). Models of heuristic teaching. In K. Marjoribanks (Ed.), *The foundations of students' learning* (pp. 73–87). Fairview Park, NY: Pergamon Press.

CHAPTER 6

Creating Student-Centered Classroom Environments: The Case of Reading

William Rutherford

In her hallmark book, *Learning to Read: The Great Debate*, Chall (1967) classified approaches to beginning reading into two categories, code emphasis and meaning emphasis. The code-emphasis approach stresses teaching children to master the alphabetic code, while the latter approach stresses meaning. Others (Hayes, 1991) have described these two approaches as bottom-up or top-down. The debate about which approach is best for teaching reading continues to this day. Paralleling this debate have been numerous studies of the effectiveness of various reading programs or approaches ranging from basal reader programs to programmed reading. In recent years the concept of whole language (Hoffman, 1992) has come onto the scene and offers another perspective on literacy instruction throughout the grades, a perspective that also creates controversy among some educators.

ELEMENTARY SCHOOLS

The elementary schools in this study were not caught up in controversy or deliberation about what is the best method for teaching reading. It was true that most of the teachers reported that they used a whole language approach to literacy instruction, but they seemed to state this in passing rather than with a passion that indicated that this was the only right approach. The teachers in these schools talked about the various things they did in literacy instruction rather than about a particular approach they followed. Although they did not state it in so many words, it seemed that the teachers in these schools were guided by general principles of effective literacy instruction that could be applied to any program.

Two of the principles of effective instruction in reading are: (1) children learn to read by reading a wide variety of materials, and (2) materials children read should be easy, but not too easy (Gunning, 1992; Guszak, 1992). Gunning (1992) offers two additional principles of effective reading instruction: (1) skills should not be taught in isolation but in relation to meaningful connected reading, and (2) teachers should help students make connections between existing knowledge and concepts and new knowledge and concepts. The importance of building bridges between the reader's knowledge and text knowledge is supported by Pearson and Fielding (1991).

A final principle offered by Gunning is that success in reading is a significant contributor to enhanced self-esteem. For many years it has been known that self-esteem is significantly related to reading achievement (Brookover, Thomas, & Paterson, 1962; Wattenburg & Clifford, 1964). Students with low self-esteem tend to achieve poorly in reading. For this reason it is important that teachers provide instruction and personal support to help students enhance their self-concept. One significant way teachers in these schools met this need was to respect and utilize the culture and the language of the students to support instruction and to build self-concept. Another principle commonly accepted is that reading and writing should be seen as complementary processes and that both should be integrated in any instructional program (Kucer & Harste, 1991). Teachers frequently engaged students in writing activities. These activities often were related to stories or books the students were reading.

The practices of these teachers reflected other aspects of reading instruction that are supported by research. Good programs utilize a variety of materials and activities. The basal reader may be a part of these materials, but it is only a part of what is needed (Au & Mason, 1989). In this variety of materials there should be a range of fiction and nonfiction books along with other forms of print material such as newspapers and magazines (Hirsch, 1987). Students are to be encouraged to read from a variety of materials and to read regularly, for students become better readers when they read more (Anderson, Wilson, & Fielding, 1988). All teachers reported that students did much reading every day and that they read from a variety of materials. Also, teachers frequently read to students, a practice that has been shown to positively affect expressive language skills, comprehension, decoding, and receptive language skills (Dickinson & Smith, 1994; Morrow, 1990, 1992).

To be an effective reader the individual must comprehend what has been read. Comprehension is a process of constructing meaning, and this requires an interaction between the knowledge or schema the reader brings to the print and the message the author intended (Rumelhart, 1984). A task of effective reading instruction is to increase the knowledge a student brings to the printed page. Reading to students is one technique that can contribute significantly to vocabulary learning (Elley, 1989; Routman, 1994). Vocabulary is best learned when new vocabulary is related to what the student already knows (Gipe, 1980; Gunning, 1992). Effective instruction constantly creates experiences for learners that activate their schemata and enlarge and enrich them so as to increase the learners' capacity for new learning (Anderson, 1984). In these schools a good portion of reading instruction time was devoted to helping students develop new meanings and understandings from print materials. To do this teachers often used both Spanish and English to relate new information to the background of the students, a practice that promotes student success (Gambrell, 1997; Losey, 1995).

Student sharing and collaboration have been found to increase student interest and curiosity and may increase their confidence in their ability to be successful in school (Schunk, 1989). Cooperative activities also promote student engagement in work (Slavin, 1987). Classrooms where cooperative learning is utilized can provide students with a greater sense of control over their learning. This has positive effects on students' interest in schoolwork and it causes them to see themselves as more competent (Ryan & Grolnick, 1986). Cooperative learning was employed widely in the elementary schools in this study. This practice can be especially beneficial for students for whom English is a second language (Guthrie & Wigfield, 1997; Kagan, 1986; Losey, 1995).

Reading Programs and Curriculum

It would be nice, and no doubt very welcomed by educators, if there were an identifiable, easily transferable program or curriculum that led to success in reading in these elementary schools. This was not the case. In these schools there was an obvious operating principle of "we will do what it takes" to help all students succeed. Teachers were ever aware of the learning needs of individual children and constantly worked together to identify learning experiences that would benefit children. Sometimes this meant modified use of published curriculum materials or use of new or different computer programs. At other times this led to developing new materials or moving a child into a different group or class. This also could mean using a completely different approach to teaching a child. To find "the secret" to teacher successes in reading, one would have to look at more than programs or curriculum in these schools. One would have to know and understand the teachers and the school climate in which they worked.

In addition to their intense commitment to student success, there were other similarities between the two schools. Both had a high degree of collaboration and cooperation among the teachers. In each school there was an expectation shared by teachers and administrators that all children could and would succeed. Throughout the faculties there was a clear and consistent commitment to teach every child so that this expectation could be met. Teachers took advantage of all opportunities to learn about techniques or programs that might contribute to student learning. It was common for teachers to spend time after regular school hours to give extra help to students, to engage in teacher planning, or to work with the parent community in some way.

There were also differences between the two schools, and three stood out. In one school teachers adhered to a practice of on-level reading at all grade levels. This meant that all students were reading and working with the same reading material regardless of their reading level. This would appear to violate the above-stated reading principle of having children reading materials appropriate to their reading level. However, teachers were very sensitive to differing student levels and used many supplemental techniques and procedures to accommodate those who needed additional assistance. In the other school there was much more attention to the identification of student reading levels and provision of instruction according to level.

A second difference was in the use of a basal reading series. The school that adhered to on-level reading used the basal reader series as the core of its reading program. Basal readers certainly were used in the second school but as just one resource among many for assisting reading instruction, not as the core of the instructional program.

A third difference was in the use of technology in support of reading instruction. Technology use was very limited in the school that used basals as its core, while technology use was rather extensive and a very important part of reading instruction in the other school.

Reading Textbooks

In each school there was an adopted curriculum series for reading instruction (but not the same series in the two schools). This formal curriculum was utilized by all teachers throughout the grades, but how it was used varied from school to school and teacher to teacher. Basic differences in basal usage between the two schools have been described above; yet, within these schools there were differences in the way basals were used. Some teachers attended closely to the scope and sequence of skill instruction proposed by the basal series but used the stories in the basal in a limited way. Others used the stories regularly but made their own determination of skill instruction that was needed. Some teachers designed thematic units around those proposed in the basal and used outside stories to enrich the unit. Other teachers built thematic units around trade books and used basal stories as supplemental. In both schools the teachers believed that to provide an effective instructional program, they had to utilize many resources and ideas beyond the basal series. They also believed that to be good readers students had to have instruction that would develop particular skills, whether that instruction came from the basal or some other source.

Supplementary Materials

In every classroom in both schools trade books were used regularly as a part of instruction. There was not a teacher who was not attempting to get the students to read regularly, in school and out, and to read a variety of books and materials. Consequently, students had easy access in their classroom to many different books as well as magazines, newspapers, and many other kinds of print sources. Both schools participated in the Accelerated Reader program, which encourages students to read from a wide choice of trade books, which in these schools were housed in the library. Regular times were set aside each week for students to read books of their choice, which could include books from the Accelerated Reader program.

Many of the stories or books housed in the classroom had accompanying audiotapes that were used to provide students with the opportunity to hear the story in addition to reading it. In some cases there were entire sets of books or stories that had accompanying tapes as well as proposed student activities. The Marie Carbo materials are an example of this. These materials are organized by reading difficulty and include activities promoting visual, auditory, kinesthetic, and tactile learning modalities. In one school a series of books by Santana was used to assist students in transition from Spanish to English. Another series, called Living Books, was used to present stories in both English and Spanish. Materials from a basal reader series other than the one adopted by the district were used in one school by some teachers to provide instruction in phonics. Some teachers developed their own "mini books" to capitalize on the interests of the students and to accommodate varying reading levels.

Teachers reported using many different kinds of hands-on materials and activities to reinforce instruction. Classroom observations verified the use of a rich array of enrichment activities available to students. Teachers or volunteers made or purchased the materials for these activities. Games, puzzles, simulation activities, and numerous other "manipulatives" were used with reading instruction as well as with other areas of literacy instruction. Many different commercial materials were used to teach the skills tested on the TAAS test. One school (actually, the entire district) had an outside consultant review its entire curriculum to see what TAAS objectives or essential elements were not covered. Based on that information, a "compacted curriculum" was developed by the teachers and used to supplement the established curriculum.

Teachers of kindergarten children in one school used a Montessori program coupled with commercially prepared Big Books to enrich their instruction. In this way they coupled the multisensory discovery approach of the Montessori system with the more traditional approach of reading books.

Technology and Tutorials

The elementary schools offered some instruction to students through the use of technology, although it was more extensive in one school than the other. A Writing to Read computer lab was available to first graders in one school for 50 minutes per day. Instruction in this lab was intended to promote all the literacy skills. Students in higher grades in this school had access to a WYCAT computer lab every other day for one period. In three schools a variety of software programs were used to promote reading skills. Sticky Bear and Kids Pick programs were used in one computer lab to teach and practice reading and writing skills. Discover English, Reading Readiness, and Initial Reading series of programs were used to assist early reading skill development and transition from Spanish to English. Reading Workshop was another program available on the computer that was intended to enhance reading performance.

The school that structured reading instruction around students' reading levels received from the computer lab on a regular basis a printout that gave the teachers the reading performance level of each child along with his or her strengths and weakness in skill areas. This information was used to guide instruction and even to assign or reassign students to particular instructional settings.

Practice for TAAS tests was provided regularly through programs such as Heart Beeps for TAAS, which focused on the reading and writing portions of TAAS. This program was used by all students, not just those who had difficulty with tests. Sticky Bear and Kids Pick also were used to practice reading and writing skills that would be tested by TAAS. One school had three computer terminals per grade level, while the other had at least two terminals per classroom. Use of these terminals was somewhat limited in the first school. In the second the terminals were used regularly for the same purposes as they were in the computer lab as well as to promote writing performance.

The Accelerated Reader program used in both schools relied on the use of computers to monitor student progress. Students would choose books that were designated as a part of this program, and after the students had read the books, they would take a computer-based test that determined whether they knew enough about the books to get credit for reading them. The program utilized a point system, and the accumulation of points could result in awards or parties or some kind of special recognition for classes or individual students. One school used a program called Books and Beyond and another called Books Around the World to encourage independent reading.

Additional instruction was provided to some students in both schools by students from middle schools or high schools who would come and provide tutorial instruction. The computer lab was open to students in one of the schools each Saturday morning for 2 hours. Students could gain additional practice in any areas where they needed support.

Instructional Support Services

Both of the schools offered a variety of instructional opportunities in addition to those of the regular classroom. There were bilingual and ESL classes to provide for students who needed language support services. There were Reading Recovery teachers who provided special assistance to first-grade students with special reading needs. Also available in one school were special reading teachers who provided specialized assistance in reading and writing for a wide range of students who had special needs in those areas. Content Mastery teachers were available in both schools to provide additional support to classroom teachers and students. How these teachers functioned differed in each school, but their primary purpose was the same—to provide additional instruction targeted to specific individual needs. Full-time personnel were assigned in the computer lab to assist and guide students as well as to work with teachers to coordinate instruction.

These additional programs and personnel were very important factors in the successes of the schools. They allowed teachers to better accommodate the needs of individual students not met in the classroom. In these schools teachers were constantly in search of ways to best meet the needs of each child, and to do this they utilized multiple resources.

Parent volunteers were another source of support in the two schools. It was not easy to identify their specific contributions to instruction, but in many ways they did things to support instruction. They helped in a classroom or lab, they helped make teaching materials, they worked in the library, they read to children, and they assisted in mobilizing parent support for reading programs.

Organizational Aspects of Instruction

Time Allotted for Reading Instruction. Reading instruction was a part of the broader period of literacy instruction. From 90 to 120 minutes a day were allocated to literacy instruction, and at least 60 minutes of this time was spent on reading instruction. This time period did not begin to cover all the time during the day that was devoted to reading of some type. Another 100 or more minutes per week, approximately, were spent on reading in the computer lab. Reading skills were used and taught in all subjects, which added to the time devoted to reading. Then there was the time spent in developing writing skills, which also involved reading. A number of teachers described the time they spent teaching reading as "all day long."

Team Planning. Teacher collaboration and cooperation was a way of life in both schools. Teachers planned and shared within and across grade levels. Teachers within a school, and particularly within grade levels, had instructional goals upon which they had agreed, and these provided the focal point for instruction. Certainly these goals included TAAS objectives and essential elements, but they included other objectives teachers felt were important. There were regularly scheduled team meetings two or three times a week, but in fact the teams met daily in informal ways. Longer meeting times were held several times each grading period in one school to permit long-term, in-depth planning. These times also were used to prepare teacher-made instructional materials.

In addition to collaborating around a common set of expectations, the teachers coordinated their thematic units so that a particular set of books would be available in sufficient quantities to meet student needs. Because the thematic units in reading incorporated other subject areas, it was necessary for teachers to accommodate the need for materials in all areas. Through their team efforts the teachers were able to look at all students under their instructional care and to shift students or share ideas or change instructional time allocations to better accommodate needs of individual students. The members of teams shared everything from lesson plans to teaching materials to teaching strategies. There was a true openness among teachers and a keen knowledge of what other teachers were doing (Guthrie et al., 1996; Wentzel, 1993).

Shared Learning Experiences

Reading was an activity that students shared in many ways. In fact, teachers relied on sharing for the development of successful readers. All classes were grouped heterogeneously, which meant that there were differences in their reading levels as well as in their skill development. To bridge these differences teachers arranged for many opportunities for students to work together. This included shared project activities, shared reading, shared writing activities, within-classroom student assistance, and cross-age tutoring (Blum et al., 1995).

The collaborative activities were not organized according to any particular principles of collaborative learning but around learning goals or objectives. In shared reading it was expected that students grouped in pairs would be better able to recognize and understand words and to comprehend what was read. Two students could help each other and engage in discussion of what was read. Furthermore, students might be asked to develop ideas that went beyond the material being read, such as creating a different ending or describing how the story might have been different if a particular character had taken a different action.

Classroom Instruction

Attempting to describe the instructional programs in these schools was as difficult as trying to describe beauty or love—there were as many descriptions as there were teachers. In general the instruction was literature-based, organized around thematic units set within a whole language framework. To elaborate, themes were developed that would be explored through the reading of stories and books, with books used as often as practical. In exploring these themes, information from other subject areas would be incorporated and suitable materials for those subjects would be included as a part of the reading students would do. The themes for the units came primarily from the basal series in one school, and were more likely to be developed by teachers independent of the basal series in the other. Regardless of the source of the theme, trade books or novels probably would be used as a major feature of the instruction. A particular theme would likely extend over a 4- to 6-week period, which meant there was time to become engaged with a variety of books and stories.

Among the teacher differences in instructional procedures, there were some important commonalities. Instructional periods usually included time when students read silently, time when they read orally to the class or in a shared reading situation, and time when the teacher read to the class followed by class discussion. The time spent on each activity each day would vary; during some days not all activities would occur, but within the course of a week all these components would be included. In most instances there were some specific purposes to be accomplished through the reading in addition to the constant purpose of becoming familiar with new books or reading for enjoyment. Always there was attention to vocabulary development, and certain comprehension skills also would be emphasized. Usually the skills to be emphasized were determined by the TAAS test, essential elements, or basal guides.

Vocabulary words either were introduced prior to reading and were discussed, or students were alerted to them and asked to try to determine their meaning from context. When teachers or students read orally, students often were asked to follow along in their books if all had copies. This process was called tracking by some teachers. The purposes, they said, were to help students recognize words they did not know, to focus on unknown words that might be discussed as the story progressed, and to hold student attention. After reading, whether oral or silent, a class discussion would take place in which the teacher would focus attention on a skill such as summarization or main idea or author purpose. Sometimes this focus on skills was in the discussion mode completely. At other times there would be written activities for students to complete. Writing assignments often were based on what had been read.

While considerable time was spent in whole group participation and interaction around a particular story or book, the entire time period was not devoted to whole group instruction. Students often read to each other in a shared reading format. Good readers often were joined with less able readers as one way of providing support for those who could not read the material on their own. Students also shared in responding to certain assignments related to the reading. As students read in various kinds of independent activities, the teacher frequently would use this time to work with small groups or individuals who needed extra help. Often there were projects connected with the thematic units. Developing a drama around the theme, a related building project that might include science or math, and a research project were some of the types of activities mentioned. These projects were always collaborative efforts among the students, calling for an application of their skills and knowledge as well as increasing their excitement about reading and its utility.

It should be stressed that there was a definite emphasis on reading skill development, but it was always done in the context of connected reading. Isolated skill instruction was not common. In the lower grades there was phonics instruction for those who needed it, but this too was accomplished within the context of reading. In the upper grades, as the need for phonics instruction diminished, there was more attention to comprehension skills, and this emphasis was always associated with the reading of stories, novels, or short selections. While there was some use of commercially prepared worksheets, it was very limited in classroom instruction. Skills were more likely taught and practiced through student–teacher interactions, student-to-student interactions, games, manipulatives, teacher-developed work activities, or computer-based instruction.

In one school, reading centers were used regularly to teach and reinforce skills. These were self-paced centers where children would listen to a story on tape while reading the printed version of the story. After listening and reading along, the students would read the story without the tape. Then there were activities to be accomplished connected with the story. These activities incorporated the use of visual, auditory, kinesthetic, and tactile modalities.

The emphasis on instruction with meaning was evident in several ways. Skills were always taught in connection with a story or book being read. Vocabulary development was based on words encountered in reading or writing. Words that were included in spelling instruction usually were drawn from words used in writing activities. In the same way grammar and the mechanics of writing were taught in relation to meaningful writing purposes. Students would not be asked to write, in isolation, a sentence with a possessive noun, for example, but this would be taught if they attempted to use a possessive noun as a part of journal writing or a story they were writing and needed assistance.

Instructional Strategies for Linguistically Diverse Students

In both schools there were many linguistically diverse students. Some spoke only Spanish when they entered and others spoke only English. Many spoke both Spanish and English. There was some relationship between their oral language and their reading skills, but not a constant relationship. Some who spoke Spanish only could not read in that language or in English. Most who spoke English only could not read in Spanish. Both schools were very sensitive to this diversity and responded to it in several ways (Moll & Gonzalez, 1994).

Many teachers in the schools were bilingual in Spanish and English and this was a tremendous advantage. More than being bilingual, most of the teachers were from the geographical region where the schools were located so they were quite familiar with the culture of the students. It was common for teachers to move from one language to another to help students to get meaning from unknown words and concepts. The teachers did this not only through verbal explanation but also by connecting the word or concept with the students' culture. Through their treatment of both languages, the teachers modeled great respect for the languages as well as demonstrated an understanding and appreciation of both cultures.

Bilingual classes were available for those students who needed them through the grades. It was common to have at any grade level students entering school in this country for the first time and speaking Spanish only. These classes were intended to help students make the transition from Spanish to English in all areas of literacy. At the conclusion of the school year all students would be tested to determine if they needed to be assigned into a bilingual classroom the next year or were ready to move into a regular classroom. There were transition classrooms that assisted students in that movement when needed. An abundance of stories and books written in both languages were available to teachers, and they were widely and consistently used.

In the classrooms students were permitted to interact in either or both languages. As a result, language tended not to be a barrier to effective communication. Acceptance of both Spanish and English meant that students could share and assist each other in whatever way language best served them.

Reading Related to Real-Life Interests

When asked, without hesitation teachers would report many ways they related their reading and writing activities to the meaningful experiences in the lives of students. Teachers spent much time developing vocabulary knowledge. If there was to be a unit on animals, a field trip to the area zoo would be planned. If students were studying food and nutrition, trips to food processing plants might be planned or a nutrition specialist might be brought in. Certainly there would be a discussion of the types of food the students ate and how that related to the unit. Audio- and videotapes also were used by teachers to develop new knowledge and build background for materials that were to be read (Baker et al., 1996; Purcell-Gates, 1996).

During the reading time, teachers often engaged students in discussions that caused them to think about how the story might relate to their life. "Do you think that would ever happen to you?" and "What would happen to your family if this event occurred?" are just two of many questions that were asked of students to connect their reading with their everyday lives. Another way of connecting instruction to life was to frequently ask students in what kind of work a particular skill or kind of information might be used or if they knew adults who used such skills and information.

A most important way teachers tried to give meaning to reading was to find out what kinds of interests individual students had and to recommend or make available books that met that interest. Through their choice of reading materials, students could bring immediate relevance to their reading. Students also were encouraged to share what they read with members of their family, which increased the potential impact of the book in the life of the student.

Assessment of Student Progress and Needs

Informal Assessments. The most commonly used assessment technique was teacher observation and judgment conducted in an informal manner. Through their daily interactions with students, teachers determined how students were performing and what was needed to move them ahead. These informal assessments included listening to students read and noting what miscues they might make, viewing their daily writing for progress in whatever skill areas might be subject to emphasis, attending to spelling and writing mechanics as teachers reviewed students' writing, and assessing performance on written comprehension tasks or other skill tasks. Traditional spelling tests and worksheet activities were other means of teacher assessment.

Semiformal Assessments. Running records and informal reading inventories were used periodically by a number of teachers as a way of assessing reading performance. In one school the computer programs available in the computer labs provided a reading-level score on each child on a regular basis. This score was based to a great extent on comprehension performance.

In the computer labs and in the classrooms TAAS practice tests were used regularly to assess student skill in the areas tested with that instrument. In most cases students and teachers maintained careful records of student progress on these tests. Because these practice tests were designed to simulate the real tests, the outcomes from these tests were useful in targeting instruction in preparation for the test.

Portfolios. Many teachers kept a portfolio of writings for each student. It was through the use of this portfolio that teachers assessed student progress in writing. Teachers were particularly careful to look at writing performance in terms of the TAAS expectations for writing, but they also used the portfolios to judge progress in spelling, grammar, and the mechanics of writing.

In a few cases, work that students did on projects also was included in the portfolios as evidence of their progress in interpreting and understanding reading as represented through different modalities and mediums. However, in most cases the projects were a part of the teacher's informal evaluation.

Middle Schools

When students enter elementary school, they, along with their parents and teachers, understand that learning to read is a most important goal. For this reason major emphasis is placed on learning to read. By the time students reach middle and high school, the nature of reading instruction shifts from learning to read to reading to learn. This shift is necessitated by the rapidly increasing learning demands faced by students in the content areas. For those students who are successful readers, making this transition is not particularly difficult. But many students reach the upper grades with limited reading skills. These students, sometimes referred to as at-risk readers (Vacca & Padak, 1990), are faced with the need to learn to read better at the same time they have daily requirements to read.

Although students in the middle schools we visited were not referred to as at-risk readers, many of them were viewed as needing special assistance to meet the academic demands of the school. TAAS test scores or lack of proficiency in English was more likely to define these students than poor performance on a specific reading test. To be sure, many of the students in the secondary schools that were a part of this study were not considered to be in need of special assistance. However, students in the ESL, reading improvement, TAAS preparation, and some of the regular English classes were thought to need extra assistance to meet school demands.

Students who have not learned to read effectively in the lower grades or who for other reasons have struggled in school are very likely to feel alienated from school (Newman, 1981). Along with this alienation they often develop a sense of helplessness in the school setting (Licht, 1983). This has been termed "learned helplessness" by some researchers (Thomas, 1979). At-risk readers typically have a poor self-image (Vacca & Padak, 1990), and students who have such a self-concept very often achieve poorly in all aspects of school (Brookover et al., 1962). It is also common for at-risk readers to view teachers as being uncaring and uninterested in their success in school (Wehlage, Rutter, & Turnbaugh, 1987).

If teachers are to be successful with all students, but especially at-risk readers, it is critical that they create a school environment where students can and do develop an enhanced self-concept and where students believe that teachers do care about them and really do want them to succeed. There are both school- and classroom-level factors that provide this kind of environment. Effective schools not only systematically address instructional practices, but also provide for the support systems students need to succeed (Winfield & Manning, 1992). Battistich, Solomon, Kin, Watson, and Schaps (1995) suggest that

> the support, commitment, and goal clarity provided in a caring school commu-
> nity may serve to compensate for the relative lack of such qualities in the
> lives of some students outside school and allow those students to develop the
> motivation and direction they otherwise might not have. (p. 650)

Success in reading is increased when the student has an enriched vocabu-lary (Davis, 1969). An enriched vocabulary is much more likely to be learned from context rather than as isolated words. At these schools teachers frequently used the reading context to teach vocabulary. When it was necessary, both Spanish and English were used to do this.

Students for whom English is a second language benefit especially from cooperative learning (Kagan, 1986; Losey, 1995). Kagan found that these students were more motivated, spent more time on tasks, and were more involved in learning activities. Appreciation and acceptance of student language use also contribute to greater student involvement in learning activities, as do challenging materials related to students' interests (Losey, 1995). Middle school students especially desire opportunities to interact with friends, as they value peer relations (Savin-Williams & Berndt, 1990). Regular use of cooperative learning in the schools investigated in this study seemed to capitalize on these values.

As will be seen in the following section, most practices shown by research to be effective for both at-risk and good readers were very evident in the middle schools.

Organizational Aspects Influencing Reading Instruction

Within and between the two middle schools that were included in this project there were variations in organizational arrangements that need to be described before the actual instructional programs are discussed. One school was formed around interdisciplinary teams. In these teams each teacher would teach the same basic subject all day, but the team would come together at least once a week to coordinate plans for the common group of students they served. In this scheme there were nine teachers who taught reading only. A similar group taught language arts only, and in these classes the focus was on writing, writing-related skills, and traditional English skills. Operating outside of the interdisciplinary team format were two teachers who taught what were called "sheltered" classes that operated in an ESL format and one typical ESL class.

Each sheltered class included students from grades 6, 7, and 8 and was self-contained, meaning that one teacher taught language arts, reading, and math to the same students in the same room. One of these classes was considered to be lower level. If students passed the TAAS test at the end of the first year, they would go into a regular interdisciplinary team. If they did not pass, they would go into the upper-level class for the next year. Eighty to 90% of the students continued in a sheltered class for a second year. Fifty-one students were enrolled in these two classes at the time of our visit. Thirteen students were enrolled in the one ESL class. This class, which was also multigrade, was taught by a fine arts teacher, with an arts emphasis in the instruction. There was one teacher who served as a special education reading teacher.

The second school had a reading department consisting of 15 reading teachers. For the most part these teachers would teach reading all day to different groups of students each period. Occasionally a teacher taught outside of the reading area for one period a day. Several types of reading classes were taught by these teachers—regular reading classes, reading improvement classes, and gifted and talented reading classes. The reading improvement classes served ESL 2 students, or advanced ESL students. In addition to these classes, there were Chapter 1 reading classes for sixth- and seventh-grade students who had failed one or more parts of the TAAS. Class sizes in the Chapter 1 and reading improvement classes were between 8 and 10 students. Regular classes were 24 or 25 students in size, and students were grouped heterogeneously.

Reading Programs and Curriculum

The nature of the classes and the curriculum followed varied between the two schools, but there were also some commonalities. In both schools all students were required to have one period of reading instruction each day. The curriculum and programs used in the two schools were determined by the teachers, who were granted considerable flexibility in the materials they used. Neither school used the basal reading program as the core of the curriculum in all classes. Stories from the basal series were used frequently in the regular reading classes in one school, but teachers tended to follow their own plans for how they taught the stories. In many classrooms reading instruction centered on novels selected by teachers. Other kinds of materials were utilized on an individual basis or according to the particular class. Preparation for the TAAS test was a significant influence on all reading classes in both schools.

In the school that had interdisciplinary teams, sets of novels were identified from which teachers might choose at each grade level for use in the regular reading classes. This was done to prevent the use of the same novel more than once with the same students. The teams were required to develop at least one thematic unit each semester. This unit would span across the subject areas. For these units there was some unity with regard to the books that would be used. The Michael Eaton reading program was used as the strategy or framework that guided the regular reading classes. Teachers of the two structured classes developed their own curriculum, which included a variety of books and practice materials. They did rely on the basal reader as a source of vocabulary words and skills that were taught and practiced. Skills taught were those required to pass the TAAS test.

In the second school, the Chapter 1 and reading improvement classes placed heavy emphasis on the skills associated with the TAAS test. Novels, basals, worksheets, and TAAS practice exercises were used frequently as instructional tools. Newspapers and magazines also were used to teach current events. While there was variety in the materials used, there was consistency in the skills taught. These skills were identified by the reading department, and all teachers were expected to attend to them in their instruction. In the regular reading classes, basal stories commonly were used as the basic reading material. Novels were used extensively in the gifted and talented reading classes, with the basal used sometimes in a supplemental fashion.

Classroom Instruction

First, the instructional processes used in the various classes in the school that engaged in interdisciplinary teaming will be described. This will be followed by a description of instruction in the second school.

Classroom Instruction—School One. Those teachers who taught regular reading classes as a part of an interdisciplinary team used the Michael Eaton approach to reading as their basic instructional strategy. The nine reading teachers used this strategy, and the classroom procedure in these classes was generally the same. As used by these teachers, the Eaton strategy emphasized connected reading in a whole language context. It stressed the application of skills over the acquisition of skills in isolation. A class period typically would begin with the teacher writing on the chalkboard the essential elements to be taught or reviewed for the period. Students would begin reading, usually a novel. As they read, the teacher would stop the process at a point when an essential element could be appropriately pointed out and taught. In most cases the skills were comprehension skills. As students succeeded in getting correct answers or responses, they would be rewarded with a coupon. TAAS skills also were emphasized, along with the essential elements.

During the time when the Michael Eaton strategy was being used, all students would read the same book, possibly reading different chapters, depending on how much progress they were making. Some days students would work in groups, reading different books by the same author. On these days the Eaton strategy was not followed. Instead the emphasis was on sharing within the group.

Every Monday a 45-minute period was set aside for sustained silent reading, a time when students in the school stopped and read books of their choice. This was a reading experience in addition to the reading class.

Reading instruction in the two ESL classes differed from that in the reading classes, but those two classes were quite similar. The second-year class did much the same work as the first-year class, except at a higher level. Preparation for the TAAS test and providing students with the ability to function successfully in English were the two main objectives of these classes. The teachers of these two classes had developed their own curriculum, which did include some attention to the basal series but actually was based on an out-of-adoption series.

Vocabulary development and writing were the two skills stressed most in these classes, for they were the skills in which the students needed the greatest assistance to pass the TAAS test. Teachers used the basal book as the source of the vocabulary instruction, but student reading was done from other books and stories. Reading materials were generally at the third-grade level. Some students could read above that level, some were below, and others were at that level. Students would read orally or chorally. All students would read aloud even if it meant rereading the story to give everyone a turn. After the reading, teachers would ask a lot of questions about the story as a means of developing students' understanding and teaching students comprehension skills. Those students who had difficulty with the reading would receive extra help from the teacher. The only silent reading done by the students was done outside of class. The reason given for this emphasis on oral reading was that the teacher needed to hear the students in order to critique their pronunciation.

A major portion of each period was spent studying vocabulary words. This was done by discussing the meaning of the words as a group, and then having the students write sentences using the vocabulary words. In connection with these sentences flash cards sometimes would be used as a different way of practicing the words. Correct spelling was emphasized in the students' writing. The primary writing activity in the class was that done in association with vocabulary development. Students would write in their journals on occasion about special events that happened. If they wished, students would read to the class what they had written.

Classroom Instruction—School Two. In the second school reading was emphasized in four types of classes. There were classes for ESL students, TAAS improvement classes, regular reading classes, and classes for gifted and talented students. All students were required to take one of the classes. Although these classes served different students, a common set of skills was taught by all teachers. These skills had been identified by the teachers in the reading department. In this school all students devoted time to reading only from 8:15 to 8:35 each Tuesday and Thursday morning.

Students in the TAAS improvement classes had all failed one or more of the TAAS tests. Instruction for these classes adhered to the objectives set forth by the reading department, but the selection of materials and teaching procedures was left to the teacher. No particular text was used, but instead a variety of materials were used. This included novels, TAAS practice worksheets, stories, and computer-based instruction.

A week of instruction in the TAAS improvement classes would look somewhat like the following: On Monday and Tuesday the focal point would be a short story, which would begin with the teacher going over selected vocabulary words. Then students might listen to the story on an audiotape and follow along in the book as they listened. Sometimes the students would read the story or parts of it chorally. After the reading of the story had been completed, students would be asked to answer questions about the story and these would be checked and graded immediately. Learning how to analyze and solve math word problems would be the instructional target for Wednesday. On Thursday students would meet with the school counselor, who would work with them on life skills they needed to function successfully in life away from school. Friday would be spent teaching vocabulary or comprehension skills. The students also might take a reading test or math test on the computer, and the grade would be recorded by the teacher. Throughout the week the teacher would engage the students in verbal interaction.

Instruction in the regular reading classes was similar across classes. All teachers attended to the same essential elements, and they all emphasized TAAS skills. All the teachers engaged the students in much reading each day, with all students reading the same story most of the time. The teacher read to students, students read orally, and students read silently. About one-half of an instructional period was teacher directed; during the other half, students worked independently. Development of vocabulary and comprehension skills was stressed consistently through the reading. Writing was a part of all classes, usually in connection with the materials being read or in journals. Teachers accommodated for the varying reading levels of students by giving some students extra help, requiring those students to read fewer pages, or both.

The teachers might differ as to the kinds of materials they used for reading. Some teachers relied more on novels, while others made greater use of basal stories. Commercial worksheets were used by the teachers, as were supplemental materials such as newspapers, magazines, or learning games. The Accelerated Reader program was available to students in sixth grade (but not seventh and eighth), and this program was used to motivate reading outside the classroom.

The classes for gifted and talented students used novels for the most part as their reading material, with basals being supplementary along with newspapers, magazines, Scholastic publications, and other print materials. The novels used were selected from a list of novels for use at the sixth-grade level. These classes had some of the same characteristics as the regular reading classes but with a strong emphasis on developing independent readers. These students were asked to do more reading on their own and to complete skills worksheets at home.

The ESL classes were not unlike the regular reading classes in many respects. Students in these classes did much reading from books or stories other than basals. To the extent feasible, teachers used high-interest materials that required lower-level reading skills. Like the regular classes, there was direct instruction and much oral interaction around reading, but there was more of both in the ESL classes. Teachers in these classes moved through the reading and learning process at a slower pace than in the regular reading classes. One feature of these classes that was a bit different was the great amount of time teachers spent building student confidence in successful literacy development. Also, there was less writing associated with reading instruction than in other classes.

Instructional Strategies for Linguistically Diverse Students

There were students in both schools who had come from Mexico recently and spoke no English at all. Other students had been in this country for several years but were lacking in their ability to read and write easily in English. There were other students who could function quite well in English but who used Spanish to explain some words or concepts.

Two basic approaches were used to accommodate the needs of each of these student groups. ESL classes were used to serve those students who needed in-depth assistance in developing literacy in English. For those in regular classroom settings the teachers provided assistance in Spanish whenever it seemed that such assistance would aid learning. This might be done on an individual basis or with the whole group. Because many of the teachers were bilingual, they could provide this assistance themselves, but those teachers who were not bilingual would use students to help other students. This might be done through daily shared learning experiences or spontaneously as the need arose (Moll & Gonzalez, 1994).

Beyond these formal and semiformal instructional arrangements, there was the informal, but powerful, climate of acceptance and respect for linguistic diversity. Students would not be made to feel inadequate or ashamed because of their differences. If anything, the students were made to feel proud of a dual language capability and of the culture that produced the diversity.

Relating Instruction to Real-Life Experiences

There was a constant effort on the part of teachers to relate what students were learning to how such knowledge was useful in their lives and to encourage students to use their life experiences to bring meaning to their reading activities. Teachers were sensitive to the differences that might exist between the language and culture of the students and those of the material being read, and the teachers sought to ensure that students could make the connections. They did this through interpretations in Spanish and through the use of many creative activities to accompany reading. For example, to develop students' understanding of a story or book, teachers would have them develop a play or dialogue to illustrate the story or depict the story through drawings or posters or even sculpture.

Teachers engaged the students in various activities in an effort to show them how the development of literacy skills could and would aid them in life outside the school. The students would write letters to request information from colleges and then talk about their own possibilities at the college level. Teachers wanted the students to believe that they could go to college and could succeed. Students would write letters to governmental leaders regarding certain issues they had been reading about and that had meaning for their lives. Through their reading the students would explore different kinds of work and the kinds of skills needed to perform that work. To make the literacy demands real to them, students would be asked to read job descriptions and even to fill out job applications. Always the students were encouraged to have high expectations for themselves.

Assessment of Students' Skills and Needs

Far and away the most frequent manners of assessment were teacher observation and judgment. Students were placed in some classes based on formal testing such as the TAAS test, and the same test might be used, along with teacher judgment, to determine when a student would move out of a class. In some classrooms teachers gave TAAS practice tests on a regular basis, and some teachers used an informal reading inventory to determine reading level. The inventory was employed with only a few students and was not done often.

HIGH SCHOOLS

Organizational Arrangements for Reading Instruction

The two high schools we visited had very similar course offerings that affected reading. There were the so-called regular English classes for English I–IV. Within this classification there were honors classes. One school offered an American College Test (ACT) class to prepare students for that exam, and the other was about to add an advanced placement component to its honors classes. Both schools offered ESL 1 classes for freshmen and ESL 2 classes for sophomores. TAAS preparation classes for those who had failed the TAAS test were used in both schools. Reading improvement classes were a part of the course offerings in one school but not the other.

Students in the ESL 1 and 2 classes in one of the high schools also would take English I or II. In the other school students in the ESL classes also took a reading improvement class. When these students had completed these 2 years successfully, they took English III and IV.

Generally class periods in the two schools were approximately 50 minutes in length, but there were exceptions. In one of the schools some of the students were on a block schedule, which meant that their classes lasted for 90 minutes every other day instead of a daily period. In the other school the ESL classes met for 2 hours per day.

Classroom Instruction

Although there were similarities in the instructional programs in the two high schools, there were enough differences to merit individual descriptions of instruction in the two schools.

Instruction in School One. ESL classes were taught by four teachers in this school. Two teachers taught ESL 1 and two taught ESL 2. Class periods were 2 hours in length. Students were assigned to these classes based on their scores on a reading level placement test. Once assigned to an ESL class, students would be in that class for 2 years. During these 2 years the students also would take an English class. After two years the students would go into regular English classes only.

There was an ESL curriculum for these classes, but it did not include books or stories. The curriculum mainly described what essential elements were to be taught. TAAS test skills also were stressed in each class. Although no two teachers taught in the same manner, all teachers included much reading and much writing in every class period. Reading typically was done from books that were of high interest but low level of reading difficulty, with all students reading the same book. Teachers frequently read to students because the books were too difficult for some. Following the reading there were discussions of what had been read, with attention given to the skills that were being taught. In addition to the teacher's reading, students often took turns reading orally to the class or with a partner, and they read silently each day. At times silent reading involved reading part of a story already read in class. Most of the time, silent reading involved students reading a new story or part of it on their own. Class discussion was always associated with the differing reading modes.

It was during the class discussions that vocabulary development was stressed. Teachers would explain new and difficult words in the books so that students could grasp the meaning of the words and then the book itself. Often the teachers used Spanish to explain word meanings. This made it easier for the students to understand the word and to associate the new word with words or concepts they already knew. Through the classroom discussions teachers helped students gain an understanding and enjoyment of books that might have been impossible to gain on their own. When students were reading novels such as *Oliver Twist* or *A Tale of Two Cities* that had accompanying videos, these were shown to the class to further develop an understanding of the story.

Associated with practice on the TAAS test were materials that teachers used for reading and skill practice. Through the use of these materials teachers were able to teach vocabulary and comprehension skills in a format like that used on the TAAS test. While there was constant emphasis on TAAS skills, the teachers also had as their goal to increase the reading levels of their students.

In each 2-hour class period approximately one-half of the time was devoted to the development of writing skills. The primary focus of this instruction was to prepare the students for the TAAS test. As much as possible their writing was related to what they were reading.

Although the students in the ESL classes were performing below grade level in terms of literacy skills, the teachers reported that they were very eager pupils who learned quickly but needed assistance in making the transition from Spanish to English.

Junior- and senior-level students who had failed the TAAS test were automatically placed in a TAAS preparation class. These classes met for 50 minutes per day, and their goal was to get the students to pass the TAAS test. To do this the students read and wrote extensively. They read novels, magazines, newspapers, or any other print documents that were of interest to them and could be used to teach the comprehension skills required to pass the TAAS test. Topical articles were read and discussed regularly since the writing topics on the TAAS test usually were taken from current events.

Students in the TAAS classes were motivated to succeed by the fact that they knew they could not graduate if they did not pass the TAAS test. In some cases the seniors had completed or would soon complete all their coursework, but they could not graduate until the TAAS was passed. Even though the students were motivated to pass the TAAS test, teachers reported that they still had to provide variety in their teaching to maintain student engagement. They did this by using reading materials of interest to the students, by varying the instruction from day to day, by keeping the instruction fast-paced, and by having students assist each other in the learning process. When students passed the TAAS test, they would exit from the TAAS class.

Regular English classes were much like the TAAS preparation classes in many respects. Preparation for passing the TAAS test was a major, if not primary, objective. All made adjustments to accommodate limited reading abilities of some students. Teachers were not bound by any particular curriculum, which was reflected in differences in their instructional practices. In some classes the adopted textbook was used extensively; one class was interested in the medieval era, so they were reading stories and plays from that time; current events and *The Canterbury Tales* were popular in another class.

Regardless of the reading material used in the classes, teachers had to provide a lot of support to help students read and understand the material. One way this happened was for the teacher to read to the students, leading them through the story or book step by step to ensure their understanding. Several teachers described their instructional process as read, stop, discuss, and explain, then repeat the process over and over. Much class time was spent in oral reading and oral interactions. Instruction tended to focus on one skill at a time but within a reading context.

Development of one research paper was required by some of the teachers, and writing of short papers describing characters read about was another writing activity used by some teachers. There was more emphasis on reading than writing.

With one exception, the teachers who were interviewed reported that they did not assign homework because the students would not do it. The one teacher who did regularly assign homework reported that the students did complete it.

Honors English classes required more independent work of the students, engaged them in reading more difficult books, and were more fast-paced than regular classes. In these classes the emphasis was on preparing students for what they might encounter in college rather than what they would be expected to do on the TAAS test. Students were required to read at least one novel outside of class each 6 weeks, and in class they were expected to read literature selections without assistance and to react to the selections in oral discussions or through writing assignments. Responses from these students were expected to be very thoughtful, creative, and insightful. One teacher reported that she would lecture twice a week for an entire period while students took notes.

Instruction in School Two. The month prior to our arrival on this campus the entire school had been working on one major project, an investigation of water quality in the Rio Grande. In connection with this project there had been numerous thematic activities that involved sharing ideas and communication across subject areas. Also, students had been engaged in many hands-on activities both off and on campus. The culminating event for the Rio Grande project was held in the school gymnasium one evening, and all parents, community members, and elected officials were invited. At this event the various classes presented to the audience their findings from this month-long study. To make this presentation, the students devised a wide variety of media approaches and devices.

This project is mentioned here for two reasons. First, virtually every teacher mentioned this project when talking about reading activities in their classroom so a description of it seemed appropriate. Second, this project was a tangible example of the extensive cooperation and collaboration that were common among the faculty of this school. While the Rio Grande project was greater in scope than most endeavors the school had undertaken, it did not require any unusual preparation on the part of the faculty, for they naturally and regularly cooperated on learning activities.

Class periods were typically 50–55 minutes in length each day, but in some cases they were 90 minutes long and took place every other day. All teachers in the reading/English area taught more than one type of class. For example, no one taught reading improvement all day or English III all day. Most teachers did teach only within the area of reading or English.

There were two senior TAAS classes that served those students who had not passed the TAAS test. Instruction in these classes was devoted completely to preparing the students to pass the test. There was extensive use of TAAS practice materials in both reading and writing. In addition, teachers would use other forms of print materials to maintain the interest of the students, but these materials would be used to focus on TAAS objectives. Over a week about equal attention would be given to reading and writing skills, although this might vary on a daily basis. Oral instruction was used frequently by teachers to help students read and understand materials that they were using and that they would be required to know for the TAAS test. Student to student interactions were used commonly as a way of reinforcing instruction.

Reading improvement classes were conducted for freshmen and sophomores who either had performed poorly on the TAAS test or had been recommended by a teacher or both. Freshmen in these classes also were enrolled in ESL 1 and sophomores were enrolled in ESL 2. The teachers who taught the reading improvement classes had the same planning period so they planned their activities together. There was a text for the classes, but the teachers used it very little because they felt it was not challenging enough for the students. Instead, they used short stories and books of their own choosing. Students seemed to prefer books to short stories.

Instruction in these classes was characterized by high student expectations and much positive feedback. Teachers felt they had to be very enthusiastic in their teaching to inspire and motivate the students. Teachers reported that the students were quite intelligent and were very willing learners. Most students had some difficulty due to transition from Spanish to English, and they needed encouragement and support to cause them to believe they could succeed. The students were especially afraid of the TAAS test so the teachers devoted considerable time to preparing them for that test. Instruction was not limited to the TAAS objectives, however.

During a typical class period the teacher would read to the students from a novel, and as she did she would discuss skills such as author techniques and recognizing plot. Prior to or during the reading, the teacher would spend a lot of time building background for understanding the story. After the reading the students would respond to comprehension questions about what was read. Responding could be accomplished through a traditional paper-and-pencil process, but more often it would take different forms, including oral responses, pictorial responses, or even written reports. On those days when the periods were short, the teacher might read all day and conduct follow-up activities the next day. For long periods, reading and follow-up activities would occur on the same day.

Students were asked to do library research on topics of interest to them as a means of developing writing as well as reading skills. Students in these classes also would read to elementary school students. (The school was just across the street from the elementary school.) This activity was another means of giving students practice in reading, and in reading books that were at their reading level. During the time when students were working individually or with partners on the activities following reading time, the teachers would give assistance to individuals. This was another means of providing for the individual reading needs of students.

A variety of practices were reported by the teachers of the ESL classes. One teacher used the state-adopted textbook to emphasize grammar development. Much of the instruction was oral in nature, with the stories in the text providing the basis for studying grammar. Each day the teacher would lead the students through a step-by-step review of the previous day's work before going on to the new lesson. Both English and Spanish were used for instruction.

In another class the teacher had just read *Moby Dick* to the students and led them through discussions of the book as she read it. A good portion of each day was spent in reading. Most of the time the teacher would read to the students, but the students read silently one day a week. Grammar was not stressed in this class. The emphasis was on vocabulary development and skill in analyzing a story through characters, title, and author. Writing was done frequently, with consistent emphasis on summarization. Writing was usually related to what was being read. Students also wrote often about current events, particularly those in their community.

Another ESL teacher balanced her time between reading and writing. To assist the students with writing, she would use many visuals. For example, the overhead projector and posters were used to provide examples of writing and to show the students exactly what they were to do and how.

Early in the year this teacher would administer informal reading inventories to the students to determine their reading level. For those who spoke little or no English she would audiotape stories using both languages as deemed necessary. She also taught students to recognize sight words through continual practice. Two students who spoke no English were working with the "Hooked on Phonics" program.

Reading was done in this class on a daily basis. The teacher would read to students, and at times students read on their own. Easy books in both English and Spanish were available in the room, as well as high-interest, low-difficulty books. In addition to this regular classroom routine, the teacher provided support and assistance to students in several other ways. Junior and senior students came to the room regularly to tutor the students one-on-one. They utilized a physical response program that had students demonstrate action words such as *stand, sit,* or *jump.* Junior and senior tutors worked with this program and they also had the students go about school and label things such as water fountains. Both languages were used by the teacher and tutors as needed.

Although all teachers taught skills that are tested on the TAAS test, they did not talk about that test being the reason for what and how they taught. In all classes the Rio Grande project was used as a focal point for both reading and writing.

In the English classes there was somewhat of a distinction between English I, II, and III and senior English classes. This was due in large part to the fact that all students in senior English had passed the TAAS test, and those in the other classes had yet to take or pass the test. Thus, in the I–III classes considerable attention was given to TAAS preparation, although this was certainly not all that was done. No particular curriculum was used in many classes, while in others an adopted literature book was used regularly. The essential elements were always a guiding force for instruction.

Every day time was devoted to reading and writing. Some teachers devoted more time to one than the other, but there was daily instruction in both. Typically there would be an objective or two for the day that guided instruction, and these objectives usually were related to the TAAS test. Part of the period would be devoted to instruction specific to the objectives. There might be a writing activity that conformed to the TAAS writing format and was based on TAAS probes. As the students engaged in the reading of a novel, they might be asked to identify TAAS objectives within the novel.

Other instruction went beyond the TAAS objectives but would emphasize them whenever possible. In connection with reading and writing activities teachers would teach grammar skills. When reading novels or stories from the literature text, poems, or plays, students would be helped to recognize and analyze various literary styles and elements. The writing of an essay sometimes would follow this kind of activity. After reading a story, students might write about it and then report orally on what they had read. In some cases students completed worksheets and discussed them orally with the class. This emphasis on presentation was intended to strengthen oral language skills. All the mechanics of writing would be stressed at one time or another as students engaged in their writing activities.

Every day some time would be spent reading with the objective of increasing reading skill and promoting enjoyment. Teachers would find out what students liked to read and would choose materials that fit the students' desires. One teacher loved to teach from the works of Shakespeare, and she would get her students excited about these materials. This led to much acting on the part of the students, along with an in-depth study of Shakespeare. In this same class students would develop their own commercials, including the props necessary to present the commercial. Another teacher would have the students make posters that would explain to someone who had not read the story what it was about. Students were called on to utilize a variety of print resources as they worked on the Rio Grande project. This required reading, writing, and oral reporting on a topic of great interest to the students.

Students in the senior English classes had passed the TAAS test so the emphasis on those objectives diminished. In these classes there was a mixture of variety and structure in the instruction. On the one hand, there was considerable attention to teaching the grammar, writing, and study skills that would be required for success in higher education. Formal, teacher-directed instruction was the preferred technique for this type of instruction, with the teacher leading the students through the learning process in a systematic manner. A textbook might be used as the basic curriculum for this instruction. On the other hand, students were involved in projects that built on their interests, such as writing a research paper on their family history, and in cooperative learning activities. For example, one teacher was working with the government teacher to have students develop a research paper on how government works. The government teacher taught and assisted the students relative to the content of the paper and the research sources, while the English teacher guided the writing process and the organization of research information. The paper was graded for content by the government teacher and for writing skill by the English teacher.

Teachers felt that the students in these senior classes were functioning on about the same level and that generally they were motivated learners. Consequently, no particular provision was made for differences in student reading level. Also, in the various projects students worked cooperatively, and this created an environment for peer assistance.

Honors English classes were available beginning at the freshman level. These classes were more challenging than regular or senior classes, and they offered more opportunity for independent student work. In this case independent meant not so much students working on their own as students working cooperatively on projects. There was a curriculum for these classes, but it was used by the teachers as they wished and certainly was not the driving force for instruction.

The honors classes required more writing than regular classes. Writing research papers was one way that the writing was carried out. Another was to have students follow up the reading of novels with various kinds of story writing such as persuasive and expository writing. Often the writing projects were followed by oral reports. Students in these classes were involved in reading more novels, especially those that might be considered classics such as *Treasure Island* and *Ivanhoe*. Several teachers used plays extensively as a way of engaging students with classic literature.

Another way that writing and reading were taught was through group projects. For example, in relation to the Rio Grande project some of the students went out into the community to interview a number of people to learn about their knowledge and feelings regarding pollution in the Rio Grande. In connection with the interviews, the students had to conduct research and then develop reports of their findings. With the reports they had to create visuals to illustrate key points.

In honors classes where students had not yet taken the TAAS test, far less attention was given to that test than in other classes.

ACT classes were for those students planning to take the ACT test in preparation for entry into college. ACT study guides were the primary curriculum used in the classes, and cooperative learning was the primary instructional technique. The students in these classes were quite motivated and would work through the study guides, focusing on each skill as it was introduced. As they did this, students constantly assisted each other. They would teach each other and test or assess each other to see if they had mastered the content and skills of the lesson. The teacher guided and assisted the students to be sure all necessary material and objectives were covered.

Supplementing Classroom Instruction

In neither school did students have easy access to computers in their classrooms. There were computer labs in each school, but there were limitations on their use. In school one English classes had access to the computer lab but ESL and TAAS preparation classes did not. English teachers used the labs primarily to allow students to complete writing assignments and for TAAS practice activities. In school two there was virtually no use of computers for literacy instruction. There was a computer lab, but it was used by other content areas. There were computers in the library that students could use when working there, and there were a few computers in classrooms that students might access during free periods or during after-school tutoring sessions. School two did have some Language Masters available for student use.

Teachers in school one reported that they had a good group of parent volunteers that assisted them. The volunteers did not work in classrooms but were available in the school to accomplish tasks for teachers. A strong PTO was operative in school two to assist in many ways. School two had tutorial classes after school that students could attend if they wished. If a teacher suggested a student could benefit by attendance, the student usually would attend. Parents were fully cooperative with this program. During the school day seniors and some juniors in school two regularly assisted freshmen and sophomores who needed extra help. Other students would go to the elementary school to assist there. A major oil company had helped school two to get televisions in most classrooms. Teachers in school two readily acknowledged that they had limited supplemental resources to work with, but claimed that they still could do what they needed to do to provide effective learning experiences for their students.

Provision for Linguistically Diverse Students

Without question both schools made provisions for linguistically diverse students. Teachers in these schools began by recognizing and appreciating the diversity, and they acted by designing and delivering instruction that accommodated that diversity. This was done not only through the various types of classes that were offered but by the way every class was taught. Never did teachers blame students for their diversity or use it as an excuse for why they would or could not teach the students. Instead, the teachers would do whatever they could in the selection of materials and in their instructional procedures to build on that diversity. Most faculty members had a command of both languages and used them for instruction when needed. Those teachers who were not bilingual would have students help other students, and they would structure their instruction so that no student was made to feel inadequate because of his or her diversity. Also, in relating schoolwork to life outside of school, diversity in families and within the community was respected. In short, students were encouraged to honor and appreciate their diversity (Moll & Gonzalez, 1994).

Relating Instruction to Real-Life Experiences

In school one, the main way of relating instruction to experience was through the use of books, newspapers, magazines, and other print materials that students found of interest. When students read novels and textbook materials, teachers would attempt to relate the setting, plot, and characters to something in present-day life so that students might see the relationship. Through the use of Spanish and English in classes, teachers were better able to help students use their own experiences to understand words and stories. Teachers in school two used these same techniques but added to them extensive use of projects involving the students in the community around them. The Rio Grande project was one example but there were many other smaller projects or field trips. A teacher of anatomy each year took the students into a major hospital in a nearby city, where each student spent 2 hours shadowing a particular medical specialist. The students observed the birth of a baby on one trip. A theater class went to see *Phantom of the Opera* in a city some distance away. As a part of a joint science and English project, another class went to a power plant to see power generated. A major museum in a distant city was visited annually by one teacher and her class. Many of the projects spanned across subject areas, with each area relating the project to something in the life of the students. This practice added realism and importance to the work (Baker, Afflerbach, & Reinking, 1996; Blum et al., 1995).

Assessment of Students' Skills and Needs

The ultimate assessment in the high schools was whether students passed the TAAS exit test. Therefore, in classes for those students who had not yet passed this test, assessment of their classroom performance on TAAS test practice activities was a common means of ongoing appraisal of student progress. All teachers observed student work habits and graded student work. Some teachers had students develop portfolios of their work, and these would be used in assessing student progress. Most often the portfolios were used to collect writing activities, but some teachers included daily assignments that had been graded and then reviewed them on a periodic basis to determine an overall grade. Performance on worksheet activities was used for assessment by some teachers at times, but this practice was limited. A few teachers reported using informal reading inventories to assess student reading levels, but they were used only by a few teachers and infrequently by them. Traditional tests covering material studied were used by a number of teachers to judge student performance. This was much more likely to occur in English classes than in reading classes (Hoffman et al., 1996).

Where projects were used, students might be assessed on the kinds of contributions they made to a project and the quality of their contributions. Since cooperative activities were used widely in both schools, assessment of individual performance within a group was sometimes problematic.

CONCLUSIONS

Reflections Across Elementary Schools

What were the ingredients for success in these two elementary schools? Many factors contributed to success in reading in these schools, and many of these were factors that might be found in other schools. But in these schools there seemed to be several distinguishing factors. First, the teachers assumed full responsibility for helping students succeed. They did not permit or accept any excuses for failure, such as poverty in the home, limited English skills, or parental apathy toward academic pursuits. Students in these schools had many needs that originated outside the school, but the schools were determined that they could and would provide whatever programs and resources were required to meet the needs for the students to succeed in school.

Meeting the need to succeed in school included the development of academic skills and student self-concept. Teachers in these schools were extremely caring and nurturing of the students. The teachers had high expectations for their students, but they were not punitive in their efforts to get the students to fulfill those expectations. Teachers believed that they were going to succeed with the students, and they constantly conveyed to the students the belief and expectation that the students could and would succeed as readers.

In any school a most valuable resource is the teachers. In these schools that resource was multiplied through consistent, intensive, and productive sharing and collaboration among teachers. It would be hard to overestimate the value of the collaborative efforts in these schools. And the collaboration was not among teachers only, but among teachers, administrators, parents, and the community. The purpose of this collaboration was not just to design instruction, but also to identify all the possible ways students could be assisted and supported.

Teachers also promoted collaborative learning among the students. Every day students spent much time working together and sharing in learning activities that involved reading. Through this sharing students were able to get help from peers, and all students engaged in more thoughtful discussions of issues related to material read as a result of this collaboration.

Teachers were consistent and intense in their efforts to make sure that all students understood what they were reading. They did this by constantly relating new concepts and vocabulary to the background knowledge the students had, thus regularly increasing the students' capability for new understanding. Teachers also used both English and Spanish to connect existing knowledge with new knowledge. This not only helped to develop understanding, but also created a stronger bond between teacher and student.

In these successful schools a wide variety of materials was readily available to students at all times. This was possible through the combined efforts of teachers and librarians. Because so many materials were available, students were always able to have books that were of interest to them and that they could read. This was an important aspect of these schools, for in them children became avid readers. Teachers constantly emphasized the joy and importance of reading, and they had an ample supply of good reading materials to offer to students to support this emphasis.

Many of the characteristics of effective reading instruction in secondary schools that were identified at the beginning of this section were in evidence in the middle and high schools in this study. Several of the characteristics stood out as being especially related to successful reading programs.

A supportive caring classroom and school environment, continuous and effective relating of instruction to student background, and regular and purposeful student-to-student sharing and cooperation were obviously related to student success in the reading program. The supportive caring environment was most evident in those schools where teachers regularly interacted with students around instructional tasks and through these interactions knew the students very well and used this knowledge to reach and teach them. When teachers exhibited enthusiasm and excitement about teaching and learning, and when they convinced students they could be successful learners, success was greater.

When students had regular opportunities to learn through collaborative activities, they were more enthusiastic about their instruction and they accomplished more. Enthusiasm and achievement were greatly increased by opportunities to participate in projects that allowed the students to be engaged in hands-on learning that had relevance for their lives (Wentzel, 1993).

Another factor that appeared to be influential in the success of these schools was the great variety of courses that were offered to meet the varying needs of the student body. This enabled the schools to provide in-depth instruction focused on specific student needs.

Utilization of both Spanish and English as needed during instruction and relating new vocabulary and knowledge to cultural background not only contributed directly to academic success but also helped create a caring environment for the students. Learning activities that spanned across content areas also added to student interest and accomplishment. Undoubtedly the respect for language and cultural diversity that existed in these schools made a major contribution to their success.

Reflections Across Middle Schools

In both schools instruction was targeted to specific reading skills, usually vocabulary and comprehension skills. This instruction was almost always based on connected reading experiences in books or stories. Isolated skill instruction was rare. Whole group involvement was the typical approach to reading instruction, but this was always accompanied by other activities and experiences intended to assist those students who needed extra help. During an instructional period there was a balance between teacher-directed instruction and students working independently. Writing activities tended to be related to reading activities in most classrooms.

In both schools there was a definite success orientation among the teachers. That is, they spoke only about the things that helped students become successful readers, not about reasons why students could not succeed. To help students succeed, teachers were sensitive to individual needs and attempted in many ways to provide for those in daily instruction. Organizationally the establishment of different types of classes was intended to offer additional support for individual learner needs. In neither school was instruction driven by a particular curriculum. Teachers began with the establishment of learning goals, and then selected materials and activities they felt helped students attain those goals (Blum et al., 1995; Cummins, 1994).

A caring community was especially evident in the schools where teachers regularly collaborated for instructional purposes and where they also developed a unified support system for students throughout the day. A sense of community within a school or classroom also is developed when teachers share control of the classroom and allow students more involvement. This, in turn, has a positive impact on students' perceptions of their competency (Ryan & Grolnick, 1986), causes them to value instruction more (Deci, Vallerand, Pellietier, & Ryan, 1991), and promotes student engagement in learning (Slavin, 1987). Many teachers regularly allowed their students the opportunity to actively participate in the instructional process within the classroom.

Effective schools systematically address instructional goals that lead to student success (Winfield & Manning, 1992). One consistent goal was to increase comprehension of what was read, whether it was in a reading class or a content area class. A technique widely used to do this was whole class discussion of what had been read, a technique that has been shown to be effective in increasing comprehension (Duffy & Roehler, 1987). Discussion allows teachers to gain insights into student thinking and to adjust instruction based on those insights. Following reading and discussion of what had been read, students often were asked to write a summary of the reading. The teaching of summarization is another effective means of improving comprehension (Baker et al., 1996; Kintsch & Van Dijk, 1978).

Comprehension also is aided when teachers establish a clear and certain connection between the material being read and studied and the community in which the students live (Pritchard, 1990). Establishing a connection between instruction and the lives of the students was a procedure used with considerable effectiveness in some of these schools.

Reflections Across High Schools

Both schools used a wide variety of course offerings as one way of accommodating the range of student needs and abilities in reading and English. Spanish and English often were used in instruction to assist students in developing increased understanding of what was read. Most teachers in the two schools taught at least two different types or levels of classes and often three. In those classes where students had not yet taken or passed the TAAS test, there was much emphasis on preparing students for this test. Teachers emphasized the need to build student self-esteem, particularly with students where language interfered with learning. Cooperation among students during learning experiences was common to both schools.

Differences in the number of students in the two schools and the communities in which they were located may have accounted for some of the differences noted in the schools. The smaller school (school two) had a high level of teacher sharing and cooperation across disciplines and throughout the school. In a like manner, student sharing and cooperation in learning activities were commonly practiced. Student discipline was not an issue of any consequence in this school. Teachers felt comfortable engaging the students in many projects and other shared learning activities. Teachers had high praise for their students as respectful individuals and for their commitment to learning. They attributed this to the nature of the community where the school was located. However, it seemed that a contributing factor was the strong relationship between what happened in classes and the lives of students outside of school, and teachers had a keen knowledge of the students and their lives. The large number of students in school one made it difficult for teachers to know students in such a close way (Baker et al., 1996; Guthrie & Wigfield, 1997).

REFERENCES

Anderson, R. C. (1984). Role of the reader's schema in comprehension, learning, and memory. In R. C. Anderson, J. Osborn, & R. J. Tierney (Eds.), *Learning to read in American schools: Basal readers and content texts* (pp. 168–169). Hillsdale, NJ: Erlbaum.

Anderson, R. C., Wilson, P. T., & Fielding, L. G. (1988). Growth in reading and how children spend their time outside school. *Reading Research Quarterly, 24,* 174–187.

Au, K. H., & Mason, J. M. (1989). Elementary reading programs. In S. B. Wepner, J. T. Feeley, & D. S. Strickland (Eds.), *The administration and supervision of reading programs* (pp. 60–75). New York: Teachers College Press.

Baker, L., Afflerbach, P., & Reinking, D. (Eds.). (1996). *Developing engaged readers in school and home communities.* Mahwah, NJ: Erlbaum.

Baker, L., Allen, J., Shockley, B., Pellegrini, A. D., Galda, L., & Stahl, S. (1996). Connecting school and home: Constructing partnerships to foster reading development. In L. Baker, P. Afflerbach, & D. Reinking (Eds.), *Developing engaged readers in school and home communities* (pp. 21–41). Mahwah, NJ: Erlbaum.

Battistich, V., Solomon, D., Kin, D., Watson, M., & Schaps, E. (1995). Schools as communities, poverty levels of student populations, and students' attitudes, motives, and performance: A multilevel analysis. *American Educational Research Journal, 32,* 627–658.

Blum, I. H., Koskinen, P. S., Tennant, N., Parker, E. M., Straub, M., & Curry, C. (1995). *Using audiotaped books to extend classroom literacy instruction into the homes of second-language learners* (Reading Research Report No. 39). Athens, GA: Universities of Georgia and Maryland, National Reading Research Center.

Brookover, W., Thomas, S., & Paterson, A. (1962). Self-concept of ability and school achievement. *Sociology of Education, 37,* 271–278.

Chall, J. S. (1967). *Learning to read: The great debate.* New York: McGraw-Hill.

Cummins, J. (1994). The acquisition of English as a second language. In K. Spangenberg-Urbschat & R. Pritchard (Eds.), *Kids come in all languages: Reading instruction for ESL students* (pp. 36–62). Newark, DE: International Reading Association.

Davis, F. B. (1969). Research in comprehension in reading. *Reading Research Quarterly, 3,* 499–544.

Deci, E. L., Vallerand, R. J., Pellietier, L. G., & Ryan, R. M. (1991). Motivation and education: The self-determination perspective. *Educational Psychologist,* 26, 325–346.

Dickinson, D., & Smith, M. (1994). Long term effects of preschool teachers' book readings on low-income children's vocabulary and story comprehension. *Reading Research Quarterly,* 29, 105–122.

Duffy, G. G., & Roehler, L. R. (1987). Improving reading instruction through the use of responsive elaboration. *The Reading Teacher,* 40, 514–520.

Elley, W. B. (1989). Vocabulary acquisition from listening to stories. *Reading Research Quarterly,* 24, 174–187.

Gambrell, L. B. (1997). Creating classroom cultures that foster reading motivation. *Reading Teacher,* 50(1), 14–26.

Gipe, J. P. (1980). Use of relevant context helps kids learn. *Reading Teacher, 33*(4), 398–402.

Gunning, T. G. (1992). *Creating reading instruction for all children.* Boston: Allyn & Bacon.

Guszak, F. J. (1992). *Reading for students with special needs.* Dubuque, IA: Kendall-Hunt.

Guthrie, J. T., Van Meter, P., McCann, A. D., Wigfield, A., Bennett, L., Poundstone, C. C., Rice, M. E., Faibisch, F. M., Hunt, B., & Mitchell, A. (1996). Growth of literacy engagement: Changes in motivations and strategies during concept-oriented reading instruction. *Reading Research Quarterly, 31,* 306–332.

Guthrie, J. T., & Wigfield, A. (1997). Reading engagement: A rationale for theory and teaching. In J. T. Guthrie & A. Wigfield (Eds.), *Reading engagement: Motivating readers through integrated instruction* (pp. 1–12). Newark, DE: International Reading Association.

Hayes, B. L. (Ed.). (1991). *Effective strategies for teaching reading.* Boston: Allyn & Bacon.

Hirsch, E. D. (1987). *Cultural literacy and what every American needs to know.* Boston: Houghton Mifflin.

Hoffman, J. V. (1992). Leadership in the language arts: Am I whole yet? Are you? *Language Arts, 69,* 366–370.

Hoffman, J. V., Worthy, J., Roser, N. L., McKool, S. S., Rutherford, W. L., & Strecker, S. (1996). Performance assessment in first-grade classrooms: The PALM model. In D. J. Leu, C. K. Kinzer, & K. A. Hinchman (Eds.), *Literacies for the 21st century* (pp. 100–112). Chicago: National Reading Conference.

Kagan, S. (1986). Cooperative learning and sociocultural factors in schooling. In California Department of Education. *Beyond language: Social and cultural factors in schooling language minority students* (pp. 231–298). Los Angeles: California State University.

Kintsch, W., & Van Dijk, T. A. (1978). Toward a model of text comprehension and production. *Psychological Review, 85,* 363–394.

Kucer, S. B., & Harste, J. C. (1991). The reading and writing connection: Counterpart strategy lessons. In B. L. Hayes (Ed.), *Effective strategies for teaching reading* (pp. 123–152). Boston: Allyn & Bacon.

Licht, B. G. (1983). Cognitive-motivational factors that contribute to the achievement of learning disabled children. *Journal of Learning Disabilities, 2,* 45–52.

Losey, K. M. (1995). Mexican American students and classroom interaction: An overview and critique. *Review of Educational Research, 65*, 283–318.

Moll, L. C., & Gonzalez, N. (1994). Lessons for research with language-minority children. *Journal of Reading Behavior, 26*, 439–458.

Morrow, L. (1990). Small group story readings: The effects on children's comprehension and response to literature. *Reading Research and Instruction, 29*, 1–17.

Morrow, L. (1992). The impact of a literature-based program on literacy achievement, use of literature, and attitudes of children from minority backgrounds. *Reading Research Quarterly, 27*, 250–275.

Newman, F. M. (1981). Reducing student alienation in high schools: Implications of theory. *Harvard Educational Review, 51*, 546–564.

Pearson, P. D., & Fielding, L. (1991). Comprehension instruction. In R. Barr, M. L. Kamil, P. Mosenthal, & P. D. Pearson (Eds.), *Handbook of reading research* (Vol. 2, pp. 815–860). New York: Longman.

Pritchard, R. (1990). The effects of cultural schemata on reading processing strategies. *Reading Research Quarterly, 25*, 273–295.

Purcell-Gates, V. (1996). Stories, coupons, and the TV Guide: Relationships between home literacy experiences and emergent literacy knowledge. *Reading Research Quarterly, 31*, 406–428.

Routman, R. (1994). *Invitations*. Portsmouth, NH: Heinemann.

Rumelhart, D. (1984). Understanding understanding. In J. Flood (Ed.), *Understanding reading comprehension* (pp. 1–20). Newark, DE: International Reading Association.

Ryan, R. M., & Grolnick, W. S. (1986). Origins and pawns in the classroom: Self-report and projective assessments of individual differences in children's perceptions. *Journal of Personality and Social Psychology, 50*, 550–558.

Savin-Williams, R. C., & Berndt, T. J. (1990). Friendship and peer relations. In S. Feldman & G. R. Elliot (Eds.), *At the threshold: The developing adolescent* (pp. 277–307). Cambridge, MA: Harvard University Press.

Schunk, D. H. (1989). Social cognitive theory and self-regulated learning. In B. J. Zimmerman & D. H. Schunk (Eds.), *Self-regulated learning and academic achievement* (pp. 83–110). New York: Springer-Verlag.

Slavin, R. E. (1987). Cooperative learning: Where behavioral and humanistic approaches to classroom motivation meet. *Elementary School Journal, 88*, 29–37.

Thomas, A. (1979). Learned helplessness and expectancy factors: Implications for research in learning disabilities. *Review of Educational Research, 49*, 208–221.

Vacca, R. T., & Padak, N. D. (1990). Who's at risk in reading? *Journal of Reading, 33*, 486–489.

Wattenburg, W., & Clifford, C. (1964). Relationship of self-concepts to beginning achievement in reading. *Child Development, 35*, 461–467.

Wehlage, G. G., Rutter, R. A., & Turnbaugh, A. (1987). A program model for at-risk high school students. *Educational Leadership, 44*, 70–73.

Wentzel, K. R. (1993). Motivation and achievement in early adolescence: The role of multiple classroom goals. *Journal of Early Adolescence, 13*, 4–20.

Winfield, L. F., & Manning, J. B. (1992). Changing school culture to accommodate student diversity. In M. E. Dilworth (Ed.), *Diversity in teacher education: New expectations* (pp. 181–214). San Francisco: Jossey-Bass.

CHAPTER 7

Using Student Advocacy
Assessment Practices

Alicia Paredes Scribner

A look at American education today shows that some form of evaluation takes place in schools on any given day. Many times such evaluations take the form of standardized tests that are unrelated to the curriculum. Although the purposes of assessment should be to guide individualized and classroom instruction and monitor student progress, what teachers teach and what is tested rarely approximate what students learn (Niyogi, 1995). Best practices suggest that rather than to judge students, assessment should be used to examine the nature of their knowledge and the manner in which they learn best (Glaser & Silver, 1994). The purposes of assessment should be to define what kind of information the educator is seeking, why the information is being sought, and, once obtained, how it is going to improve student learning. Assessment should define expectations for students, teachers, schools and school districts, as well as educational agencies.

To consider effective assessment practices for Hispanic, limited English proficient students, one is compelled to begin by looking at the classroom, for the classroom is the setting where teaching and learning take place (Garcia, 1994; Perrone, 1991). Studies indicate that Hispanic students learn better when high expectations are set by their teachers, when new learning theories guide instruction, when teaching and learning are collaborative, and when there is abundant opportunity for listening, speaking, reading, and writing (Cummins, 1984, 1986; Duran, 1989; Figueroa, 1990; Garcia, 1994). In the absence of these conditions, a student's lack of skills may be interpreted as lack of ability instead of lack of opportunity to learn or lack of access to effective instruction.

Traditional classroom task-specific assessment practices underestimate what a student knows. A language-minority student enters the schooling process without the language in which the process is embedded (Figueroa & Garcia, 1994). Much of what occurs in the teaching, learning, and testing processes requires effective communication of facts, concepts, ideas, and problem-solving strategies. Students who are learning English as a second language may be perfectly able to participate in the aforementioned cognitive processes in their native language, but may lack the communication skills to perform the same type of processes in the code of a new language. As a result, norm-referenced, standardized objective tests used in schools yield deficient profiles for language-minority students in language, cognition, memory, perception, learning ability, and aptitude (August & Garcia, 1988). In other words, reliance on standardized testing presents a picture of below-average ability in growth and development that is unfair and harmful. In contrast, authentic, performance-based assessments engage the student in hands-on activities that take many forms. Such alternatives hold the instructional setting accountable for student learning. One example of authentic, performance-based assessment is portfolio assessment, based on a collection of the student's work over time reflecting the student's growth and potential.

The literature reviewed for this research addressed teacher competencies, curricular modifications, and flexibility in the delivery of instruction as key elements in the academic success of Hispanic students. Effective teachers were found to be knowledgeable in instructional methodology and had graduated from teacher-training programs that emphasized multicultural education. These teachers were able to articulate educational philosophies that guided their instruction and were competent instructors in their respective content areas. Skills were taught using a thematic curriculum, and instruction was integrated across a variety of subject areas. Opportunities for active learning were the rule rather than the exception. Collaborative and cooperative interactions among students were encouraged. Creativity, resourcefulness, and commitment were defining attributes characterizing effective teachers. Finally, delivery of instruction reflected a mode that facilitated authentic, performance-based assessment appropriate for what students learned, and promoted communicative interaction among students and between students and teachers (Alvarez, 1991; Cummins, 1984, 1986; Duran, 1989; Figueroa, 1990; Garcia, 1994; Hamayan & Damico, 1991; Paredes Scribner, 1995b; Valencia & Aburto, 1991).

When effective instruction is lacking, Hispanic students will exhibit difficulty acquiring the necessary skills in English. Teachers who do not know what to do refer to assessment specialists for solutions. The way in which linguistic ability is assessed may preempt special education placement for these students. Experts in speech and language assessment caution about the use and interpretation of discrete-point, standardized tests with LEP children. They recommend supplementing standardized tests with various informal procedures involving test content, administration procedures to compensate for the tests' cultural biases, or both. Many experts also recommend the use of qualitative measures (i.e., observations, reports, and interviews) to complement standardized test scores and further reduce bias. Such alternative procedures result in more realistic information, more naturalistic data, and the integration of cultural, linguistic variation (Cummins, 1984; Damico, 1991; Erickson & Iglesias, 1986; Langdon, 1992; Peña, Quinn, & Iglesias, 1992).

Promising practices in psychoeducational assessment of LEP students propose a more advocacy-oriented approach to assessment. An advocacy-oriented approach to assessment takes into consideration the ecology of the learning environment; effectiveness of classroom instruction; level of skills in the native language as well as English; background and culture; expectations of teachers, parents, and students themselves; and results of systematic observation(s) (Cummins, 1984; DeLéon, 1990; Duran, 1989; Figueroa, 1990; Garcia, 1994; Paredes Scribner, 1995a; Valencia & Aburto, 1991). Advocacy-oriented strategies for LEP students test the tests. If it is determined that assessment results undermine a student's potential, then advocacy-oriented approaches to assessment involve strategies that assume that (1) something must be wrong with the test, rather than the student, and (2) learning (classroom) conditions, criterion (testing) conditions, and antecedent (home or environmental) conditions can be altered to meet the student's needs.

The use of informal procedures along with formal measures allows the examiner to assess the student's learning capacity and degree of modifiability. In this manner, the psychoeducational evaluation is more likely to link assessment to instruction and provide the teacher(s) with relevant and direct interventions to improve learning. Thus, in this study the argument can be made that in high-performing Hispanic schools where students achieve in spite of the odds, a broad, encompassing concept of assessment and its relationship to instruction exists. This assumption sets the stage for the most basic type of educational reform at the classroom level (Niyogi, 1995).

THE SCHOOLS

For the sake of anonymity, the campuses selected for this study have been given fictitious names. Calles, Obregón, and Carranza were the three elementary schools in the study. There were two middle schools and one junior high school—Francisco Villa, Madero, and Huerta, respectively. The two high schools were Benito Juarez and Porfirio Diaz. A description of these schools, their faculty and administrator characteristics, and other pertinent information can be found in Chapter 1.

Three clusters surfaced in the data analysis. The first cluster is instructional interventions and modifications, representing the value that change is for the student's sake. The second cluster converges on the maximizing of resources. Through collaboration and consultation, professionals work together for the child. Professional growth and empowerment is the third cluster, representing professionalism, self-efficacy, and the characteristic of teachers and other school professionals feeling in charge of their own destiny.

Five themes were reflected across the three clusters: (1) the philosophy of the school, (2) the cohesiveness and collaboration among school professionals, (3) the understanding of learning difficulties as they relate to language proficiency, (4) the use of alternative assessment methods, and (5) the personal goals set to improve one's professional skills.

Cluster 1: Instructional Interventions and Modifications

One of the critical concerns in misdiagnosis of language-minority students as learning disabled is the manner in which learning difficulties are evaluated. In most schools, learning difficulties of LEP students were addressed through modified instruction referred to as prereferral intervention. Although the term "prereferral" implies a stage in the formal assessment process, in practice the term identifies options that school professionals consider before assuming that a learning disability exists. Services in special programs varied as a result of English language proficiency and grade level—the lower the grade level, the more mechanisms existed for prereferral options. For example, students who were English speaking rarely were referred at the junior high school level; junior high Hispanic, English-speaking students in special education programs had been referred prior to junior high school. The vice principal at Huerta Junior High School, and a member of the multidisciplinary team at the school, stated, "Sixty to 70% of LEP kids are receiving services—not necessarily because they were identified here. A lot of kids are identified in elementary school—most of them are. There are not too many kids who are identified that come from English-speaking homes."

At Francisco Villa Middle School, the prereferral process works relatively like an Individual Educational Plan (IEP) that gives objectives for the child and is distributed to a team of teachers. The team of teachers attempt the instructional modifications for 6 to 8 weeks. If the student makes the desired progress, there is no need to refer further. Team planning periods greatly facilitate this process. A special education teacher at Madero Middle School, in another district, commented that being able to plan together for a student or a group of students, meet with one or more students for instruction or assessment purposes, or meet as a group with the parents was beneficial.

Instructional modifications in the regular education program also were developed in the form of an IEP at Madero Middle School. This IEP was circulated to all the teachers working with the student, and interventions were implemented over a 6- to 8-week period. For those students whose difficulty was clearly limited English language skills, intensive ESL instruction was planned. A teacher at this school reported:

> At this middle school, we have an ESL program. ESL 1 means students are placed with the teacher for three periods per day and that teacher teaches language arts. ESL 2 is for two periods per day, and these students go to another teacher for reading improvement. ESL 3 is in the regular classroom with ESL-certified teachers. Once exited from ESL programs, the students are followed for 3 years by the Language Proficiency Assessment Committee.

Concern for the student appeared paramount at the elementary level. At all campuses, prereferral interventions were in place. Prereferral checklists were used and the staff recognized the need to assess students' abilities in English and Spanish. Since the majority of instructional personnel at these schools was bilingual in English and Spanish, teachers felt competent differentiating between a language difference and a language disability. In addition, teachers were required to describe in the referral packet what modifications and teaching/learning strategies had been tried. The period of time allowed to determine whether modifications had positive results was a minimum of 6 weeks. Typically, input from parents regarding developmental information had been part of prereferral interventions and occurred at the beginning of the process.

At the elementary level, the referral and eligibility rates were very close and within expected parameters. Assessment personnel at the elementary level appeared to be sensitive to issues of acculturation, adjustment to new school systems, and familiarity with stages of second-language acquisition. The educational diagnostician at Obregón Elementary School said, "The referral rate and qualifying rate has been good, very close. The only time they [teachers] refer a child who's a recent immigrant is when they suspect mental retardation."

At all the schools, language proficiency was established by using the Language Assessment Scales (LAS) (De Avila & Duncan, 1977, 1986), per guidelines set by the Language Proficiency Assessment Committee. This committee typically comprised the ESL supervisor, an administrator, bilingual/ESL teachers, and parents. A trained clerk, who administers the LAS at Obregón Elementary School, said:

> I usually give kids a week or so to adjust to school, then I go to the classroom and pick them up individually. I gather all the information and then the LPAC gets together. Then the decision is made whether the child is a bilingual student or a regular student. Further testing and monitoring is also done to allow the child to transfer or transition to other programs.

The question of supervision arose at this point. It appeared that contrary to state guidelines, a certified speech/language pathologist did not provide regular supervision to the language assessment clerk.

The educational diagnostician at the same junior high school added, "We are not concerned about misidentifying kids because a child who is language delayed is going to be language delayed in his native language also. If it's only in English, then it's really a matter of a language barrier."

Identification of learning disabilities proceeded with caution at these schools. A comment made by the vice principal at Huerta Junior High said it all: "We consider our students all regular students, and then from there, we check to see if there is a language barrier or what. . . . We don't treat them differently because most of our students are LEP."

The diagnostician at Huerta Junior High said that visible handicaps were addressed immediately. Other learning problems were treated with caution: "If we suspect a learning disability, we first see how the kid does by comparison."

At Obregón Elementary School, the educational diagnostician said, "I consider information I get on the referral, and information I get from the parents and teachers."

Interventions considered for LEP students who were exhibiting learning difficulties varied across grade levels. The vice principal at Huerta Junior High School discussed how block scheduling solved some problems.

> With language-minority kids, all teachers working with a given grade or program have the same planning period and they discuss learning problems at this time. This is a time also when parent meetings are scheduled. The other thing we do is have a program for our new students, who came straight from Mexico, called High Intensity Language Development [HILD]. We have two dynamic teachers in this area—one is a special education teacher.

The HILD program was, indeed, exceptional. This program offered instruction in the content areas in Spanish to students new to this country. Groups of students of varying degrees of English proficiency worked together. The more advanced students helped those who needed more direction. When students were ready to move on to instruction in English, their progress was monitored closely. Once in English instruction, students were taught from regular curriculum materials, but teachers used ESL techniques to make the material comprehensible. According to the vice principal at this school, "Teachers motivate these kids so that they want to learn."

Another aspect of the HILD program was that student performance was assessed using portfolio assessment. A visit was made to the HILD classroom while a science lesson was in progress. The sophistication of the assignments and student products was impressive. When the students' portfolios were shared with a member of the research team, it was evident that a variety of strategies were employed to evaluate student work over time and that learning was taking place.

Reaching out to the parents also was a practice at these schools. A counselor at Obregón Elementary School said:

> Home visits? Yes, we all make home visits. We even have multidisciplinary team meetings in the homes. Teachers make frequent home visits—all of them do. We are all very good in that respect. We try to be. Just recently, we had a meeting on a Sunday morning. We had the teacher, the administrator, and the assessment person.

Porfirio Diaz High School had two bilingual counselors who work with LEP students and their families. The principal closed the discussion on prereferral interventions by saying:

> All factors are taken into consideration. We try alternatives, modify instruction in the regular classes. The problem might be stemming from the home. We get the counselors to work with the student and the family. There is a mechanism—we have a team and we have an intervention.

A summary of the prereferral instructional interventions and modifications are delineated in Table 7.1.

Cluster 2: Maximizing Resources: Consultation and Collaboration

Across school levels, assessment personnel worked closely with teachers in consultation to maximize resources. The collaborative relationship that

TABLE 7.1. Cluster 1 Summary
Highlights of Best Practices in Instructional Interventions and Modifications

Context	Best Practice
Prereferral Practices	Instructional modifications Team planning/teaching Intensive ESL instruction ESL-certified classroom teachers
Language Assessment	Adjustment period Intensive language development Team planning/teaching Coordination of instruction
School Philosophy	Collaboration Commitment to student learning Familiarity with LEP student needs Bilingual staff Parent involvement

was reported and observed indicated the sense of teamwork that takes place on behalf of students. Team planning offered the opportunity for a group of teachers to meet with selected professionals for consultation. These meetings sometimes resulted in home visits. A counselor at Carranza Elementary School reported, "Sometimes it is necessary to meet with parents if we have concerns about a student. If they can't come to school, we go to them."

The speech/language therapist added, "I can consult with other diagnosticians, the counselor, teachers, whenever I need extra information. Or I can visit the parents if sometimes I'm not sure that they have given all the information and I suspect there are some medical problems I need to explore."

Most of the schools visited had principals who supported staff and faculty, saw themselves as professional mentors, and were open to suggestions from all school personnel. Instructional and other personnel were supported and encouraged to institute innovations and participate in local and regional workshops. A vice principal at Huerta Junior High said, "Our school supports its teachers within the system and offers information and updates as needed. . . . The principal is the one who gets all the conference information. He decides who should go to those meetings and makes it possible for us to go."

Assessment personnel in general appeared to play an important role in consulting with teachers when an LEP student was suspected of having a learning disability. The educational diagnostician at Huerta Junior High School commented:

> When lack of educational opportunity is suspected, we try to tell the teachers that they need to keep that kid in their classroom for at least a year while trying different instructional modifications, and then the following school year if the kid is still having problems, then we go to the referral process.

Team planning was favored by teachers at all levels. Teachers at the middle schools and the elementary schools had team planning periods in which they could plan specific strategies for one student or a group of students. The team could meet with an individual student, a group of students, or parents during this time. Assistance also was sought from other teachers or staff. Before a student is referred at Huerta Junior High School, experienced teachers are asked to review the student's work and are asked their opinion and recommendations.

Generally, school faculties felt comfortable determining whether a student's learning difficulty was due to a language difference or an academic problem. In this respect, block scheduling and a team planning period were very helpful, according to teachers across levels. From the administrator's perspective, troubleshooting was done easily as a team. The vice principal at Huerta Junior High School noted discussion of particular learning problems and suggested interventions that helped teachers understand similar situations in the future. In fact, many administrators reported that more consultation with teachers occurred when a student was found ineligible for special programs. The team discovered what the student could and could not do. The counselor at Obregón Elementary School remarked on the degree of interaction she had had with the speech/language therapist: "We can ask the speech/language therapist about where a child is as far as language goes. We know we can ask for help anytime—we go back and forth. We work real well together. They're doing the best they can for kids. . . . The same thing with parents."

The speech/language therapist at Porfirio Diaz High School also offers consultation to teachers. A teacher observed, "The speech/language therapist is very good about going in and observing in the classroom. She is bilingual and makes suggestions for interventions in the classroom."

The high school principal at the same school added, "Our basic philosophy is that all students should learn. . . . Here, it is a team effort. We don't believe any one person can do everything."

The educational diagnostician at Francisco Villa Middle School described her consultation with teachers: "There is a lot of teamwork here.

TABLE 7.2. Cluster 2 Summary
Highlights of Best Practices in Maximizing Resources:
Consultation and Collaboration

Context	Best Practice
Consultation	Teaching/learning technique
	Medical concerns
	Cultural aspects
	Team instructional planning
	Language development
	English as a second language
Collaboration	Home visits
	Professional mentoring
	Sharing of resources
	Sharing of perspectives within and across disciplines
School Philosophy	Commitment to students
	Commitment to faculty/staff
	General responsibility for new hires
	Mentoring administrators

Teachers will come to me and tell me to be on the lookout for whatever problem a student may be having. I make myself very available to the teachers."

Teamwork and collaboration also were evident in the sharing of resources. The principal at Carranza Elementary commented: "When we hire a new teacher or staff person, I want my teachers to also meet and interview the prospective hire. After all, they are going to be working together."

In relation to sharing of resources, the same principal said, "Our teachers do a great job keeping each other informed. We have a budget for sending teachers to workshops out of town and they come back and share their information with other teachers." Table 7.2 illustrates best practices used by assessment personnel in consultation and collaboration with teachers and others to maximize resources.

Cluster 3: Professional Growth and Empowerment

Formal preservice training in bilingual assessment was limited. How, then, did it happen that many individuals appeared to be intuitively using best practices in the assessment of language-minority students? Perhaps what made the difference was the fact that a large majority of professionals in this study were bilingual, with backgrounds similar to those of the students. Professionals respected the language and culture of the students and recognized the value of bilingualism and biculturalism. The high degree of collaboration and administrative support also may lead to the use of best practices in bilingual assessment. The counselor at Benito Juarez High School commented: "This area is very different from Central Texas. Here there is still a lot of respect for speaking Spanish. Our students feel good about their background, who they are, and are not intimidated if they speak Spanish."

The principal at Porfirio Diaz High School observed:

> You know, I started my teaching/coaching career in a little town close to Kingsville. I was really surprised because they [other Hispanic professionals] tried to assimilate and become part of the group. I was Roberto and all the others used names like "Robert" and "Joe," and they did it out of survival. Through my training, I believe that it is important to keep our culture. In this school, I encouraged the teachers to help the kids be proud of their background.

Inservice professional development occurred mostly at the regional level. The local education service center was the source of most professional training in matters related to assessment. By and large all professionals interviewed belonged to their respective regional and/or state associations. Few reported membership in national professional associations. The educational diagnostician at Huerta Junior High School commented, "Continuing professional development is encouraged. We attend seminars and workshops, also conferences. I had some courses that addressed bilingual assessment, but most of the diagnosticians that did not go to school in this area do not attend professional development activities."

The principal at Porfirio Diaz High School said:

> I'm a member of the Texas Association of Secondary Principals and also the National Association of School Principals. Being a principal, I get lots of literature and I like to be a good mentor. We go to lots of training. I also belong to a group that monitors schools. I get a chance to see what others are doing that works. Sometimes I get my teachers to visit these schools and network with colleagues. If we can work together as a team, we will be better off.

He continued:

> People who conduct language assessment are trained at the regional service center and are bilingual. When we hear about any training,

we try to get the appropriate person involved. We try to do a lot of in-house training and updating. When there is something available in training centers or workshops, we attend it as a district.

The counselor at the same high school stated: "We go to the education service center for workshops and seminars. If all of us can't go, then one will go and come back and share the information."

Many of the assessment personnel agreed with the comment made by the speech/language therapist at Obregón Elementary School: "We have had no formal training on cultural bias and assessment instruments, or alternative means of assessment. We use informal procedures we have learned through the education service center."

For example, the diagnostician at Porfirio Diaz High School commented:

One of the main concerns is that there aren't too many tests in Spanish. We use things like the Woodcock–Muñoz, the Bateria in Spanish. We also use a lot of teacher information because that is very valuable. A lot of times we can't assess a student using Method I, so we use Method II a lot. Some people think that there needs to be one standard deviation [for discrepancy], but this is not my opinion. With the students we are describing, sometimes you do not get a clear profile and yet professionally you feel there is a need for services. In such cases we use Method II, and there is a lot of discussion with counselors, teachers, and administration to see what is best for the child.

At Carranza Elementary, the principal shared the following:

We use informal measures such as observations and question and answer all the time. As a matter of fact, we are undergoing extensive training in portfolio assessment. We have teachers who are traveling to the regional service center to train and have been sharing the information with other faculty.

A teacher at the same school added:

For language testing, we use the LAS to indicate different levels of English proficiency. We have a home language survey that indicates whether a child comes to us with a home language of either English or Spanish. We rely on the home language survey. We test in English and Spanish to determine if they are going to participate in the bilingual program or an oral language program.

A speech/language therapist at Madero Middle School said:

I use formal tests but also informal observation. I might see if the student knows analogies, past tense verbs, irregular plurals, if they can repeat sentences, understand time, general language concepts. Sometimes we use adaptive behavior measures as well.

A teacher at Porfirio Diaz High School shared: "I came here 7 years ago (from the midwest). I took classes in bilingual education while at my other school. They prepared me a little bit, but experience has prepared me the most. I've learned a lot on the job."

The counselor at the same high school said: "In my formal education, I studied a lot about multiculturalism and assimilation. My own family came from Mexico and I feel for these kids, because I know how I felt."

One of the educational diagnosticians serving Francisco Villa Middle School said:

I have gone to various workshops over the years and have been introduced to a variety of instruments and procedures. Most of our tests are in English. Even though I am not bilingual, over the years I have learned to use alternative procedures. Most of our training we get at the service center.

The diagnostician at Huerta Junior High commented: "I often go to conferences, seminars, or inservices. We have monthly meetings to talk about what is new. I am constantly attending conferences on assessment-related issues."

Obregón Elementary School employed a supervisor's clerk who was trained by the district to administer language proficiency tests for early childhood students. This individual was an instructional assistant for 14 years and had been in her current role for the past 5 years: "The only training I've had is here in this district. The bilingual director has helped us a lot, inservicing us with the LAS. I do the pre-LAS for the lower grades."

A number of interviewees noted that the opportunity to observe other schools and other programs had been of great benefit. Likewise, a principal at Carranza Elementary School expressed the benefits of sharing information: "Two of our special education teachers do a great job keeping us informed. They attend many conferences and keep us informed."

The need for training outside the domain of assessment personnel, but related to student progress, was also noted. A teacher at Porfirio Diaz High School said:

> We have an active parent teacher organization. That's rare at the high school level. We try hard to get vocational people—people from the Texas Rehabilitation Commission, Mental Health/Mental Retardation and other agencies. We send parents notices and try to work closely with them so they will understand what is available for their kids.
>
> We also have a parent trainer on our advisory committee who provides training for parents. Our PTO chapter is very active. Graduating seniors are informed about programs available for student loans and college programs.

Along with training, research team members were interested in finding out what recommendations were made in a student's IEP for additional services. Interviewees talked about the language of instruction. For example, if the student was eligible for special education in a bilingual setting, then such a recommendation was made. It was not uncommon to find that, in addition to academic need for modification, counseling was recommended. At Obregón Elementary, a teacher said, "If appropriate, we refer for bilingual counseling. Our counselor speaks excellent Spanish."

The principal at Porfirio Diaz High School explained:

> Counseling objectives are written into IEPs. We have three counselors, and we have more counselors than other schools. Counselors should counsel, not do paperwork. This is a big concern of mine. A lot of these kids have some tough problems away from the school. I would like to have some group counseling and address issues of HIV and teenage pregnancy. Next year, we are going to have all our teachers be advisers, where each teacher would have 15–20 students assigned to him or her. Sometimes the most influential adult is that one teacher.

For students in special education programs, recognition of the need for more frequent monitoring of their progress was evident in the following statements. The speech/language therapist at Obregón Elementary School said:

> Re-evaluations prior to 3 years do occur, but it's mainly for different placement, when we see the child hasn't progressed any. We've just had a few cases where they've transferred from another campus, or

TABLE 7.3. Cluster 3 Summary
Highlights of Best Practices in Professional Growth and Empowerment

Context	Best Practice
Training	Mentoring Professional development Regional inservice workshops Alternative assessment procedures Training encouraged and facilitated
Advocacy	Prereferral intervention Avoidance of deficit model Learning environment considered Understanding of linguistic issues Understanding of cultural issues Alternative assessment procedures
Empowerment	Freedom to try alternatives Collaboration/consultation Professional respect Commitment to students Commitment to professional growth

another district, so we do some further assessment here. If kids have met the goals, we have dismissed them.

The diagnostician at the same school added, "When they have mastered IEP goals, when we see that they've carried over their IEP goals into the classroom, the teacher doesn't have any questions, then I retest them. We meet as an ARD committee and dismiss them." A range of training, advocacy, and empowerment opportunities were provided to the professional staff in the high-performing Hispanic schools (see Table 7.3).

CONCLUSIONS AND RECOMMENDATIONS

The literature review conducted for this research reflected an ever-growing interest in the best ways to teach and assess students from culturally and linguistically diverse backgrounds. A large number of studies and journal articles have isolated characteristics of effective instructional and assessment practices for Hispanic LEP students. Many of these characteristics were found in our research of effective assessment practices in border district schools.

Teachers and school administrators who believe students can achieve despite their background set high expectations for them (Collier, 1994; Garcia, 1994; Lucas, Henze, & Donato, 1990). Successful schools have principals who are supportive of their staff and give their teachers autonomy while maintaining curriculum and academic accountability. Successful teachers are expert instructional leaders who emphasize functional communication and organize instruction of basic skills and academic content around thematic units (Garcia, 1994). Functional communication is emphasized between teacher and student, and among students (Garcia, 1991). In fact, pervasive in the literature was the recommendation that language development should be the primary goal of instruction (Hafner, 1995).

Language proficiency and the manner in which it is assessed remains a critical concern in effective instruction. The number of students for whom language is a factor in assessment is greater than the number identified as LEP. Although students may develop sufficient proficiency to move out of the LEP category, the influence of language remains (Cummins, 1984, 1994). One of the problems may be that school systems have varying definitions of language proficiency. As students move from one district to another, or as they transition from one level to another, their language proficiency status may qualify them for different instructional programs. Language proficiency constitutes a confounding variable that differentially influences the scores students achieve on tests in general. The manner in which language proficiency is assessed may indicate that we are failing many students. It points to the problem of potential misidentification and misdiagnosis when students in middle, junior high, or high schools receive services in special education over time without substantial changes in the type of instruction they receive.

Psychoeducational assessment practices in this study do not differ greatly from the traditional assessment practices considered to be biased for language-minority students. Prereferral intervention and consultation, between and across disciplines, appeared to help reduce the number of referrals to special education. Assessment personnel who were interviewed recognized the pitfalls of using only standardized measures in their assessments and advocated alternative methods that would render more relevant information for instructional modifications.

The schools investigated in this study are exemplary in that they are posting educational gains for Hispanic LEP students. The best practices identified in assessment procedures in the educational context, language proficiency, and psychoeducational evaluation will provide other schools and other professionals with alternatives to improve the education of language-minority students. Recommendations for professional development in this area include the following.

Instructional Strategies and Curricular Modifications. The philosophy that all children can learn should guide instruction that teachers deliver to enhance student understanding and language development. Teachers must become knowledgeable and current in instructional methodology known to be effective for second-language learners. Teachers need to feel and be competent in their area of instruction and use a thematic curriculum that is integrated across content areas. Second-language learners perform better when opportunities exist for active learning, and when cooperation and collaboration are encouraged and rewarded. Authentic and purposeful communication should be used to teach language skills. Interventions should be centered on effective communication and learning, rather than on deficits.

Language Assessment. Language assessment should examine the way in which students process language to determine specific situations in which they perform as expected and others where they demonstrate difficulty. Such a holistic communication evaluation would consider multiple naturalistic observations, language use questionnaires, culturally appropriate narratives, and spontaneous language samples in English and the primary language.

Alternative Assessment Procedures for the Classroom. Alternative or informal assessment procedures in the classroom give more accurate information that relates directly to the curriculum and instructional strategies. Alternative assessment procedures also reflect literacy learning across content areas more effectively than do standardized measures. Teachers should be instructed in portfolio assessment, curriculum-based assessment, whole language instruction, informal reading inventories, using metacognition for assessing reading comprehension, and informal procedures for assessing competencies and weaknesses in writing and spelling.

Formal Assessment Procedures. After a period of instruction during which appropriate interventions and modifications have been provided and no progress is noted, it is appropriate to consider formal assessment procedures. Formal assessment should be advocacy-oriented and may include some or all of the following approaches: performance-based assessment, test–teach–test strategies, curriculum-based assessment, and dynamic assessment.

Consultation to Maximize Resources. Definitions of consultation in the schools all stress using problem-solving techniques and view participation as voluntary. As the principal of one of the high schools said, "We have a team effort. . . . We don't believe any one person can do everything." The needs of language-minority students are great and the number of appropriately trained teaching and assessment personnel currently serving this population of students in schools is limited. Efforts should be made to maximize school resources by improving teaching/learning techniques, the learning environment, our knowledge of cultural and linguistic issues, and alternative assessment procedures, to name a few. These difficult tasks may be accomplished by learning from each other and crossing over professional boundaries to enhance professional competencies for the benefit of students.

REFERENCES

Alvarez, M. D. (1991). Psychoeducational assessment of language minority children: Current perspectives and future trends. In A. A. Ambert (Ed.), *Bilingual education and English as a second language: A research handbook* (pp. 299–345). New York: Garland.

August, D., & Garcia, E. (1988). *Language minority education in the United States: Research, policy and practice.* Chicago: Charles C. Thomas.

Collier, V. (1994, March). Promising practices in public schools. Paper presented at the annual meeting of the Teachers of English to Speakers of Other Languages, Baltimore.

Cummins, J. (1984). *Bilingualism and special education: Issues in assessment and pedagogy.* San Diego, CA: College Hill.

Cummins, J. (1986). Empowering minority students: A framework for intervention. *Harvard Educational Review, 56*(1), 18–35.

Cummins, J. (1994). The acquisition of English as a second language. In K. Spangenberg-Urbschat & R. Pritchard (Eds.), *Kids come in all languages: Reading instruction for ESL students* (pp. 36–62). Newark, DE: International Reading Association.

Damico, J. S. (1991). Descriptive assessment of communicative ability in limited English proficient students. In E. V. Hamayan & J. S. Damico (Eds.), *Limiting bias in the assessment of bilingual students* (pp. 157–218). Austin, TX: Pro-Ed.

De Avila, E. A., & Duncan, S. E. (1977). *Language Assessment Scales I.* San Rafael, CA: Linguametrics Group.

De Avila, E. A., & Duncan, S. E. (1986). *Scoring and interpretation manual for the Language Assessment Scales.* San Rafael, CA: Linguametrics Group.

DeLéon, J. (1990). A model for an advocacy-oriented assessment process in the psychoeducational evaluation of culturally and linguistically different students [Special Issue]. *The Journal of Educational Issues of Language Minority Students, 7,* 53–67.

Duran, R. (1989). Assessment and instruction of at-risk Hispanic students. *Exceptional Children, 56*(2), 154–158.

Erickson, J., & Iglesias, A. (1986). Assessment of communicative disorders in non-English proficient students. In O. L. Taylor (Ed.), *Nature of communication disorders in culturally and linguistically diverse populations* (pp. 181–217). Austin, TX: Pro-Ed.

Figueroa, R. (1990). Assessment of bilingual children. In A. Thomas & J. Grimes

(Eds.), *Best practices in school psychology II* (pp. 93–106). Washington, DC: National Association of School Psychologists.

Figueroa, R., & Garcia, E. (1994). Issues in testing students from culturally and linguistically diverse backgrounds. In F. Schultz (Ed.), *Multicultural education, 95/96,* (2nd ed.; pp. 147–156). Guilford, CT: Duskin.

Garcia, E. (1991). Bilingualism, second language acquisition in academic contexts. In A. Ambert (Ed.), *Bilingual education and English as a second language: A research handbook* (pp. 181–217). New York: Garland.

Garcia, E. (1994). *Understanding and meeting the challenge of student cultural diversity.* Boston: Houghton Mifflin.

Glaser, R., & Silver, E. (1994). Assessment, testing, and instruction: Retrospect and prospect. In L. Hammond (Ed.), *Review of research in education* (Vol. 20; pp. 393–419). Washington, DC: American Educational Research Association.

Hafner, A. (1995, April). Developing and modifying statewide assessments for LEP students. Paper presented at the annual conference of the American Educational Research Association, San Francisco.

Hamayan, E. V., & Damico, J. S. (1991). *Limiting bias in the assessment of bilingual students.* Austin, TX: Pro-Ed.

Langdon, H. W. (1992). Speech and language assessment of LEP/bilingual Hispanic students. In H. W. Langdon & L. L. Cheng (Eds.), *Hispanic children and adults with communication disorders: Assessment and intervention* (pp. 201–271). Gaithersburg, MD: Aspen.

Lucas, T., Henze, R., & Donato, R. (1990). Promoting the success of Latino language-minority students: An exploratory study of six high schools. *Harvard Educational Review, 60*(3), 315–340.

Niyogi, N. S. (1995). *The intersection of instruction and assessment: The classroom.* Princeton, NJ: ETS Policy Information Center.

Paredes Scribner, A. (1995a). Advocating for Hispanic high school students: Research-based educational practices. *The High School Journal, 78*(4), 206–214.

Paredes Scribner, A. (1995b). *Psychoeducational assessment of linguistically diverse students in Texas Borderland Schools* (Effective Border Schools Research and Development Initiative). Austin: The University of Texas at Austin.

Peña, E. D., Quinn, R., & Iglesias, A. (1992). The application of dynamic methods to language assessment: A nonbiased procedure. *Journal of Special Education, 26*(3), 269–280.

Perrone, V. (Ed.). (1991). *Expanding student assessment.* Alexandria, VA: Association for Supervision and Curriculum Development.

Valencia, R. R., & Aburto, S. (1991). The uses and abuses of educational testing: Chicanos as a case in point. In R. R. Valencia (Ed.), *Chicano school failure and success* (pp. 203–251). New York: Falmer Press.

CHAPTER 8

Creating Learning Communities for High-Performing Hispanic Students: A Conceptual Framework

Jay D. Scribner and Pedro Reyes

INTRODUCTION

There were lessons learned from this research. In this final chapter we will share why we think schools enrolling primarily low-income, linguistically diverse students can be created where every child can succeed. After an extensive search for a conceptual framework that would assist us in describing, interpreting, and understanding the success we found when we visited and studied these high-performing schools, we were taken by the ideas Peter M. Senge sets forth in his best-selling classic, *The Fifth Discipline: The Art and Practice of the Learning Organization* (1990). These schools, like Senge's learning organizations, provide a true alternative to our time-worn authoritarian hierarchies. These schools, like the private-sector organizations Senge describes, maintain their competitive advantage through the ability of their members (their learning community) to learn together, and faster than the other schools around them.

The people who had a stake in what took place in the schools we studied maintained their advantage over other schools by truly focusing on what mattered to them—the students. Thus, the first thing learned from our studies was that the reason these schools stayed on a steady course, creating a learning community that produced high-performing Hispanic students, was that they embraced a shared vision of success for all students. Their personal outlooks were to emphasize everything positive related to the learner, the learning conditions and characteristics of their students and the home environment. They simply ignored the "barriers to learning" so often associated with deficit thinking (Valencia, 1997). An attitude prevailed that all environmental factors associated with low-income, linguistically diverse Hispanic students can be shaped in ways that ensure that all students will succeed. Their shared vision acted "as the rudder of their ships" in ways that encouraged team learning and created a place, as Senge (1990) describes so eloquently, where people are continually discovering how they create their reality. And how they can change it.

To clarify the meaning of what our adaptation of Senge's learning community is about, we should begin by saying that the stakeholders in the learning communities we studied, the teachers, parents, students, school staffs, administrators, and their surrounding communities, undoubtedly would discourage any reader from directly adopting what they do. Adopting our depiction of the best practices found within their schools would be just another exercise in mindlessly adding the latest fad, newest technological widgetry, or novel idea. Three decades ago, Downs (1968) forewarned us of such behavior when he came to the conclusion that disjointed incrementalism had never worked. This is particularly poignant among those who remember the heyday of the late 1960s and early 1970s when there were change agents galore and schools were buried in deluges of innovations, few either to be remembered or to exist today (Fullan, 1991). Disjointed incrementalism becomes insufficient as a management strategy when institutional change of a fundamental nature is necessary.

A CONCEPTUAL FRAMEWORK

To create schools that are learning communities requires, first, what Senge (1990) refers to as five component technologies. These five components or disciplines are indispensable in the building of organizations in which all members can truly learn. Each is embodied in theory and must be mastered to be put into practice. Unlike traditional management disciplines, these are personal, as Senge suggests:

> Each has to do with how we think, what we truly want, and how we interact and learn from one another. In this sense, they are more like artistic disciplines than traditional management disciplines. (p. 11)

They are described for our purposes as follows:

1. *Systems thinking* calls for a mind-set that allows for seeing the whole, as well as the parts, penetrating beyond the obvious, and

distinguishing between what works and what fits, and what impedes the pursuit of high-performing schools as learning communities.

2. *Personal mastery* implies an ability to create tension within the school's learning community, to set high expectations, to produce the results we hope for, and to achieve personal and professional success within a high-performing school.

3. *Mental models* require deeply ingrained beliefs, such as the belief that all children can succeed in school. These encompass assumptions, values, and visions that lie beneath the surface level and that affect the way we view and understand the world within which we work.

4. *Building shared vision* incorporates a capacity to inspire loyalty and commitment to a vision of all members of the learning community, to translate personal ideals into a shared vision of what a high-performing school ought to be, and to create bonds among all members of the learning community.

5. *Team learning* comprises the practice of dialogue, as opposed to discussion, suspending judgment for the genuine interchange of ideas, tapping into a broad array of alternatives, and innovating in coordinated ways. (Senge, 1990)

The high-performing Hispanic schools discussed in this volume represent learning communities in which, to varying degrees, these five disciplines are practiced. We believe that to understand the meaning of the true nature of a learning community, is to become engaged in what recently has been coined as indigenous innovation (Heckman & Peterman, 1996). Members of the learning community (the school) examine their own beliefs about what they do, how it gets done, their students, their students' parents, each other, and the larger community within which they work. They work from within, creating their own innovative solutions (Blase & Blase, 1997). They focus and refocus on what they truly want. They strive to do their personal best. They welcome challenges and exhilarate over discovery of the solution to an intractable problem. They collaborate and maximize their human and material resources, however adequate these resources might be, to ensure that every student succeeds—no exceptions. And most important, the locus of their creativity and the change that they initiate, implement, and institutionalize comes from within their own learning community.

Figure 8.1 illustrates a framework for creating learning communities for Hispanic students. At the center of the framework is our primary target, high-performing Hispanic students. The framework consists of four broad categories that are requisite to the development of the capacity within a

FIGURE 8.1. Creating Learning Communities for High-Performing Hispanic Students: A Conceptual Framework

school, as a learning community, to provide outstanding results for all students.

Our first category focuses on *the knowledge required* to develop a high-performing learning community, particularly what we know about the learning conditions of Hispanic students (e.g., the home/community, the classroom/learner, and assessment conditions). The second category of our model draws attention to the shared values, assumptions, beliefs, and expectations that affect how knowledge is understood, whether it is used effectively or not, how verbal and nonverbal statements are interpreted, and what written documents leave out, or say or do not say "between the lines." These are the cultural elements of the learning community, the deeply rooted, invisible forces that define those tangibles that affect all decision making and action taking of *a responsive school culture*. More important, however, whether these cultural elements become barriers to success or not has much to do with how well all members of the learning community practice *the disciplines of a learning organization*, which constitute the third category found in our model. Finally, the fourth category concerns making *what we know* and *how we think and feel* contribute to *how we work together* in ways that ensure that *what we do* produces outstanding results for all students. This is *the action dimension*, those lessons learned from the "best practices" addressed in the research reported in this book and this final chapter. The four action dimensions derived from our research are as follows:

> *Action Dimension I.* Community and family involvement are essential to the development of a high-performing learning community for Hispanic students.
>
> *Action Dimension II.* High-performing learning communities for Hispanic students depend on leadership at all levels that supports collaborative governance that enables every student to succeed.
>
> *Action Dimension III.* Culturally responsive pedagogy is required for students to succeed in a high-performing learning community for Hispanic students.
>
> *Action Dimension IV.* Advocacy-oriented assessment that motivates the individual learning of the student is crucial to sustaining a high-performing learning community for Hispanic students.

We found numerous examples of actions taken within the high-performing Hispanic schools that contribute to student success. However, each school, as a learning community, creates its own culture, its own past, present, and future. Clearly, these schools have their imperfections, but, as stated at the outset, they are among the best schools in Texas and the predominantly Hispanic region of the Rio Grande Valley region of the state. The stakeholders involved in creating excellence in these learning communities sought to overcome their imperfections and continue to do so. Cloning an exact replica of any of our schools would be a futile exercise. All we attempt to do here is to offer our insights into what we think are useful practices found within the eight unique cases we studied. Our hope is that once a shared vision has taken root in the learning community of those school practitioners who read this book, the practices presented here will become useful within their own realities, as they seek their own futures.

Action Dimension I. Community and Parent Involvement

Community and parent involvement are essential to the development of a high-performing learning community for Hispanic students. While there is clearly uniqueness, the schools tend to be seen as centers of learning for all. Community and parent involvement represents an integral part of relationship building for the borderland schools we studied. Proactive measures are taken to create a sense of community and purpose among members of the larger community, including local business leaders, governmental and service organization leaders, citizens without school-age children, and students' parents, who in our study included *la familia*, the extended family. Consciously planned efforts of school staff to personalize interactions and facilitate community members and parents getting to know one another, teachers getting to know parents, and the school getting to know the community through outreach activities, are manifested in culturally appropriate and effective ways. Five lessons emerged that we thought best described what it takes to create a sense of community and purpose among the entire school's community.

1. Supportive, personal relationships that reinforce a feeling of belonging to the "school's family" (school, home, and community) are nurtured by school staff. Personal contact and familiarity lay the foundation for a collaborative relationship among school, home, and community. Transportation is provided in order for professional staff to meet students' families and maintain direct personal contact with parents throughout the year. Educational staff members also assume personal responsibility for establishing links with parents and the community at large. They do this by generating commitment, initiative, and "a broader and deeper sense of responsibility for their work" (Senge, 1990, p. 143). Frequently, educational staff members take responsibility for drawing up a personal plan of action stating what each person will do during the school year to engage families and the community at large in learning events taking place in the school. The parent specialists, where they are found, and teachers share this personal responsibility with the school nurses, counselors, administrators, and others. This is a deep-seated assumption of responsibility that acts as a covenant between the organization and the individual within it. No formal binding contractual arrangement (i.e., "an honest day's pay in exchange for an honest day's work") is necessary (Senge, 1990). The staff we observed share an unconditional commitment to their schools' communities as resources.

2. Community members are encouraged to contribute to the school in ways the community considers important. In most schools, fund-raising goals are set exclusively by the school staff, parents raise the money, and school staff, in turn, decide how it is to be spent. However, for the most part, in these high-performing Hispanic schools, it is made abundantly clear by administrators and staff that the funds parents raise should be used to support projects parents themselves value. Clearly, the schools we studied are atypical. Fostering a climate in which those who have a stake in making students as successful as they can be, and holding the highest expectations for all students, means granting autonomy to parents and other community stakeholders. By empowering community members in this way, collaboration not only has relevance for the learner within a learning community, but benefits the students within the school in ways parents and other community groups feel are personally relevant to them. Giving a sense of autonomy to community members is an expression of respect that is highly valued in the Mexican American communities we studied.

3. Parents are encouraged to become involved in both formal and informal activities associated with schooling. Both parents and staff describe parent involvement activities as formal and informal, but each holds distinctively different views on the kinds of activities they value. In the high-performing schools we studied, parents engage in formal activities such as attending parent–teacher conferences, participating in site-based, decision-making teams, and running for office, and likewise in informal activities, such as simply making informal contacts with school staff when dropping children off at school, checking children's homework, getting help for a child when needed, making appointments with teachers, and cooperating with the school when called upon. We found these involvement activities to be parent initiated, school initiated, or initiated collaboratively by both parties.

4. Access to needed information is provided for community members and parents in ways that facilitate a culture of respect and collaboration. As indicated above, an underlying belief within these high-performing schools was that information about the school and the community not only empowers, it is a "right." Since these schools' communities included many families who had limited experience in the dominant culture, school counselors, teachers, and parent specialists emerged as "culture informants" and sought creative ways to forge links to information exchange networks that not only would facilitate an understanding by school staff of the cultural context of their community, but, equally important, would empower the parents to effectively utilize services at their school and within their community. This greatly increased the use of integrative services within the community and community participation in an institution that represents the dominant culture. The high-performing schools embrace the local culture. Not only do they embrace the culture and first language of the student, they are successful in creating learning communities in which little separation between the school and the community cultures can be found.

5. Adult education opportunities are used to enhance the skills of community members and parents and to enable them to help their children and other children within the school. Opening computer labs on weekends, providing health information and immunization requirements, training in English as a second language, supplying information on how to keep students away from drugs and out of gangs, and changing the mind-sets of parents about the role of the school in their lives and their children's lives were among the broad array of adult education activities furnished by the school. Parents and community members from each school's community, as well as the *colonias* (depressed barrios with few of the amenities found in a school's immediate neighborhood), want to understand how the school system works, how it is governed, and how they can improve their lives through education.

These adult education opportunities were handled in a way that assisted in the development of both participative and reflective skills, or what can be referred to as the two faces of *openness* (Senge, 1990). The former concerns involving people in decision making and the latter calls on people to look within themselves to challenge their own thinking, and to dialogue and deal with defensiveness. As our findings revealed, once school staff, community members, and parents interact on some regular basis around specific activities, such as those provided in adult education opportunities, mutual reservations and fear become transformed. Positive results accrue for the personal and academic development of students, as well as for the perceptions and predispositions of parents, community members, and school staffs.

In summary, high-performing schools tended (1) to capitalize on their community's resources, collaborating with community groups and businesses to garner material resources and support; (2) to establish strong working relationships among staff and with central office personnel, parents, and the community at large, providing opportunities for acquiring new skills, accessing information, and developing an understanding of how to work with school bureaucracies and community infrastructures; and (3) to serve as centers of learning for their local communities, integrating local cultural values into the school culture. Now let us turn to issues concerning the internal governance and leadership of these high-performing Hispanic schools.

Action Dimension II: Collaborative Governance and Leadership

High-performing learning communities for Hispanic students depend on leadership at all levels that supports collaborative governance and, ultimately, success for all students. Senge (1990) submits that learning communities (or learning organizations) tend to be "localized" places. In our study, these are places where learning is acquired more rapidly because people enjoy a genuine sense of responsibility for student success. The members of the high-performing Hispanic schools have developed a strong sense of community by embracing a caring environment that is strongly collaborative and collegial, rather than adversarial. All learning community members, including students, parents, teachers, and staff, as well as principals, were empowered by central administration and their school boards to lead and collaborate. Team learning was prevalent and open dialogue and discussion prevailed. At all levels leadership that supported collaborative governance (enabling student success) was accomplished in an open environment where no one cornered the market on wisdom and intelligence with respect to what it takes to make every student succeed. Indeed, support for these schools transcended the local school context to the central administration and school board. These schools were allowed to be visionary islands comprising individuals who replaced the dogma of managing, organizing, and controlling with the new dogma of vision, values, and mental models (Senge, 1990). Thus, principals shared their leadership in ways that demonstrated a strong vision of high performance of all students in their mutual quest for student success. What were some of the lessons we learned about collaborative governance and leadership?

1. The human potential of all involved with the high-performing learning community takes precedence over traditional notions of bureaucracy. The high-performing Hispanic schools we describe are places where the potential of all learning community members, including students, teachers, staff, and administrators, takes precedence over traditional notions of bureaucracies. Notions about hierarchies where judgments about what is right and what is wrong are left to the principal, where moral judgments and feelings atrophy, and where judgments about staff members' performance are left to supervisors, principals, and other external stakeholders, simply do not exist within a learning community where everyone cares for one another. Moreover, students are central to this concept because all adults in the learning community believe the primary reason for their existence in the lives of their students is to see that each and every student learns and is cared for within an environment where affection, caring, and collaboration prevail. With the assumption that all children, with no exceptions, can learn, embedded deeply in the culture of the school, energies, emotions, and relationships become focused very narrowly on enabling all members of the learning community to succeed in what they are good at.

2. Everyone is willing to engage in and to be held accountable for innovative practices that will improve learning conditions for their students. Principals support and guide change within the high-performing schools we studied. We found extraordinary flexibility in programs; schedules; working relationships with teachers, administrators, and parents; curriculum innovation; planning time; and interdisciplinary instructional patterns. Principals made it possible for all participants in the change process to feel potent, to become "change agents who believe in the change(s), who feel they have an important part to play in [their] achievement and who feel valued and respected by others" (Blase & Blase, 1997, p. 89). Teachers reflected on this flexibility in terms of their freedom to be truly creative within nonrestrictive and safe environments. New ideas, innovations, programs, and materials were adopted only after much reading, visiting, and training. Within these high-performing Hispanic schools, innovative practices rarely are undertaken because of the appeal of the latest widget or whim, and this holds true whether it is the result of a state mandate or simply something aboard the latest "bandwagon." Research is valued, and sharing with faculty and staff the knowledge gathered from a seminar, workshop, or recent reading reinforced the emphasis on teamwork and peer support. School staff held themselves accountable for the changes underway in their schools and their classrooms. They analyzed, discussed, and made decisions on the top-down mandates for change in terms of effects they perceived would enhance or inhibit learning and the overall development of the students for whom they were accountable. Thus, they were neither driven to teach to the tests nor held hostage to tensions these external demands placed on them. Rather than being victims of high-stake testing policies, their students were empowered within the learning community to become the best they could be. Creative tension caused by societal pressures only served to close the gap between their vision and current reality (Senge, 1990).

3. All members of the learning community are empowered to make fundamental decisions about what is to be done to ensure student success. Governance in these schools begins with a clearly established vision and mission. Organizational goals and individual goals are congruent (Beck & Murphy, 1996). School boards and superintendents articulate a vision and mission that permeate the entire school district. Unflinching support for site-based decision making by school boards, superintendents, and central administrations was also apparent where these high-performing learning communities prevailed. A common vision of all students succeeding, and all staff contributing to this success, is the driving force behind those schools in which principals and their staffs generate their own vision concerning curriculum, teaching, and learning (Blase & Blase, 1994; Senge, 1990). School board and superintendent commitment is critical for success in these schools. Extensive work at this level, sharing the concepts associated with the learning community, enables high-performing schools to develop. The board sets the tone by taking a hands-off posture to school management.

By focusing on policy making, school boards allowed their schools to experiment with shared decision making, facilitating the caring cultures and expressions of empowerment (Blase & Blase, 1997; Bredeson, 1994; Lightwood, 1986). These school boards and superintendents refrained from involvement in day-to-day decisions, viewing the administrators and teachers as the experts.

4. Because leadership is a pervasive concept shared by all, all members of the learning community became self-actualized. In the high-performing Hispanic schools, the principals were more interested in empowering others and building a learning community (Blase & Blase, 1997) than in relying on charisma, tradition, and control over critical resources as the basis for their authority and influence. In these schools, the principal facilitates the self-actualization of individual members of the learning community by allowing them to realize their own potential.

The key to self-actualization is embedded in two underlying assumptions. As mentioned earlier, within the high-performing Hispanic schools it is assumed that everyone succeeds. For this to occur, principals do whatever it takes for teachers to be successful in teaching and, likewise, whatever it takes for students to succeed in learning. For example, the principals ensured, among many other things, access to the best instructional strategies, newest materials, or extra help when needed, such as tutorial assistance. Support was provided to make sure that not only each staff member, but each student reached her or his potential. There was little, if any, tracking of students. Instead, heterogeneity of grouping was promoted. When asked what makes this school so great, staff said, "Kids first, then the principal."

The second assumption underlying the key to self-actualization was effective leadership practices. It used to be said that an effective principal was "driving"; a more accurate description of the principals we studied would be "steering." Sharing leadership; creating a culture of caring; instilling trust, authenticity, and pride; extensive reading; sharing information with others; and actively seeking the resources, both monetary and material, needed by staff are among the many leadership initiatives that help the principal steer the school toward higher performance levels (Beck & Murphy, 1996). However, the most effective principals we observed did more than this. They worked persistently and quietly to get everyone to transcend their own self-interest for the sake of the team, the school, and the larger community. These principals undoubtedly would be overlooked by those who hold a traditional perspective on leadership. These principals were engaging, active, and involved in their schools, yet more often than not they remained in the background. What we learned about principals who have the capacity to transcend their own self-interest for the good of the school and the self-actualization of all members of the learning community corresponds directly to Senge's (1990) keenly sensitive description of an outstanding leader.

> Most of the outstanding leaders I have worked with are neither tall nor especially handsome; they are often mediocre public speakers; they do not stand out in a crowd; and they do not mesmerize an attending audience with their brilliance or eloquence. Rather, what distinguishes them is the clarity and persuasiveness of their ideas, the depth of their commitment, and their openness to continually learning more. They do not "have the answer." But they do instill confidence in those around them that, together, "we can learn whatever we need to learn in order to achieve the results we truly desire." (p. 359)

5. An essential function of collaborative governance and leadership is the principal's capacity to communicate meaning and to inspire people to become active participants in collegial and collaborative processes. No one segment of the learning community controls another. The climate, or visionary leadership pervasive in the school, is modeled by the principal. The principal communicates meaning by modeling behavior conducive to facilitating substantively meaningful dialogue among all members of the learning community. Principals model open communications, enable others to learn, work long hours, and "listen–listen–listen." Collegiality and collaboration are the key words describing communication. Site-based, decision-making committees at the high-performing Hispanic schools enact important decisions, and opportunities are created for finding out from other teachers, staff members, and students about student needs. The principal fosters an atmosphere where all is aimed at student success. Principals recognize their role as teachers, listening carefully to what others say, fostering a problem management culture, giving everyone the opportunity to participate, and constantly attending to building collegial and collaborative relationships. In short, principals of the schools we studied do not assume that collegiality and collaboration exist without their nurturance.

Action Dimension III: Culturally Responsive Pedagogy

Culturally responsive pedagogy is required for students to succeed in a high-performing learning community for Hispanic students. The classroom is a central place within the high-performing learning community for Hispanic students. Teachers, parents, students, and community members take responsibility for the learning of all. No one is excluded from this responsibility (Senge, 1990). Teachers create disciplined dialogues on subject matter. They critique and help each other become better teachers and they conduct research and question their teaching practices, with an eye toward constantly improving student learning. Students themselves critique their own work, review their performance, and know exactly where they stand in relationship to standardized test performance. Parents come to the classroom to learn and to share their life experiences with teachers and students; members of the business community come to the classroom to share with children their knowledge of work and its relationship to schoolwork. They all connect in the classroom. They relish opportunities to learn and share knowledge. The students absorb similar attitudes, beliefs, and actions, which are reflected in their work and relationships with others. In summary, teachers use a pedagogy that establishes the relevance of classroom activities for students, responding to the students' culture and needs. This is what stimulates students to *engage in learning activities* within democratic classrooms (Beyer, 1996). Following are five ways in which this, perhaps the most critical, action dimension is put into practice.

1. Teachers believe every student has the ability to achieve, and they communicate this belief to students, parents, and colleagues. These teachers accept students as they are. In everything these educators do and say, they communicate the belief that all students can learn. These educators never mention that their students are difficult to teach or are deficient in any manner. On the contrary, they view their students as a valuable resource, unique not only in who they are, but also in what they have to offer in terms of knowledge, understanding, and expertise.

Teachers even go so far as to recognize that many students view their own behaviors, mannerisms, and interaction modes as affirmations and outward expressions of who they are and what they stand for within their peer group or home community. For that reason, a culturally responsive teacher interprets the individual's behavior and manner of speaking as a part of the whole student and inventories these attributes as contributing to the positive inherent qualities of each and every student. Students who use nonstandard English, Spanish, or other forms of language or culture to express themselves are honored and respected. A culturally responsive educator believes that every aspect of the individual has value and worth, and refuses to categorize or label students as low-achieving or lacking in ability.

2. Teachers provide a caring environment in which students are viewed as the most valuable resources of the school. In the high-performing Hispanic schools we studied, teachers care about what students are thinking, what the students know, and what they consider to be important. In fact, the students themselves are viewed as the most valuable resources of the school. Instructional practice is premised on the realization that student learning never ceases. Teachers assume student learning occurs constantly—both inside and outside the school. When students enter the classroom, teachers listen to what they are talking about. If the students refer to what they did with their families or discuss specific school activities, culturally responsive teachers treat what students say as more than just topics of conversation. Such conversations represent potential student projects and inroads through which teachers connect with or get to know their students as a basis for developing curriculum material and identifying student expertise.

In a culture of caring, teachers do not expect students to repress their own background knowledge. Rather than forcing students to respond to questions or activities that fit into the traditional framework of the classroom, teachers are willing to design their curriculum and classroom agendas to correspond with and complement the knowledge and understanding of the students they serve. Furthermore, classroom norms and behavior give voice to the interactional norms and behavior that students have learned from their families and peers. The overall culture and official rules of the classroom are structured to embrace the ideals of caring and inclusion. Every student belongs and is a legitimate member of the class.

3. Teachers empower their students, providing opportunities for experimentation, innovation, discovery, and problem solving. As the culture of caring is established, students begin to expose themselves to activities that involve experimentation and discovery. They experience the personal satisfaction gained from constructing their own knowledge in a social environment or contributing to another's knowledge base and understanding. The realization of the value of shared knowledge leads to collaboration. Because students realize they are indispensable resources to each other, they replace previously held assumptions about who can teach and what constitutes knowledge and understanding. They are armed with the powerful realization that they are the most important participants in the teaching and learning process!

Ultimately, students are treated as the most essential agents of the educational process. Students are encouraged to select relevant information from their environment, interpret it through what they already know, and construct new meaning or apply what they have learned to new and different situations. Together, teachers and students develop a conceptual understanding of the subject matter and create new understandings through goal-directed activities. Instructional goals concentrate on helping the student develop learning and thinking strategies that are appropriate for working within a variety of settings and subject areas. In the end, students are empowered because they experience the reality that who they are, what they think, and what they have to say has legitimacy and value. Because students are empowered by their school experiences, their academic performance and social and emotional identity are enhanced.

In short, everyone has a function and purpose in the teaching and learning process. The teacher acts as a facilitator, helping students as they share and negotiate specific meanings and construct their own mental models for learning. The students themselves serve as the primary mediators of their own learning. Because they are given a larger and more active role in the teaching and learning process, they also become more involved in the day-to-day activities of the school or classroom. They begin to take responsibility for the everyday affairs of the class and help to select appropriate topics for learning. When students are given a voice in deciding what and how they should learn, they begin to expect more of themselves and one another.

4. Teachers make use of two-way "instructional conversations" with students that encourage goal-directed activity and the use of higher-order thinking skills on the part of students. Instructional conversations involve a teacher-modeling approach that arms students with knowledge of the learning process and specific strategies they can use in and out of the classroom. The term *instructional conversation* refers to the type of dialogue that takes place between the "teacher" and "learner" as the teacher strives to help the student achieve or perform beyond his or her current capacity. In addition to classroom activities and instruction that assist students in their learning, dialogue helps students develop thinking skills and learn how to form, express, and exchange ideas in speech or writing. In other words, teachers and students question and share ideas and knowledge through interaction. Thus, through conversation, students learn new skills and concepts.

Teachers who apply the concept of instructional conversations embrace the philosophy that talking and thinking go together, and assume that the student may have something to say beyond what the student's "teacher" or "peer" is thinking or already knows. Together, they develop higher-order thinking skills by questioning and sharing ideas and knowledge through conversation. As students participate in conversations with one another, they continually learn new skills and concepts. As the student engages in goal-directed activities, the teacher or student-peer works with and listens to the student. The teacher is aware of the student's continually changing relationship to the subject matter and responds when the student needs assistance. As the two continue to interact, the teacher and student build even stronger trust relationships.

5. Teachers use students' funds of knowledge as the basis of their instructional strategies. In the first few years of life, most students learned how to obtain the necessary economic, social, and physical resources that they need to survive. Resources are obtained through intimate and informal interactions and social functions that occur between and among family, friends, or acquaintances. By exchanging different skills and resources, they develop ways to enhance their ability to survive and prosper from day to day. By the time students come to school, many have already acquired a wealth of knowledge and skills that they need in order to make it in the "real world." We refer to this type of knowledge as funds of knowledge (Moll, 1991). The student is recognized as possessing funds of knowledge that form the foundation for student learning and understanding.

The knowledge possessed by students, their families, and friends provides teachers with a major social and intellectual resource for classroom instruction and student-engaged learning. Students, parents, and other community members can make intellectual contributions to the development of lessons. Their background knowledge can supplement and strengthen the instruction of basic skills and academic content. A culturally responsive pedagogy is structured to empower students and members of their various social networks. Teachers use appropriate student background knowledge and concepts and apply what students already know to new learning and skill development.

Teachers never limit their understanding of what a student may know to the context of the classroom. Teachers expand the arena in which students' learning experiences take place beyond the resources of the school. They allow students to use their native language as tools for inquiry, communication, and thinking. They use the students' funds of knowledge and outside resources (such as parents or family members, friends and other teachers, members of the school or business community), and any other resources that may connect with the students' funds of knowledge and learning style.

In summary, a culturally responsive pedagogy is one that is structured to connect what is being learned with students' funds of knowledge and cultural backgrounds. Teachers take advantage of the social and cultural aspects of their students' lives and use students' social relations as a motive and context for acquiring and applying knowledge in the classroom. Students' vast reservoirs of knowledge and skills are used as powerful curricular resources. Many of the topics or reinforcements for teaching and learning are initiated by students' interests and their questions (rather than imposed by adult teachers). Students are allowed to bring in their own stories or experiences and, as a class, they are encouraged to search for ways in which each subject can be applied to a particular situation or event.

Action Dimension IV: Advocacy-Oriented Assessment

Advocacy-oriented assessment that motivates the individual learning of the student is crucial to sustaining a high-performing learning community for Hispanic students. While norm-based, high-stakes assessments have put many schools enrolling low-income, linguistically diverse students on notice, and subjected many of these students to unfair testing practices, no one in the schools we studied concentrates on this issue. School personnel use a diverse array of assessment data to promote the individual learning of students. Again, the focus is on what it takes to facilitate individual student success, rather than to assign grades, to see how their schools compare with others, or simply to determine how effective their overall curriculum was. Moreover, they know their students can learn and are unimpressed with assessment results from tests that ignore their students' bilingualism and diverse cultural background. As indicated in the previous discussion, teachers focus on culturally responsive pedagogy and curriculum and instruction that work with their students' cultural background. What students learn from their unique cultural background, and from using two languages to process information, is seen as producing greater learning. And whenever learning problems occur teachers focus on early intervention. Thus, believing all students can succeed, the schools we studied have adopted advocacy-oriented assessment practices and hold the instructional strategies employed by educators accountable, assessing their impact on the learner. From our research, we learned several lessons about how advocacy-oriented assessment, the fourth and final action dimension of our framework, contributes to creating learning communities for high-performing Hispanic students. Examples of these most promising practices are delineated below.

1. Advocacy-oriented assessment is practiced through the understanding of cultural and linguistic diversity and its relationship to academic achievement. We found that in schools where advocacy-oriented assessment prevails, all members, and especially teachers, of the learning community communicate positive attitudes towards the students' culture. Teachers understand that cultural diversity means that different students hold different world views, influencing how they perceive the world around them. Each student's history, family structure, communication patterns, religious influences, and related factors are considered in the interpretation of assessment results and ultimately in the instructional decisions based on those results. That nonverbal communication styles, dialectical differences, and language patterns attributed to different cultures can influence student performance differentially not only appears to be well understood by these teachers, but results in flexible criteria for assessing student learning potential, raising expectations for individual student performance and growth.

All school staff—principals, teachers, school psychologists, special education personnel, and other service personnel—believe that student performance can reflect language status rather than cognitive ability. Knowledge of the process of second-language acquisition is shared by a majority of teachers and assessment personnel in these schools. These *professionals* are familiar with the stages of learning a second language, the teaching practices that promote the learning of a second language, and the difference between a language disorder and a language difference. These teachers do not find it unusual for students learning a second language to suffer a "loss" in their first language. Clearly, it is possible that due to the exposure to two languages, neither of the languages develops as rapidly in a bilingual speaker. These teachers understand that linguistically diverse students may temporarily exhibit learning difficulties, and that they can make a difference by improving instruction in ways that enhance linguistic competence and thus academic progress. Consequently, assessment results from norm-referenced tests, for example, are used as a small part of a much more inclusive picture of the student and never to categorize or lower expectations for students.

2. Language assessment is conducted to determine linguistic competence in the native language and English. Contrary to the goals of formal assessment, establishing language dominance is not seen as important in assessing many of the Hispanic students in the schools we studied. Establishing which language is dominant and proceeding with formal assessment in the "dominant" language is seen as risky because the student may possess conversational linguistic ability in one or both languages, but not the cognitive academic language proficiency skills necessary to deal with abstract academic language. Language proficiency levels in both languages, however, allow the examiner to determine whether the student has a fundamental understanding of concepts and skills in the native language. If so, limited ability in English is seen as a temporary condition. Thus, teachers are aware that this will improve as the student's English proficiency improves. In short, by determining the linguistic competence of their students in the native language and English, those responsible for the students' success in school are able not only to validate the importance of both languages, but ultimately to expand the students' potential for cross-cultural and cross-lingual knowledge (Miramontes, Nadeau, & Commins, 1997).

3. Teachers and assessment personnel use instructional interventions and modifications to address learning difficulties. In the schools we studied, learning problems of limited English proficient students are considered transitional. There is a mechanism in place that makes the teaching setting and instruction accountable to these students. The first step taken in consideration of student progress is to consider whether the student's instruction is appropriate for his or her level of language skills. If not, consultation among teacher(s), assessment personnel, and program coordinators occurs to design a plan of instruction that meets short-term goals that ultimately support the student's progress toward proficiency in English. Strategies and procedures are documented much like they are in an IEP developed by a special education multidisciplinary team. A period of time is agreed upon during which the student's progress is monitored closely. The collaborative, consultative, and mutual learning on the part of all the professionals advocating for the student exemplifies what it means to be a member of a learning community, as conceived by Senge (1990).

Tracking students as fast or slow learners is never considered by these professionals as an appropriate alternative. They do not take kindly to setting arbitrary criteria for exiting students from native language instruction, or any other language support program, on the basis of a specified length of time designated for language support. In these schools, instructional interventions and modifications are applied creatively to ameliorate any detrimental effects resulting from the misinterpretation of the source of learning problems, such as linguistic competence.

4. Teachers and assessment personnel work together through collaboration and consultation to set high expectations for linguistically diverse students. At the schools we studied, the observation was made that no one individual can single-handedly serve the academic needs of limited English proficient students. Principals, teachers, and supportive personnel recognize that professionals have to work together to improve the academic opportunities of students. This means that collaboration and consultation among professionals are very important. Garcia (1994) underscores the "need for leadership that welcomes, adopts, nurtures, celebrates, and challenges our culturally diverse students. . . . 'They' must become 'we'" (p. 68). In these schools, the principals, teachers, and assessment personnel often reverse their roles, each leading, examining, and interpreting data; consulting; learning; and collaborating with others. The underlying condition of collaboration and consultation among these professionals is their unflinching commitment, regardless of their *professional role*, to advocate for all students. Thus, as we consider these schools as learning communities, we find these examples of collaboration and consultation, or stated another way—team learning. As one of the five disciplines, team learning emulates the principles and practices of becoming a lifelong learner. As Senge (1990) puts it, "Team learning is vital because teams, not individuals, are the fundamental learning unit in modern organizations" (p. 10).

But how do they find time to meet as teams and to create opportunities for analyzing student assessment data and coordinating instruction for the benefit of all their students? One of the most successful interventions was found to be *block scheduling*, which provides time for team planning for teachers working with a given child or group of children. During team planning, teacher(s) consult with each other and/or assessment personnel to target areas of academic weaknesses and coordinate instruction in ways that can improve student learning. Teachers count on the support of bilingual counseling staff, diagnosticians, speech pathologists, school psychologists, parent specialists, and others to work with them as a team on issues dealing with the learning conditions of their students (see Figure 8.1). This support makes it possible for the teachers to concentrate on the classroom context and the individual students' academic needs, while other support personnel concentrate on the coordination of appropriate instructional support, ameliorating student discipline issues, assessing language development, making home visitations, and, in the case of secondary students, guiding them concerning their postsecondary possibilities.

5. There is a commitment to authentic assessment procedures for the benefit of linguistically diverse Hispanic students. Although the majority of assessment professionals have not received formal training in bilingual assessment, it is our observation that alternative assessment procedures are in place. For those high school-age recent immigrant students, instruction is conducted in the native language in content areas. These students are evaluated with the use of portfolios (Paulson, Paulson, & Meyer, 1991), which includes samples of student work, team progress reports, teacher comments, and other relevant data on individual students. It is evident from a review of such portfolios that the students are staying abreast of grade-level content while simultaneously acquiring better English skills. Regular professional development in *authentic assessment* procedures is available to teachers and other professionals in the region where these schools are located. In fact, professional development in the area of authentic assessment is encouraged by the school principals, who expect those attending training workshops to return to their schools (learning communities) and share their new knowledge with the rest of the faculty.

REFLECTIONS ON RELEVANCE AND THE DYNAMICS OF CHANGE

Based on our personal observations and collective experience, the research we conducted in the eight high-performing Hispanic schools, and our own summary of these studies in this volume, what kind of conclusions might we reach about what it takes to create learning communities that result in high-performing Hispanic students? Before answering this question, however, we should make it clear that we are fully aware that the research results reported in this volume would apply to other schools with non-Hispanic low-income, linguistically diverse students, and, for that matter, many of our findings are applicable to schools in general. Also, we share a certain reluctance to state definitive conclusions here because, to us, much of what we could say about these high-performing schools is acutely obvious, has been discussed in the literature often, and already exists in many other schools throughout the nation. But as we indicate at the outset of this book, Hispanic students are among the most likely to drop out of school, to endure low expectations, and to be misdiagnosed, misplaced in special education programs, and tracked as slow learners; rarely are Hispanic students diagnosed as gifted or talented. For these reasons alone we think it is important to consider what it takes to create high-performing learning communities in predominantly Hispanic schools. Our research underscores our essential conclusion—that there are no excuses for anything other than high-impact schools and high-performing Hispanic students.

We believe the key considerations to be taken into account when making a conscious effort to create high-impact schools and high-performing Hispanic students, revolve around issues concerning the students' instructional environment and how it relates to two other environments, the home and community, and the school's organizational culture. The home and community relationship concerns the issue of *relevance*. Relevance is the ultimate determinate of stakeholder engagement in the Hispanic student's educational experience. It is clearly an important factor to consider in establishing the school as a center of learning for all, including parents and community members, students, teachers, school staff, and administrators. When a conscious effort has been made to empower all the stakeholders responsible for the Hispanic student's success, including the students themselves within democratically run classrooms; when a deliberate attempt has been undertaken to draw on the rich traditions, histories, and artifacts found in the Hispanic student's home and community environment; and when a genuine offer has been made to make the school the center of community activity, integrating social services, expanding accessibility, and the like, the *relevancy question* for the student about "Why are we doing this in school?" or for the parent or community member about "What pertinence does this school have for me, the students, or the community at large?" becomes moot.

The school's organizational culture concerns an equally important consideration, the *dynamics of change* within the learning community. This is an issue that is inextricably intertwined with the human and technological components found in the instructional environment. A view of these dynamics that penetrates beyond the obvious, deep within the school's organizational culture, is necessary before the creation of a learning community for high-performing Hispanic students can be realized. Throughout the studies reported here certain themes pertaining to the high-impact Hispanic school prevail. For example, it is essential to establish a shared vision of success and a fundamental belief that opportunities, not barriers, exist and that environmental factors associated with learners, learning, instruction, curriculum, home, and community can be purposively shaped to benefit the students. A commitment must be made to do whatever it takes to alter "deficit thinking" and create new "ways of thinking." The dynamics of change reflected in these schools result from establishing a change environment that fosters collaboration, participation, and the confidence to fail because ultimately everyone succeeds.

Thus, engaging in the creation of a school, as a community of learners, means all participants share a common goal to ensure that all students become high performers. It means dealing with the issue of relevance and the dynamics of change within the learning community. And it means modeling cooperative learning among all participants and establishing a school culture where pervasive leadership, indigenous innovation, and team learning are the necessary norms for developing high-performing Hispanic students.

REFERENCES

Beck, L. G., & Murphy, J. (1996). *The four imperatives of a successful school.* Thousand Oaks, CA: Corwin Press.

Beyer, L. D. (Ed.). (1996). *Creating democratic classrooms: The struggle to integrate theory and practice.* New York: Teachers College Press.

Blase, J., & Blase, J. R. (1997). *The fire is back!* Thousand Oaks, CA: Corwin Press.

Blase, J. R., & Blase, J. (1994). *Empowering teachers: What successful principals do.* Thousand Oaks, CA: Corwin Press.

Bredeson, P. V. (1994). Empowered teachers—empowered principals: Principals' perceptions of leadership in schools. In N. A. Prestine & P. W. Thurston (Eds.), *Advances in educational administration* (Vol. 3; pp. 195–220). Greenwich, CT: JAI Press.

Downs, A. (1968). Alternative futures for the American ghetto. *Daedalus, 97,* 1331–1378.

Fullan, M. (1991). *The new meaning of educational change.* New York: Teachers College Press.

Garcia, E. (1994). *Understanding and meeting the challenge of student cultural diversity.* Boston: Houghton Mifflin.

Heckman, P. E., & Peterman, F. (1996). Indigenous invention: New promise for school reform. *Teachers College Journal, 98*(2), 307–327.

Lightwood, S. L. (1986). On goodness in schools: Themes of empowerment. *Peabody Journal of Education, 63*(3), 9–28.

Miramontes, O. B., Nadeau, A., & Commins, N. L. (Eds.). (1997). *Restructuring schools for linguistic diversity: Linking decision making to effective programs.* New York: Teachers College Press.

Moll, L. (1991). Social and instructional issues in literacy instruction of "disadvantaged" students. In M. S. Knapp & P. M. Shields (Eds.), *Better schooling for the children of poverty* (pp. 61–84). Berkeley: McCutcheon.

Paulson, L., Paulson, P., & Meyer, C. (1991). What makes a portfolio a portfolio? *Educational Leadership, 48*(5), 160–163.

Senge, P. (1990). *The fifth discipline: The art and practice of the learning organization.* New York: Currency Doubleday.

Valencia, R. (Ed.). (1997). *The evolution of deficit thinking: Educational thought and practice.* Austin: The University of Texas at Austin.

Index

About the Contributors

Pedro Reyes, Ph.D., University of Wisconsin

Professor at The University of Texas at Austin in the Public School Executive Leadership Program and associate dean for Graduate Studies. Professor Reyes's teaching and research publications center on administrator and teacher behavior, student outcomes, and educational policy. He is past president of the University Council for Educational Administration and fellow of the National Academy of Education. Dr. Reyes was co-director of the South Texas Effective Border Schools Research and Development Initiative. He is co-director of the Migrant Education Policy and Practices Project. He is also the author and co-author of more than 50 books, monographs, chapters, and articles related to his research interests.

Jay D. Scribner, Ed.D., Stanford University

Professor at The University of Texas at Austin in the Public School Executive Leadership Program, where he is the College of Education's Kenneth E. McIntyre Professor for Excellence in School Leadership. Dr. Scribner is also the director of the Educational Policy and Planning Program. Professor Scribner's teaching and research focus on educational politics, policy, and school leadership. He has served as president of the Politics of Education Association and the University Council for Educational Administration. Joining the University of Texas faculty in 1989, he previously had served as dean and professor at Temple University. Dr. Scribner co-directed the South Texas Effective Border Schools Research and Development Initiative and currently is co-directing the Migrant Education Policy and Practices Project.

Alicia Paredes Scribner, Ph.D., Temple University

Associate professor of School Psychology at Southwest Texas State University. She has been a bilingual elementary school teacher and school psychologist in the School District of Philadelphia and has served as associate director of the Multi-Lingual Educational Research, Information, and Training Center and director of the Personnel Preparation Project for Hispanic Women at Temple University. More recently, her experiences include clinical supervision and research in the area of bilingual special education at The University of Texas at Austin. Her teaching and research interests focus on assessment of language-minority school populations. She provides consultation and training to districts in state educational agencies on issues related to practices and procedures used in the psychoeducational assessment of language-minority students.

Ann K. Brooks, Ed.D., Teachers Colleges, Columbia University

Associate professor in the Adult Education and Human Resource Development Leadership Program at The University of Texas at Austin. Professor Brooks has more than 15 years of international teaching and consulting experience in business, industry, and higher education. Her publications include *The Emerging Power of Action Inquiry Technologies*, a book on action research.

Lance D. Fusarelli, Ph.D., The University of Texas at Austin

Assistant professor of Administration, Policy and Urban Education at Fordham University. His research interests are state-level policy making and urban educational reform.

Paul C. Kavanaugh, Ph.D., The University of Texas at Austin

Received his Ph.D. from the Adult Education and Human Resource Development Leadership Program at The University of Texas at Austin. At the present time he is the interim director of Professional Development and Evaluation at the University of Texas at Brownsville/Texas Southmost College.

Barbara Pazey, Ph.D., The University of Texas at Austin

Vice principal at Reagan High School in the Austin Independent School District in Austin, Texas. Her research interests pertain to communication, urban issues in education, youth leadership, and special populations.

Anna Pedroza, Ph.D., The University of Texas at Austin

Director of Special Populations for the San Marcos Consolidated Independent School District. She was a researcher during the South Texas Effective Border Schools Research and Development Initiative and is interested in educational program practices and policies affecting achievement in predominantly Mexican American schools. Her educational experiences include teaching bilingual, gifted and talented, and migrant students.

William Rutherford, Ed.D., The University of Texas at Austin

Associate professor in the Department of Curriculum and Instruction at The University of Texas at Austin. Professor Rutherford's teaching specializations are literacy development and the management and evaluation of change in organizations. He has 40 years of teaching experience ranging from elementary to university level.

Lonnie H. Wagstaff, Ed.D., University of Oklahoma

Professor at The University of Texas at Austin in the Public School Executive Leadership Program. His teaching specializations are organizational behavior, the principalship, and school restructuring and renewal. Dr. Wagstaff was dean of the College of Education, University of Cincinnati; chair of the Department of Educational Administration, Ohio State University; associate superintendent of Schools, Fort Worth, Texas; a principal; and a public school teacher. He currently holds the M. K. Hage Centennial Professorship in Education, The University of Texas at Austin.

Michelle D. Young, Ph.D., The University of Texas at Austin

Assistant professor in the Division of Planning, Policy, and Leadership Studies at the University of Iowa. Her areas of specialization are research paradigms and methodology, educational politics and policy, home–school relationships, and administrator preparation and professional development.